"WHO IS A JEW?"

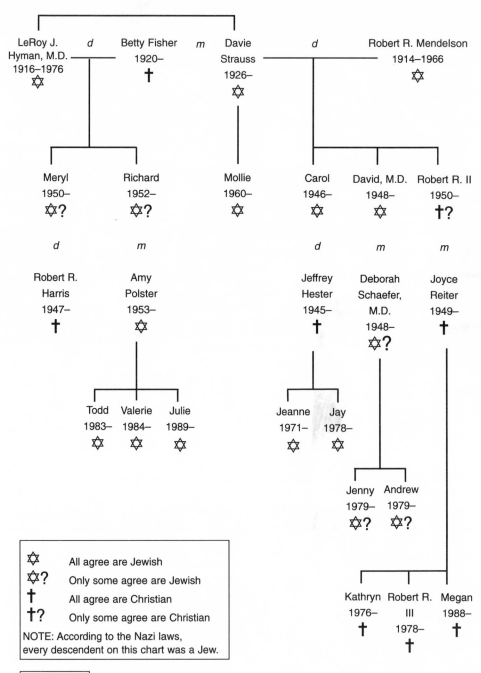

✡	All agree are Jewish
✡?	Only some agree are Jewish
✝	All agree are Christian
✝?	Only some agree are Christian

NOTE: According to the Nazi laws,
every descendent on this chart was a Jew.

d = divorced
m = married

"WHO IS A JEW?"

Conversations, Not Conclusions

Meryl Hyman

JEWISH LIGHTS PUBLISHING
Woodstock, Vermont

"Who Is a Jew?": Conversations, Not Conclusions

Copyright © 1998 by Meryl Hyman

Grateful acknowledgment is made for permission to reprint from the following works: S. Zalman Abramov, *Perpetual Dilemma: Jewish Religion in the Jewish State*, Cranbury, N.J.: Associated University Presses, Inc., 1976; Jacob Neusner, *The Mishnah: A New Translation*, New Haven, Conn.: Yale University Press, 1988; David Hartman, *Conflicting Visions: Spiritual Possibilities of Modern Israel*, New York: Schocken Books, 1990; *Report of the Committee on Patrilineal Descent on the Status of Children of Mixed Marriages*, New York: Central Conference of American Rabbis, 1983.

Library of Congress Cataloging-in-Publication Data
Hyman, Meryl, 1950–
    "Who is a Jew?" : conversations, not conclusions / by Meryl Hyman.
        p. cm.
    ISBN 1-879045-76-1 (hc)
    1. Jews—Identity. 2. Judaism—Essence, genius, nature.
3. Judaism—20th century. I. Title.
DS143.H96   1998
909'.04924—dc21   98–10686
                                                                                      CIP

First Edition

10 9 8 7 6 5 4 3 2 1

Manufactured in the United States of America
Text design: Sans Serif, Inc.

Published by Jewish Lights Publishing
A Division of LongHill Partners, Inc.
Sunset Farm Offices, Route 4
P.O. Box 237
Woodstock, Vermont 05091
Tel: (802) 457-4000   Fax: (802) 457-4004
www.jewishlights.com

In memory of

LeRoy J. Hyman, M.D.
1916–1976

This book is for his family.

Contents

Acknowledgments

This book was blessed by many people whose enormous generosity will be apparent to the reader. To those in particular who overcame doubt that a book on this subject was possible, or even desirable, my great thanks. If it has even partially succeeded it is only because they took the time to help the reader understand the issues.

Others whose help was immeasurable are less obvious. Throughout the world are a legion of, mostly, women, identified as secretaries and assistants who keep the great institutions (and their leaders) running. Invariably, they make themselves known only by first names, and only when asked. To all of them—Iris, Irit, Dot, Malka, Jean, and many more—my thanks and admiration. So too my thanks to extraordinary people who devote themselves to the care and use of Jewish libraries, among them Henry Metzger and Roy Segal.

I am blessed with intelligent and caring family, friends, and mentors whose belief in this book and time-consuming help played as great a part in its accomplishment as anything I did.

My thanks and love to Amy Hyman, who, when she married my brother, did not know she was also marrying this book, which would not have happened without her transcriptions, research, commentary, advice, and enthusiasm.

And to Moshe Samet, whose research and discussions on the "Who Is a Jew?" issue gave me a place to start.

Thanks for their help and guidance to Dr. William and Gloria Lewit, Rabbi David Ellenson, Diana Marshall Weissberg, Rabbi Louis Jacobs, Rabbi Lionel Blue, Shoshana Cardin, Rabbi Amy Klein, Rabbi Shaul Feinberg, Marilyn Henry, Debra Nussbaum Cohen, Ira Rifkin, Anat Ben-Dor, Sasha Treuherz, Victor Gelb, Manfred Moses, Mark Michaels, Karen R. Klestzick, Susan and Augie Hasho, Davie Hyman, Seymour Feldman, Bette Greenfield,

Daniel and Wendy Greenfield, Nancy Q. Keefe, Mary Carr, Jonathan E. Freeman, Kim Kavin, Louise Tutelian Morgenstern, Jean Patman, Elemir Horvath, and Janet and Loring Pratt. And to my mother, Betty Fisher Grundies, who lovingly answered my questions and supported me in this quest though it renewed sometimes painful memories.

My thanks to Gary Sherlock, Robert W. Ritter, Kenneth Paulson, Laurie Thomas, Bill Madden, Jeff Walsh, and all the staff, managers, and executives of Gannett Newspapers who extended themselves to give me time for this book.

At Jewish Lights, special thanks to Antoinette Matlins, Arthur J. Magida, and Sandra Korinchak.

When I mentioned to Stuart Matlins, the publisher of Jewish Lights, that I was thinking about writing a work of fiction on the subject of "Who Is a Jew?," he said, "It's too important to be a novel." May all writers know the pleasure of working with a publisher whose first goal is to change the world.

Some may take issue with all or part of this book. Such complaints should be directed to me. The persons who helped with this book are in no way to blame for its shortcomings.

Jews live throughout the world. I chose to look at this question intensely in three places: Israel for obvious reasons; the United States because it contains the greatest number of Jews and because I am American with a particularly American identity problem; and England because, while its Jewish population is small, it is a highly visible minority in an overwhelmingly Christian society.

A note about the conversations:

I do not speak Hebrew. Fortunately for me, and for the reader, educated Israelis speak wonderfully colorful English, generally with American accents and idioms, and Hebrew-Israeli inflections and cadences.

Almost everyone included in this book was interviewed in person, with few exceptions. Because these were conversations rather than straight question-and-answer interviews, I deleted most of my own statements and queries except in those cases where clarification was necessary or the conversation veered suddenly. I have edited the conversation transcripts for length. I showed transcripts to Rabbis Bulman, Sacks, and Lamm as they requested. I strove to represent fairly and accurately the many generous people in Israel, Europe, and the U.S. who took time to educate me, and to let me see the humanity and passion at the heart of their difficult responsibilities.

Introduction: A Jew's Daughter— A Personal Quest for Identity

Israel: Nobody belongs here more than you.
—Motto of the Israeli Tourist Board

IT IS FRIDAY in Jerusalem. On Ben Yehuda Street, American, English, French, Japanese, German, and Russian tourists wear ineffective windbreakers. They are surprised by the cold. The Israelis are prepared for a bitter Jerusalem winter, even so late in March when history tells them the high sun will heat the hills. Civilians and soldiers are wrapped in wool, their baby strollers are battened in plastic. Arms filled with flowers, they set their courses and unremittingly stride, refusing to give way on the sidewalk, their handbags and Uzis colliding as they rush to beat the dark.

Sabbath, which in Hebrew is Shabbat, does not begin until sundown, but by four o'clock, with three hours of light left, most storefronts are gated. The ultra-Orthodox Jews, in their long black Old World coats and big hats, set up booths on the streets and stop men in modern dress to offer phylacteries, black boxes containing four biblical passages bound with leather straps to the left arm and the head during prayer. They take their leave before the sky grows dark. A shrieking siren calls Jews to begin Shabbat observances—the same siren used in war. Five times each day the Muslims are electronically called to prayer from the city's minarets. The Jews are called just once a week, on Friday.

The country that broke the rules has lots of its own. At the Lev Yerushalayim Days Inn hotel, a chicken meal, cooked before sundown, is served to the ultra-Orthodox travelers who pray standing at their tables, then wash their hands at the sink in the center of the dining room before breaking bread for the Sabbath. I feel a little silly among them, and sillier still after dinner when, impatient for the elevator door to close, I stab at the buttons. A young

Chasidic woman in a beautiful long brown suit, her hair covered by a fashionable hat and snood, speaks to me in English. "This is the Shabbat elevator," she says. "It goes by itself." It is set to automatically stop, open, and close on each floor so that no one need ignite a spark of electricity, which would break the Sabbath injunction against lighting a fire.

Willingly, sometimes ignorantly, I break the rules, but I know better than to drive tonight through Me'a She'arim, where the ultra-Orthodox live and pray and throw stones at cars on Friday nights. They want vehicles off the street on Shabbat, and, eventually, they will succeed, not because they throw stones, but because their political power will increase as it did in Safed, 124 miles to the north, the bustling hilltop artists' colony that is shut up tight tonight, and every Friday now.

Arabs throw rocks at Jews in the Gaza Strip, Jews throw rocks at Jews in Jerusalem and into my heart. I have come to the land of my fathers to be told I am not a Jew, though I can just as easily be told the same thing at home, in the Diaspora, the term used to denote all Jewish communities outside of Israel. I am one of perhaps hundreds of thousands who are members of Jewish families, but who are not Jewish according to Judaism's ancient legal code because our mothers are not Jewish.

At the conclusion of my formal Jewish education when I was a teen-ager, my rabbi in Cleveland suggested I convert to Judaism so that "there would never be any question." Fine, I said. I'll convert to being a girl at the same time so there will never be any question about that, either.

Here, as I stand on Ben Yehuda Street on a Friday night thirty years later, Americans at home ask the questions and explode with the anger that had long seemed mine alone. "Who Is a Jew?," the puzzler central to my life and periodically to Israeli politics, now threatens to break the Jewish people apart.

On Ben Yehuda Street in Jerusalem, I think of my father. As he was dying, he asked for three things: that cars of mourners be parked in the big field at the side of the house; that none of us indulge in guilt—he'd loved his life and he and we had nothing to be sorry for; and that someone say Kaddish, the Jewish prayer for the dead, on his behalf.

He married my Christian mother in a civil ceremony during World War II. He would stake his claim and work the rest out with the rabbis later. My parents were married by a naval officer in Washington, D.C. The only photo of the event I've seen is of bride and groom standing beneath the crossed swords of my father's shipmates.

My father's family in Asbury Park, N.J., had qualms about their favorite son's unconverted bride, but were soon won over by her beauty, humor, and devotion to her new husband, the headstrong son. My mother's family in New Philadelphia, Ohio, never voiced a doubt about the marriage. Her father and his new son-in-law liked each other. I suspect her parents were pleased that this defiant daughter had found herself a doctor with a will equal to hers.

After the war, my parents moved to Novelty, Ohio, a farm community thirty-five miles from Mount Sinai Hospital in Cleveland, where my father set up practice because, as a Jew, he was denied privileges in hospitals in Colorado, where he really wanted to live. In those days, discrimination in the medical profession was legal. He had simply come too late; the Jewish quota was filled. Though forced to live too far east for his taste so that he could be near Jewish hospitals, he would live the country life he dreamed of, even though that meant a then unheard-of daily drive of thirty-five miles to Cleveland from a community in which he was the only Jew. From the classiest house on the street, he ruled one of the biggest spreads in the community, and he trained show horses.

I was born in 1950, but it wasn't until the birth of my brother in 1952 that my father was forced to face the first of many consequences of his marriage: the Reform rabbi in Cleveland refused to perform a ceremony accepting the child as a son of Israel because his mother, my father's wife, was not Jewish. It was not arrogance that drove my father to insist his son be recognized. I think rather it was a kind of hopeful denial, an almost willful ignorance by this Conservative bar mitzvah—whose mother kept kosher except for bacon, because "anything that good can't be *treif"* ["unclean," not to be eaten]—that Reform Judaism had any rules at all. But it was a lesson bitterly learned. Once a supporter of Israel, awed by its existence, my father now understood that his children might be accepted in its safe haven because they were children of a Jew, but they would not themselves be identified as Jews. In defiance of his fellow Jewish surgeons, who took pride in the money raised for Israel in Cleveland and forged their social and professional lives at events dedicated to the Jewish homeland, my father made his donations to individuals and local welfare organizations instead. Some American Jews are now beginning to do this for the same reason.

But my father did not renounce his Judaism or his children's. At night, when we said the *Sh'ma,* "Hear O Israel, the Lord our God, the Lord is One," the core statement of Judaism, my father talked of ignorant people who would call us names. Be proud, he said. They did, and we were.

If at the age of five I had the honor of explaining Judaism to my best friend's Baptist Sunday school class, this was at least a religious distinction I understood. I was ashamed when in 1956 I had to explain divorce to the same friend.

My father remarried, this time to Davie, a Jewish divorcee, and this time in a synagogue by the very rabbi who had refused to accept my brother as a Jew.

In the course of an eight-year custody battle, another thing that was virtually unknown in those years, my brother and I went to live with my father and his new wife, her children, and their child. We now had four more brothers and sisters. We all went to the Reform temple, but a different one now, though my father liked this rabbi no better than the one before.

At the dinner table, my father held discussions, seemingly Socratic:

"If Hitler asked you if you were a Jew, should you tell him?"

Or, "Is Judaism a race or a religion?" But no matter what the topic was, somehow he always got it around to: "A little bit Jewish is like a little bit pregnant."

Though we all knew ourselves to be Jews, we represented most of the permutations of heredity that face American Jews now, those happenstances of birth that set us in different castes. Unlike most such families, we have been at it so long that I can tell you what became of the next generation, too:

Carol, the daughter of a Jewish mother and a Jewish father. A Jew by any standard. Her children, because they have a Jewish mother, are Jews, although their father is not.

David, the son of a Jewish mother and a Jewish father. A Jew by any standard. David married a Christian, who converted to Judaism after their children were born. Because they attend an American Reform temple, his twins were considered Jews at birth by virtue of their patrilineal Jewish descent. Now, five years after their b'nai mitzvah coming-of-age ceremony, they would be considered Jews for purposes of citizenship in Israel, but they would certainly be denied the right to marry as Jews there.

Reed, the son of a Jewish mother and a Jewish father. Reed was born a Jew by any standard. His three children, because they had a non-Jewish mother, were not Jews, and never thought they were. Reed himself converted to Episcopalianism, but considers himself a Jew by nationality and culture. His family celebrates Passover so that he can explain to his children that the Last Supper of Christ was a traditional Passover meal, a seder, during which the story of Israel's deliverance from Egypt is told.

Rick, the son of a Jewish father and a Christian mother, is by Orthodox and Conservative standards not a Jew. His children, however, are Jews by any standard because their mother is.

Mollie, the daughter of a Jewish father and a Jewish mother. However, because Mollie's Jewish mother married a second time without a Jewish divorce, she was technically an adulterer in religious terms. By the Orthodox standard, Mollie is a *mamzeret,* the child of a forbidden relationship. She is not eligible to marry most Jews, though she may marry another *mamzer* or a convert and live happily ever after. She has no children yet, but when she does they, too, will be *mamzerim,* as will all her descendants for all time.

And me. The daughter of a Jewish father and a Christian mother. I was for many years married to a non-Jew. If we'd had children, they would not have been considered Jews by Conservative or Orthodox standards. Nor would any children I might have had with a Jewish husband. Had I undergone Reform conversion, as my rabbi suggested, my children might be considered Jewish in this country but would have trouble being considered Jewish in Israel. Had I undergone Orthodox conversion, they might have a better chance at being considered Jewish in Israel, but even then it would not be a sure thing.

Though our family's Jewish batting average is on the high side—of the ten grandchildren, seven consider themselves to be Jews—this working of the math was troublesome for me. That was, I am sure, because my Judaism was first defined by gentiles, from whom I was "other," and later by Jews, from whom I was another kind of "other." I lived in my own very small Diaspora.

My brother didn't seem to have these problems. His connection to people was through sports and boy stuff, and the question of his Judaism never came up. Ask him now why he married a Jew and he will tell you it is because he happened to fall in love with her. Ask him why he sends his children to temple, he says all children need a religion to reject. He grumbles to me about having to have a seder. I remind him it is a good story. "I've already heard it," he says, missing the point of his own explanation: He and his family are living a Jewish life.

I was not an athlete and could not seek common ground with other kids through sports. My connections with people were verbal, and so my differences from other children were never put aside. Like many children, I would have been grateful to give up one difference at least, and I was given that chance when my mother took me to church after the divorce. I was about eight years old and tried to be a Christian like everybody else. More important, I wanted to please my unhappy mother, to make things better for her and for us all. "Dear Jesus," I prayed, "please let me believe in you. I think you are a nice man. But I don't think you are God's son. I'm glad you're Jewish." But it didn't take, any more than did the Hebrew classes I had earlier, briefly, endured from a severe Orthodox teacher who had no sympathy for my being six months behind the rest of the class.

I loved my mother. I identified with my father. As a teen-ager in my father's house, I was able to glory in the religion, the history, the joy of being what I was born to. But unlike my stepbrothers and stepsisters, I hadn't been steeped in Jewish Cleveland. I was as uncomfortable with my Jewish friends as I had been with my Christian ones.

Nevertheless, I was confirmed (in those days, Reform Judaism seldom performed bar or bat mitzvahs) and, after receiving the award for "most improved" student in the confirmation class, I was selected by the latest rabbi my father didn't like for further improvement in Israel as an Eisendrath International Exchange Student. My father and I thought then the rabbi chose me to tell me I was a Jew. I now think he was hoping I'd become one.

Just weeks before I was to leave, the Six-Day War was fought and my father refused to send me to Israel. A veteran of the Pacific theater, he would send no child of his to an unstable country. The exchange-student organization arranged instead for me to go to Amsterdam, where I lived with Rabbi Jacob Soetendorp and his family and attended the synagogue at which Anne Frank and her family had worshipped. Now twenty years after her death, her father, Otto, was a frequent visitor to the Soetendorp home.

Anne's picture hung on the wall of the temple, and Rabbi Soetendorp and his friend Otto—whom I could not help thinking of as Pim, as Anne called him in her diary—told me a story: When Otto returned from the camp after the war he went to his old friend Soetendorp to tell him Anne's diary had been found and he thought perhaps it should be published. "Ach!" said the rabbi, "no one wants to read that!"

I spoke only prayer Hebrew and dirty Dutch, but the long days we spent at the synagogue were for other reasons unlike anything I knew at home. This was a more traditional Judaism, and several of the people around me had numbers tattooed on their arms. What was left of Dutch Jewry had come home to this place, to each other. Rosh Hashanah and Yom Kippur, the High Holy Days, were for them more than services to be gotten through until dinner. I learned there what it was to be a Jew of the world and in some small way what it was to be a child of the Holocaust, though my grandparents had escaped Lithuania during the earlier pogroms.

One night after dinner, the rabbi called us all to the TV set. On the screen was a documentary about the Nazi trains rolling into Amsterdam. The rabbi and his wife pointed out people they knew who were being loaded into box cars. The Soetendorp children recognized people they knew at the synagogue. No one knew exactly who the emaciated bodies were when the photos of Dachau appeared, but I screamed, "You are all sick! How can you watch like these are home movies!"

The rabbi followed me to the room they called mine, and held me as I cried. "Meryla," he said softly, rolling the "R" in his big throat. "These *are* our home movies. We have to watch. And so do you. You must tell the world that you have known these people so that it never happens again."

He told me something about his war, about sending his baby, Awraham, now the Liberal rabbi of the Hague, to live with a family in that city as a gentile child. The rabbi and his wife had ultimately hidden in the dirt, with straws in their noses to draw air from the surface. After the war, they managed to find Awraham, no longer a baby, and bring him home. For years, little Awraham did not know his parents and cried for his "mommy."

And so I returned home, not "more Jewish," but a smarter Jew.

After college, I moved to New York City and found, for the first time, total acceptance as a Jew because there were so many there, and because I could think of no reason to tell people that my mother wasn't Jewish. But I did tell the young man I thought I loved, and, in time, he used my mother's Christianity as an excuse to end the romance. I married the next man I dated, the first gentile I had dated since high school, in the process dashing my father's hope of finding a rabbi to perform a marriage under a *huppa* (a ceremonial canopy under which the bride and groom stand).

Perhaps my decision not to have children was in some way based on my not wanting them to work the math and find that they were merely one-quarter Jewish, and the wrong quarter at that. To my gentile husband's way of thinking, any children we might have would be Jews; they could not escape their heritage and they should never want to try. They would be reared as proud Jews, he said, because I would endow his children with a marvelous heritage. The Jew who came before thought I would contaminate his; he had history on his side.

Though the status of a child was in early Judaism determined by the status of the father, as early as the sixth century B.C.E., the prophet Ezra expelled the non-Jewish wives of Jewish men who had intermarried during the Babylonian exile. By the second century C.E., Jewish law defined a Jew as someone who had a Jewish mother. It was at this time, too, that standards of conversion were incorporated into Jewish law, though these principles were "in force before the rise of Christianity. . . . The rabbis . . . would apply these rules to the determination of the identity of the early Christians, both Jewish and Gentile, and to the question of whether Christianity was to be regarded as a Jewish sect or a separate religion," wrote Lawrence H. Schiffman in *Who Was a Jew?: Rabbinic and Halakhic Perspectives on the Jewish Christian Schism.*[1] As Schiffman also pointed out, "Jewish status could never be canceled, even for the most heinous offenses against Jewish law and doctrine," although over the generations rabbinic

---

[1]Lawrence H. Schiffman, *Who Was a Jew?: Rabbinic and Halakhic Perspectives on the Jewish Christian Schism* (Hoboken, N.J.: KTAV Publishing House, Inc., 1985).

authorities viewed some as heretics, refusing their entry into the quorum *(minyan)* needed for certain prayers and Jewish burial, for example. This fundamental principal of Judaism has continued through today.

Even early Christians of Jewish descent were still Jews. "Judaism had long been accustomed to tolerating both differences of opinion and deviation from the norms of observance by its members," wrote Schiffman.

With the destruction of the Temple, smaller sects of Jews and the once powerful group of Jews known as Sadducees were lost to the Pharisaic approach to Judaism, which ultimately saw Christianity as a separate religion. Indeed, by the time of the ultimate break between Judaism and Christianity, most, or virtually all, those who were identified as Christians were probably not of Jewish lineage, Christianity itself having purged Jews from its ranks. Schiffman concluded his fascinating study with a profound understatement: "From then on, Christians and Jews began a long history of inter-religious strife which played so tragic a part in medieval and modern history."

In the twelfth century C.E. there was again a marked divide in the practices of the Jewish communities, as seen in Constantinople, according to Paul Johnson in *A History of the Jews*. At this point in Jewish history, the question of conversion was not so much of getting *into* the Jewish people, but of getting *out*. For while the Byzantine "law specifically forbade anti-Semitic acts," wrote Johnson, "Jews were second-class citizens, scarcely citizens at all." Jews were now a tiny minority in a Christian world, and the law of the land—Christian law—"made it as easy as possible to convert Jews. . . . Any Jew caught molesting a convert was burned alive, and a converted Jew who reverted to his faith was treated as a heretic." Clearly, then, from a Christian standpoint, Judaism was a faith, rather than a nationality to be measured by genealogy.

By the fifteenth century, that had changed in Spain, in great part because of what Johnson called "the hemorrhage of converts as the Christian pressure increased." Johnson wrote, "Converting

Jews did not solve 'the Jewish problem.' What it did, as the Spanish authorities rapidly discovered, was to present it in a new and far less tractable form. For the problem now became racial as well as religious."

The local majority knew that many converts secretly practiced Judaism, that they had "converted" out of fear or to gain advantage, Johnson wrote. No longer easily recognized, Jews were then seen as "a hidden danger."

"A Spanish Jew found he could not evade anti-Semitic hostility by converting," Johnson wrote. "With conversion, anti-Semitism became racial rather than religious, but the anti-Semites found . . . that it was exceedingly difficult to identify and isolate Jews by racial criteria. They were forced back . . . on the old religious ones. In fifteenth-century Spain, a Jew could not be persecuted on religious grounds, because he was born a Jew, or his parents were; it had to be shown that he was still practicing Judaism secretly in some form." Ultimately, 32,000 people were killed by burning, most of them suspected of being secretly Jewish. In 1492, any Jew who would not accept immediate conversion to Christianity was expelled from Spain.

Yet the Jews of twentieth-century Germany were not able to escape their faith, or their fate. For a time, Hitler's Nazis gave some privileges to Jews who could prove they did not practice the faith, but ultimately the distinction between Jew and Gentile was, for these Germans, racial. The Reich did not accept the Jewish matrilineal standard of "Who Is a Jew?," but defined as Jewish anyone who had a Jewish grandparent. For the sinister purposes of the Nazis, it did not matter what any such Jew believed or in what way he or she practiced religion. Judaism was a racial distinction; it was no longer possible for a Jew to "escape" from Jewishness in the hostile non-Jewish world.

Against this background, and facing rising intermarriage in the United States, American Reform Judaism in 1983 decreed that all children of Jewish patrilineal descent who practiced Judaism were Jews. It was a radical move, the ultimate break from traditional Judaism. It would also turn out to be a continuing source of enmity from Conservative and Orthodox Jews, and even from some Reform Jews.

In 1997, newly divorced with my maiden name, Hyman, reattached, I would reveal the caste system that splintered my culture and my life. Yet that part of my mission was accomplished by others before I began. The week I arrived in Jerusalem, a bill about conversion was brought before the Knesset by the ultra-religious political parties. It stated that conversions performed in Israel were valid for citizenship purposes only if deemed appropriate by Jewish rabbinical authorities in Israel, which is to say the ultra-Orthodox. While technically a conversion performed by a Conservative or Reform rabbi in the Diaspora could qualify someone as Jewish and entitle the convert to citizenship in Israel, the greater truth is that the validity of such conversions is frequently denied on technicalities on a case-by-case basis when the ultra-Orthodox are in power in the Interior Ministry.

In matters of personal status—such vital determinations as whether a person is Jewish; legally married, never-married, or divorced; where they may be buried, and other matters that determine rights and obligations to the state or to other persons—the ultra-Orthodox had always held complete control in Israel. Under previous administrations when the ultra-Orthodox did not hold governmental positions, it was possible for virtually any person who had been converted by any rabbi anywhere under any Jewish denomination to make *aliyah,* the Hebrew word for the process of immigrating to Israel and becoming a citizen. Yet such a person could be denied the right to marry a Jew in Israel or be buried as a Jew in Israel. The conversion bill would grant the ultra-Orthodox the right to deny the rights of automatic citizenship to those who had been converted to Judaism in Israel under any but ultra-Orthodox auspices. Technically, those converted to Judaism outside of Israel under any denomination would still have rights as Jews. But with their qualifications to perform conversions in the Jewish homeland denied, Reform and

Conservative rabbis around the world were delegitimized as a matter of law, as they had for fifty years been delegitimized in Israel as a matter of tradition. They had never been permitted to perform valid marriages in Israel, and had themselves been married by Orthodox rabbis in Israel, or been married outside of Israel by rabbis of their own movements, in ceremonies that were then recognized in Israel under international law because they were deemed legal by another government's authority.

If I chose to convert in Israel under the bill pending in Israel, I would be forced to live the life of an Orthodox Jew, or to lie by promising I would try to live such a life. The Orthodox insist that strict adherence to their version of Jewish law is necessary for proper conversion. While most of my family would never be asked what they believed, I would be forced to commit not only to a certain type of belief in God, but to keeping kosher, to not touching my husband in public or directly handing him an object when I was menstruating, to not driving on the Sabbath, to hiding my elbows in long sleeves, and, if I were married, to hiding my hair beneath a hat or a wig in public. Unless I made these promises, I would not be accepted as a Jew, and would not necessarily be entitled to automatic citizenship and the rights and stipends of a Jew. Without conversion, I could become a naturalized citizen after about seven years, but my identity card would state that I am a non-Jew. A similar card in an earlier time in another place would have insisted I was a Jew—and marked for death.

Were I to convert under the auspices of a Reform, Conservative, or even some Orthodox rabbis anywhere but Israel, I might be permitted to become a citizen of Israel, even to carry a card saying I was a Jew. But that would not obligate the official rabbinate in Israel to let me marry there.

While I sipped latte on Ben Yehuda Street—a few months before it was struck by three Arab suicide bombers—rabbis in the U.S. prepared speeches and letters of outrage, provoked further by a group of American Orthodox rabbis who seized the occasion to declare Reform and Conservative practices "not Jewish."

The Chief Rabbi of England had refused to enter a Reform temple to attend the funeral of a leading Reform rabbi. While extolling his office as representing all English Jews, the Chief Rabbi told an ultra-Orthodox colleague that Reform had "no enemy or opponent equal to the chief rabbi."

I had come to Ben Yehuda Street to define my own Jewish identity at the very moment that Jews throughout the world began "the process of redefining what constitutes the Jewish identity," as Rabbi Prof. Jonathan Magonet, a leading English rabbi, was soon to tell me.

The ax I brought to grind became a tool of entry. I knew what to ask because I lived the question.

A life led to the writing of this book, but this is not a life's work. I want you to hear what I heard as I traveled for a few months through Israel, England, and the United States. I told people my story. I listened to their responses. Now and then, I argued with them, sometimes perhaps more strongly than an ostensibly objective reporter should.

You will meet, as I did, some of the spokespersons and leaders on all sides of the "Who Is a Jew?" question who officially represent their organizations' points of view. You will meet others whose voices are representative of a body of thought, and some whose points of view are singular. You will not like some of these people, but I don't know which ones.

"Are you aware that if you write this book everyone will hate you?" said Rabbi Nachman Bulman, the rabbi whose fiery defense of ultra-Orthodoxy formed the basis for many of the conversations I would later engage in. "Do you know that if you give me a fair shake the other side will hate you; and if you give them a fair shake, I will?"

From whichever side you enter the "Who Is a Jew?" argument, you will find your enemies here, as well as your allies. But you may learn, as I did, that they all speak with integrity. There are no monsters here.

1

An American, a Russian, and an Israeli go to a restaurant.
The waiter says, "I'm sorry, there is a shortage of beef."
The American says, "What's 'a shortage'?"
The Russian says, "What's 'beef'?"
The Israeli says, "What's 'I'm sorry'?"

—*A joke*

IN MY LIFETIME, which already spans one-quarter of the history of
the United States, the amalgam in the American melting pot cur-
dled. My Jewish Lithuanian immigrant ancestors to New Jersey
were among those who thought that to be an American meant
speaking the single language, dressing in the single fashion, and
dreaming the American dream. That insistence was a reason they
became integral to their new culture. Yet once that integration
was achieved, these Jews, like other groups, awoke to a sense of
loss—of custom, of language, of all that had let this tiny group
survive for so many centuries. In just a few generations, the new
group—Americans—had broken back into the parts of its sum:
Jew, German, African, Italian, Scandinavian, Irish, and English,
all seeking a way to live together rather than a way to live alike.
Within those groups are smaller ones still, their differences usually hidden to outsiders, and generally to good purpose.

We hide the cracks along which we can be broken. As Jews, we
have various beliefs and backgrounds, and divide ourselves into
groups as disparate as the twelve tribes from which we are said to
descend. Ultra-Orthodox, Orthodox, Conservative, Reform, Reconstructionist, unaffiliated—these are terms that define our belief systems. "Ashkenazi" and "Sephardi" denote our physical

1

and cultural heritages. "Diaspora" and "Israel" denote our current places of residence. However much these terms divide us, we are also stuck together at the edges. Whether our attachment to the past and present members of our group is religious, cultural, national, historical, practical, or sentimental, we work fairly well together in the face of larger adversity. When there is no pressure from without, we break apart.

When the question of "Who Is a Jew?" is asked, it is always followed closely by its companion question: Are We *One* People? At this point in our history, I don't think we are. Perhaps we never were.

As early as the first century C.E., the Jewish community known as the Sadducees rejected the oral law (*halakha*) as binding just as Reform Jews do today; however, Reform Jews do not reject the *halakha* as a source of Jewish authority, teaching, and inspiration. *Halakha* is said to be based on laws given orally by God to Moses at Sinai. This, with the written law of the Bible, is the twofold revelation of Torah, the body of "teachings." The oral laws were written down and analyzed by sages of the second and third centuries C.E., who also prescribed additional blessings, called *mitzvot* in Hebrew, such as lighting candles on Shabbat, the Jewish Sabbath. The Orthodox consider *halakha* "fixed," for while various Orthodox communities interpret the *halakha* in various ways, they attempt not to stray from its specific, literal injunctions. Of the 613 commandments, 248 are positive, prescribing actions to be taken; 365 are negative, prescribing actions to be avoided. These are the specifics of prayer shawls with long fringes, dietary laws that declare pork is unclean, or *treif*, and therefore not to be eaten, and various stipulations concerning marriage, sex, and the Sabbath.

Modern Orthodox and Conservative Jews, who interpret the *halakha* differently from the ultra-Orthodox, seek to apply strict adherence more precisely to the modern world. Modern American Reform Judaism does not subscribe to the body of ancient rabbinic law as binding, contending that a code written for a people thousands of years ago is no longer strictly appropriate, and that *halakha* is not fixed, but fluid and changeable as the world changes.

It is *halakha* that discounts my own Jewishness, in language that is almost always contradictory. The sages differed in their interpretation of laws that were passed down in what might be called the ultimate game of telephone. Their current meaning is then in the hands of the rabbis, who continue to search for a concrete, binding resolution to their own debates. On the subject of my place in the universe, and my brother's and half-sister's and step-siblings' and our offspring, the halakhic rules generally hold together. In a recent English translation of the Mishnah, the Oral Law, by the noted American Talmudic scholar Jacob Neusner, these read, in part, like this:

> Ten castes came up from Babylonia: (1) priests, (2) Levites, (3) Israelites, (4) impaired priests [unsuitable for service], (5) converts, and (6) freed slaves, (7) *mamzers*, (8) *Netins* [temple slaves], (9) silenced ones , and (10) foundlings.
>
> Priests, Levites and Israelites are permitted to marry among one another.
>
> Levites, Israelites, impaired priests, converts, and freed slaves are permitted to marry among one another.
>
> Converts, freed slaves, *mamzers*, *Netins*, silenced ones, and foundlings are permitted to marry among one another.
>
> And what are silenced ones?
>
> Any who knows the identity of his mother but does not know the identity of his father.
>
> And foundlings?
>
> Any who was discovered in the market and knows neither his father nor his mother . . .
>
> He who marries a priest girl has to investigate her genealogy for four generations via the mothers . . . :
>
> Her mother, and the mother of her mother, and the mother of the father of her mother, and her mother, and the mother of her father, and her mother, and the mother of the father of her father and her mother.

And on it goes, winding through the various permutations of genealogy and caste, asking questions, denying unions or permitting them, defining outcasts, in some ways making the more outlandish cases clearer than the common ones: *If a man married overseas and his wife dies and he returns with children he says are hers, he must have proof . . .*

From such minutiae was Jewish civilization built. From such minutiae my family, and millions of other Jews, fled in the belief that this obsession with detail would, in the end, kill us in a complex world. It is to such minutia that millions of Jews are now returning by degrees, to keep us together, to declare once again a separation from the rest of the world that might keep us whole. Yet such a notion is inherently dangerous, for it comes with the inevitable human quest for power. And it raises the inevitable question: Whose Judaism will survive?

In the Diaspora, particularly in the U.S., such a question might never be asked were it not for the rebirth of Israel, the homeland to which all Jews are entitled to return. There are enough Americans of every stripe and variation to form a group, a community, a congregation based on a singular need, or set of beliefs. Were it not for Israel, my identity crisis might now be solved: I am an American Reform Jew. I belong to this one group of Jews by its own definition. Were I tied only to the United States, where many Jews and all gentiles accept my definition of myself, it could be enough. Yet I am tied to Israel too, and if I am the only member of my family who is not permitted to love and be loved by our other homeland as a Jew, the only one who may not express my Judaism in Israel and contribute to the culture of my forebears and the well-being of my contemporaries there, I am unmarked baggage, lacking symbols to identify my destination.

While I have lived quite well without Israel, and it has lived quite well without me, I am inextricably linked to Israelis whose laws might exclude me from my extended family, whom I hold most dear. That is an easier truth to live with than the fact that among Israelis it is perhaps only ten percent who are ultra-

Orthodox, who do not accept me, and who are trying to decide my fate as a Jew.

It is not easy to know exactly who speaks for the ultra-Orthodox world, because it is not one world. Each community has its rabbis, and each of these is a disciple of the community *rebbe,* the grand leader, whose teachings may be carried on after his death, most often by his sons or sons-in-law. In some cases, the rebbes were once close, sometimes related, and eventually they split on theological or political lines. Outsiders who attempt to sort them out will find it like bird-watching through a camera that sees plumage only in black and white. Secular Israelis are better at sorting them out than are many American Jews, who see only black hats and black coats and beards that copy the look of the nineteenth-century Russian or Polish or Lithuanian villages their grandparents fled. They see Jews who dress funny, set themselves apart and shun modernity and the mildest forms of assimilation. Israelis can look at a hat and know the particular Orthodoxy it represents. I never learned to do that, but then, I never learned to distinguish a modernly dressed Arab from a secular Jew at a glance, either.

This did not, however, prevent my being offended when cab drivers in Israel asked me, as they all did, if I was a Jew. In the first place, the question was inappropriate, downright undemocratic, maybe even racist. But worse, how could they question this Jewish face, this *punim?* Of course I was a Jew, and I was insulted that the question was asked. Yet, if Judaism is a race, as my father seemed somehow to believe, I can't describe it. Even Hitler required armbands to tell us from the rest.

Distinguishing among the ultra-Orthodox was more perplexing, but I knew I wanted to speak with those who affiliate under the umbrella of Agudath Israel, an organization formed before World War II to protect and advance adherence to Orthodoxy. At the creation of the State of Israel, the organization became a political party. Its rabbi leaders disagree on big issues and small

ones, but they are the rabbis who represent grass-roots ultra-
Orthodoxy, and promote the fundamentalist view of the "Who Is
a Jew?" issue. Depending on political factors within the Knesset
and power plays among the ultra-Orthodox political parties and
coalitions, Agudath rabbis frequently take a lead in the debate on
the issue.

Other ultra-Orthodox communities—such as those who lived in
Israel for centuries under Arabic, Turkish, and British rule and still
do—thought the creation of the Jewish state was a spit in God's
eye. If Israel is to be redeemed by the Messiah, as the Bible states,
then the Messiah will not be rushed by the creation of some
phony country called "Israel." So rash an act might even delay
the coming of the Messiah, who will be offended by the insolence
of people who make decisions in God's place. Still other ultra-
Orthodox opposed the Jewish state because the borders were not
Israel in its Biblical entirety.

The Agudath rabbis chose not to oppose the State of Israel, but
to see it as a beginning of the redemption of the Jewish people.
Their decision was, to my mind, a practical one. In a Jewish
country, people have less opportunity to stray from God's path.
The Orthodox do not deny that their methods are coercive. They
know that is what God told them to do. They do not want to destroy modern civilization, but to save it. But when I approached
Agudath rabbis to discuss these issues, they politely suggested I
look elsewhere, explaining that they had been misrepresented by
reporters for years and weren't about to go through this again, especially now that they were so close in the Knesset to accomplishing a conversion bill that they had designed.

Most American Jews did not know how close the ultra-
Orthodox were to accomplishing the bill. I was one of those
who failed to see that, in 1996, an election half a world away
would have great significance in our lives. But in that year the
ultra-Orthodox, many of them holders of dual citizenship in the
Diaspora and Israel, came by the planeload from around the
world to vote for Binyamin Netanyahu in Israel's first direct election of a prime minister.

Had Netanyahu looked like his ultra-Orthodox supporters, I might have paid more attention to Israeli politics. But Bibi, as he is called, is modernly debonair, sportily dressed, and, by virtue of his American schooling, speaks English with an accent that might be from Cleveland. He was a hard-liner in matters of war and peace with Arabs, and, if that is what Israelis felt they needed, it had nothing to do with me.

Running for leadership in Israel, Netanyahu had to be seen as a world leader, to be photographed with the mighty, and to curry the favor of influential Americans so that they, in turn, could influence the U.S. government to work with him. He worked American cities like the host of a cocktail party. Savvy, sophisticated, he made hay of a hidden resentment, a nearly silent five-year backlash that pitted Jew against Jew after a fast war in the Middle East that was spun to commercial perfection in 1991 by the Pentagon. Even its name was ad-wise: Operation Desert Storm. When Iraq, under Saddam Hussein, invaded Kuwait, Israel found itself aligned with its traditional Arab enemies, who heard Saddam declare—after the fact—that his invasion had been a message to Israel—and then he sent missiles to Tel Aviv to prove it. The United States led a coalition of Western and Muslim armies against Saddam, and drove him back to his own piece of the desert.

The rules had changed sufficiently so that later that year in Madrid, Israeli Prime Minister Yitzak Shamir, Palestinian leader Yassir Arafat, and representatives of Syria, Jordan, Egypt, and Lebanon talked officially for the first time, with the U.S. acting as father figure. Israelis responded by electing a peacemonger, Yitzak Rabin and his Labour Party, thus ending a fifteen-year hold on the government by the Likud party, which had been staunch in its defense of post-1967 borders.

In 1993, Rabin and Arafat shook hands at the White House as they signed the so-called Oslo Accords that over five years would trade Israeli-held land for peace. Sinai, the West Bank, and Gaza would be returned to the Arabs. The enemy would become a good neighbor, if never a good friend. For some, then, the Oslo

Accords meant giving up land, houses, cities, and strategic hills for which so many had died. The renegotiated borders were seemingly impossible, or too costly, to defend. But for many, peace was worth the price, and Rabin was the modern-day Moses who would lead them to freedom from war.

While Israelis and Jews around the world were learning to live without a common enemy for the first time in fifty years, or, perhaps even two thousand years, there were still no guarantees that the peace would hold. Palestinian refugee camps on the West Bank were an enormous problem for Israel, and international pressure—much of it from American Jews—on Israel to provide in some way for the Palestinians was proving an embarrassment for many in Israel, which had built a reputation for seeking a higher moral ground. Likud candidate Netanyahu represented those who maintained the hard-line, defended the need for isolating the Palestinians, and, while not openly defying the Oslo Accords, objected to the way that Labour was implementing them. The land had been won, and the land would be kept. He made the international rounds, and dealt quietly but not secretly with Israeli religious parties, which were needed to form a coalition government. If, in the end, he could not win over all American Jews, or even most Israeli ones, he could cobble a government from the minority parties, including the ultra-religious coalition parties, which had been placated or ignored for several years.

Israel is democracy at its purest, but it is also democracy at its most absurd. It has no weighting of states, no winning of districts, just a simple counting of all the votes in the country for a particular party. The percentage of votes a party receives is the percentage of votes it will hold in the national government—a system that promotes minority parties and makes national consensus almost impossible to achieve. Even Arabs sit in the Knesset. The Jewish religious parties, who agree on very little else, agreed to combine forces behind Likud. Most secular Jews pinned their hope for peace with the Arabs on the incumbent, Prime Minister Yitzak Rabin.

Then, a young, fanatical, well-educated modern Orthodox Jew

who was an army veteran and former emissary for Israel in Russia murdered Rabin for giving the country away.

I told a Tel Aviv cab driver who insisted on taking me to the spot where Rabin was murdered that America, too, had such a death. The driver could not believe my stupidity. We should have expected John F. Kennedy's assassination, he said. America was a violent place, unlike Israel where it is safe to walk the streets at night.

Israel is built on twenty layers of irony. Rabin's widow blamed Netanyahu for the rhetoric a young man, her husband's assassin, took too far. And yet, following renewed Arab terrorism against civilians, Bibi was elected in Israel's first direct election of a prime minister, with 50.4 percent of the vote against Shimon Peres, Rabin's successor. The religious parties took 20 percent of the vote. This gave them a total of 23 seats in the Knesset. Though only about 10 percent of the total Jewish population is religious, an additional 10 percent voted with the religious parties. This was their statement for a renewed hard-line policy against the Arabs, a challenge to the Oslo Accords and the entire peace process. Though the majority of non-Orthodox Jews did not vote for the religious parties or for Bibi, neither did they oppose him strongly enough to prevent his election, perhaps hoping that if nothing else they could rely on his strength. If that meant they had to give in a bit more to the ultra-Orthodox rabbis, it was only in a theoretical sense.

Lifelong Israelis had known nothing but the "status quo," the brilliantly executed sidestep that united Jews long enough to liberate and build their homeland. In 1948, Israel's founders had attempted to avoid writing new laws and even declined to write a constitution, declaring instead temporarily to maintain the "status quo," the legal practices of the hated British who had ruled by mandate of the League of Nations. Only religious leaders, through ecclesiastical courts, could perform marriages and divorces and determine other matters of family law including adoption and conversion. In a hurry to declare independence and prepare for the inevitable war with neighboring Arabs, the Jews staked their claim and would work the rest out later. The result was—and is—a democracy in which there was no civil marriage, divorce, or burial. The Orthodox rabbis had what amounted to full control over what in other democracies are personal rights free from religious influence.

Few Israelis have real problems about such matters. They seldom marry non-Jews or adopt non-Jewish children who need conversion. The exception is in matters of divorce, which is an even more complicated business than marriage. By halakhic standards and Israeli practice, women who have undergone Jewish marriages may not remarry without a *get*, as a Jewish divorce is called. This is an emotional issue in Israel where unfreed wives are forced to remain alone by recalcitrant or vengeful, often remarried, ex-husbands who are willing to go to jail rather than yield to a court order to deliver the paper freeing their not-quite ex-wives. Women who have never worked at anything but homemaking are then left without provision or protection. (Muslim marriages are also recognized in Israel and can be dissolved only according to Muslim custom.)

According to a study by The Louis Guttman Institute of Applied Social Sciences in Israel in 1992, 25 percent of 2,540 respondents said they attended synagogue regularly and 56 percent said that they sometimes attend. More than half of those asked in the study favored or "leaned toward" separation of synagogue and state.

Yet most could not see that, in 1996, with the election of Netanyahu, religion and state would, in some ways, form an even stronger alliance that could have an impact on their daily lives.

It is difficult now to understand why more Jews did not see a need to establish secular rights from the beginning. But this was a new, unbuilt, raw, poor country in the throes of reclaiming Jews from Hitler's savaged Europe, the survivors of families who had died by order of the Reich because they sought to live by the orders of the rabbis. The Reich's point of defining a Jew was to exclude—and worse. The Jewish country would have to define a Jew for the widest possible inclusion, taking in all those whom

Hitler would have destroyed without lending credibility to his definition. In other words, while I was not considered by Jews to be one of them, I was eligible for the concentration camps because I was in some way *of* Jews. Israel would have to find a way to bring me in, while not allowing the greatest enemy of the Jews to destroy Jewish unity by forcing me upon them.

While speaking of Jews as a "race," Hitler's definition was based on matters of heritage rather than physical traits of any kind. In formulating German citizenship laws and in court cases in which persons tried to prove themselves not Jewish, Jewishness was defined by degree. A full Jew was a person with three or four Jewish grandparents, or a member of the "Jewish Religious Community," or one who was married to a Jew. Such persons were barred from German citizenship.

A person who identified with the Jews was classified as a Jew. That would have included me. Had I not been a practicing Jew and sought to pledge my allegiance to the Reich early in its development, I might have sought refuge in the category of *Mischlinge,* which was devised for those who were not of 100 percent Jewish blood and whose ties could be mitigated by acts promoting the Reich. According to *The Destruction of the European Jews* by Raul Hilberg, a *Mischlinge* of the "first degree" was one with two Jewish grandparents, who did not belong to the Jewish religion, and was not married to a Jew. A *Mischlinge* of the "second degree" was a person with one Jewish grandparent. They were not exactly Jews, but they were excluded from the civil service and the Nazi party, could serve in the army only as common soldiers, and could not marry Germans without official consent. A friend might appeal to the government for special treatment of such a person if it could be proved, for example, that a grandparent was not religious or that the subject did not think of himself as a Jew. Eventually, the authorities concluded that such applications were handled too "softly" and Hitler declared that "blameless conduct" was not in itself sufficient grounds to mitigate inherently Jewish defects. "The *Mischlinge,*" wrote Hilberg, "had to show 'positive merit,' which might be proved if, for example, without awareness of his ancestry, he had fought for the party uninterruptedly and for many years."

In the end, any Jewish tie was sufficient for inclusion in the gas chamber. A person with Jewish family members, any percentage of Jewish blood, or any religious connection to Jews, even if he had sought release from his heritage, was among the six million who were murdered because they were Jews. For Jews who fought their way to Israel during and after World War II, governmental definitions of Judaism were of less importance than the fact that they had a country to call their own.

Israel's 1950 Law of Return, under which every Jew in the world has the right to immigrate, and the Citizenship Law of 1952 under which all Jewish immigrants have a right to Israeli citizenship under the Law of Return, did not initially define a Jew. An immigrant had only to declare himself a Jew to be granted citizenship and enjoy the specific rights of Jews in the new homeland. In fact, Israel's standard of Jewishness and conversion was so much more lenient than the Orthodox standard in the Diaspora that some people who married into Jewish families and were denied conversion in the Diaspora came to Israel to be certified as Jews.

A wave of immigration to Israel from Eastern Europe in 1956, which included large numbers of mixed couples, and an increasing vocal opposition to assimilation by Orthodox rabbis in the Diaspora, led to something of a crackdown on who was to be considered a Jew. The door to Israel was still open, but the passageway was narrowing, not because the laws were changed, but because their interpretation was. By 1957, the director of the Registration Department of the Interior Ministry ordered that the questions of religion answered by new immigrants be verified. The director was a member of the National Religious Party.

The battle was on. In 1958, the Attorney General and the Interior Minister issued written guidelines—not laws—to defend immigrants from a harsh search of their backgrounds. They put into writing what had always been an informal policy: It was sufficient for a person simply to declare that he or she was a Jew. They succeeded, temporarily. The religious party withdrew from the government. But the internecine war was not over. David Ben-Gurion called together fifty rabbis and intellectuals whom he called the "Sages of Israel" to settle the matter of "Who Is a Jew?" in Israel. More than eighty percent of the sages advocated the halakhic standard, which requires a Jewish mother or traditional, which is to say Orthodox, conversion.

In 1959, another set of guidelines, which was not written into law, was issued: For the purposes of the population registry, a Jew was a person whose mother was a Jew or one who had been converted according to the Orthodox halakhic standard, which requires circumcision for males, immersion in a ritual bath for males and females, and, most important, a promise to live by Orthodox rules. A deal was struck to make that definition a law of the land, but it failed again.

Enter Brother Daniel, a most interesting chapter in the history of the modern "Who Is a Jew?" question, and a fascinating story by any standard. Here it is, as told by S. Zalman Abramov in his definitive history of the relationship between religion and the state in Israel, *Perpetual Dilemma: Jewish Religion in the Jewish State:*

"Brother Daniel was born a Jew with the name Oswald Rufeisen, and was brought up as a Jew in Poland by his parents. . . . In his youth, he was active in the Zionist movement, and after completing his secondary school education he underwent training for pioneering work in Palestine. With the outbreak of the German-Russian war in June 1941, he was imprisoned by the Gestapo but managed to escape; he succeeded in obtaining a certificate to the effect that he was a German Christian, and as such he became secretary and interpreter at a German police station in the district of Mir, Poland. While there, he established contact with the Jews of the town, and would inform them of German designs against them. When he learned that the Germans were about to exterminate the local ghetto, he reported this to the Jews and supplied them with arms, so that many of them were enabled to join the partisans. Some of them survived and eventually settled in Israel. His true identity was later discovered by the Gestapo, but he again escaped and hid for some time in a convent. Before long he joined the partisans, and was finally awarded a Russian decoration for this services with the fighting underground.

"In 1942, while in the convent, Oswald Rufeisen embraced Christianity, and at the end of the war became a monk, entering the Order of the Carmelites. He chose this Order deliberately because he knew that it had a chapter in Palestine, which in due course he hoped to join. During the [Israeli] War of Independence and several times thereafter, he sought the permission of his superiors to emigrate to Israel. In 1958 he obtained that permission.

"After the Israeli consulate in Warsaw informed him that he would be granted an entry visa into Israel, he applied to the Polish authorities for a passport in the following terms: 'I, the undersigned, the Rev. Oswald Rufeisen, known in the monastic order as Brother Daniel, hereby respectfully apply for permission to travel to Israel for permanent residence, and also for a passport. I base this application on the ground of my belonging to the Jewish people, to which I continue to belong, although I embraced the Catholic faith in 1942, and joined a monastic order in 1945. . . . My national allegiance is known to the Church.'

"The Polish authorities agreed to comply with his request, after he waived his Polish citizenship. On his arrival in Israel he applied for an *Oleh* status [immigrant with right to citizenship] and for registration as a Jew on his identity card. This application was refused on the basis of the government's decision of July 20, 1958, which provided that 'anyone declaring in good faith that he is a Jew, and does not profess any other religion, shall be registered as a Jew.'

"The attorney for Brother Daniel took the position that the term Jew in the Law of Return should be given its halakhic interpretation. . . . The State Attorney, in opposing this position . . . [argued] that a Jew converted to another religion may not be considered a Jew, or should be considered at most a partial Jew, that is, one who is not entitled to all the rights accorded to full Jews under the *halakha*."

A "partial Jew." A *mamzer*. A *Mishlinge*. As my father said, "A little bit Jewish is like a little bit pregnant."

Brother Daniel lost his case. The majority Israeli Supreme Court opinion, written by Justice Moshe Silberg, stated that under the halakhic standard, Brother Daniel *was* a Jew. But, he said, the Law of Return was a secular document, and Brother Daniel was not a Jew as far "as it is usually understood by the man in the street."

"There is one thing shared by all Jews who live in Israel," Silberg wrote, "and that is that we do not detach ourselves from our historic past, and that we do not deny our heritage. . . . Whatever national attributes may be possessed by a Jew living in Israel, whether he is religious, non-religious or anti-religious, he is bound by an umbilical cord to historical Judaism, from which he draws his longings. . . . I have not the least doubt that Brother Daniel will love Israel. This he has proved. But the love of this Brother will come from without. . . . He will not be a true part of the Jewish world. His living in Israel in the midst of the Jewish community, and his sincere affection for it cannot take the place of identification that can come only from within, and which here is absent."

Although agreeing with the majority, Justice Zvi Berenson pointed out that Brother Daniel's conversion would not have kept him out of Hitler's death camps. "And now that the petitioner comes knocking at the gates of Israel, can it refuse to recognize him as a Jew?"

Yes, apparently it could. The Orthodox were pleased with the decision, but not pleased by the criterion, which had circumvented *halakha*.

In a case resolved in 1970, an Israeli naval officer, Binyamin Shalit, tried to register his children with the Interior Ministry as Jews and, in the process, to define being a Jew as a nationality. He insisted that his children not be required to register a religious identification for the Population Registry. All who live in Israel are issued identity cards, on which, while religion is not cited, "*Leom*" must be declared. *Leom* means "nation" or "ethnic group"—not country or citizenship. Under directives of the Minister of the Interior, people could not register as Jews, either by religion for the Population Registry or by ethnic group for the identity card, unless they had a Jewish mother. Shalit's wife was born a Christian. The couple were both atheists, and she did not wish to convert. Shalit therefore asked that the identity cards label his children Jews by nationality (*Leom*), but that the Population Registry leave blank the answer to the question about religion.

The Interior Ministry refused and Shalit appealed to the Israeli Supreme Court that it was not the responsibility of a registry official to decide if his children were Jewish as a matter of religion. The Supreme Court began hearings in 1968. The Israeli Orthodox, with full backing of the two chief rabbis of the country and from Diaspora Orthodoxy as well, announced that they would withdraw from the government if the strict guidelines were not upheld. The Attorney General argued that religion and nationality were one, that "a person's subjective feelings about his national or religious affiliation were irrelevant, since there were objective criteria that determined one's status as a Jew. . . . In brief, it was the religious criterion that regulated one's entry into and one's exit from the Jewish people."

Shalit argued his own case, in naval uniform. His position was that identity was a matter of personal interpretation. He drew on the case of an Arab terrorist whose mother was a Jew. The terrorist "is entitled to call himself a Jew; and I, a native of the country, and my wife who regards herself a Jewess in all respects, may not register our children as Jews?" Shalit apparently meant that his wife identified herself as a Jew, although she had not converted from her childhood religion and did not believe in God.

The court asked the government to delete the nationality ethnic group (*Leom*) question from identity cards, in hope of settling the matter without further struggle or declarations in the "Who Is a Jew?" question. The government refused. The court postponed its decision until January of 1970, when Shalit won, in a vote of 5–4.

In America, this might have been the end of it. Not so in Israel. The Orthodox refused to abide by the court's decision and threatened to leave the coalition and bring down the government. A compromise was found by Prime Minister Golda Meir and the Labour Party: The child of a non-Jewish mother would not be registered as a Jew, though non-Jews in the family of a Jewish immigrant would have the right to benefit from the Law of Return in all ways.

The Law of Return was amended: "For the purposes of this law, 'Jew' means a person who was born of a Jewish mother or has become converted to Judaism and who is not a member of another religion." Further, "The rights of a Jew under this Law . . . are also vested in a child and a grandchild of a Jew, the spouse of a Jew, the spouse of a child of a Jew, and the spouse of a grandchild of a Jew, except for a person who has been a Jew and has voluntarily changed his religion."

The population registry law was amended as well, to bring it into line with the Law of Return. Registry officials now had the right to inspect an applicant, and to reject applicants who did not have papers of authentication, or anyone who could be proven by documentation to be not Jewish. Had I come with my father to live in Israel, I would not be registered as a Jew. Though I would be an automatic citizen and could take advantage of certain monetary allowances afforded Jews for a new start in the homeland, I could not marry a Jew in Israel or be buried in a Jewish cemetery. Had I come on my own as an adult, I might be entitled to citizenship because I am, as the law says, "a child and a grandchild of a Jew." Or, depending on who was in charge, I might become a citizen by the process of naturalization, which is how anyone else might become a citizen of the state. And, of course, I would, in either case, not have the status of a Jew.

By virtue of the Brother Daniel case, a person could, of his own free will, opt *out* of Judaism. By virtue of the Shalit case, a person did not have the right to opt *in*.

Religious law prevailed. But this was Israel. The question was not really settled, because, although the Orthodox hold on personal-status laws was solidified, it was not absolute until one further question was answered: Whose conversions abroad would be acceptable in Israel for purpose of the Law of Return?

The question then, as now, was far more complicated and important than it might at first appear. On the surface, it seemed to be a matter of procedure: A conversion must include immersion in a ritual bath, called a *mikvah*, circumcision for a male, and a promise to live a Jewish life. When I was a child, Reform rabbis were indeed far more lenient, almost always foregoing the ritual bath, for example. Many mainstream Reform rabbis and courts of Jewish law *(bet din)* now insist on all the rules. The problem then is beneath the surface, but visible from the shore. For conversion is also understood to include a course of study about Judaism and Jewish history conducted by accepted teachers. Orthodox rabbis argue that because Reform is not Judaism, its rabbis are not acceptable teachers. That is why you will hear people say that the question is not "Who Is a Convert?" or "Who Is a Jew?," but "Who Is a Rabbi?" The issue is further complicated by the promise to live a Jewish life, and to accept and perform *mitzvot*. But by whose standard? If only the Orthodox may perform valid conversions, then only adherence to Orthodoxy is acceptable. Others argue that a promise to keep *mitzvot* was not a traditional requirement of conversion.

Clearly, then, when American and Israeli Orthodox demanded in May 1970 that the words "by the authorized religious body— the Chief Rabbinate of Israel" be added to the Law of Return in the portion concerning converts, it had every intention of denying all but Orthodox conversions. Further, it demanded that the words "according to *halakha*" be added as a written stipulation for conversion in the Law of Return, and the official registry law.

While these words have not been added to law, the government that is in office has essentially had control of who is accepted as a Jew in Israel. This means that when governments dependent on ultra-Orthodox parties are in power, the religionists hold sway. Both Golda Meir and Menachim Begin lost favor with American Reform when they made deals with the religious parties that might have tipped the balance permanently by changing the citizenship law itself rather than adhering to temporary, not binding, "guidelines" or "directives." Neither side, Orthodox or non-Orthodox, is happy with the "status quo," a limbo that leaves personal status in terms of religion, marriage, and divorce in the hands of the ultra-Orthodox rabbis. The Orthodox rightly feel that their power is usurped according to political winds and that binding law must be enacted. The Reform feel, also rightly, that the threat of a permanent and all-encompassing hold by the ultra-Orthodox is possible unless they are specifically written out of the law.

The political games over the issue have been intense. They have brought down politicians and governments, and thrown seemingly immovable blocks between the Diaspora and the homeland, though in a curious way they brought the Reform and Conservative movements closer. Conservative Judaism maintains *halakha*, but does not agree that the Orthodox interpretations are definitive, though, like Reform, it does see Judaism as historically developed. While in practice and principle Conservative Judaism sees itself as closer to Orthodoxy than to Reform, it has for purposes of fighting Orthodox domination created an uncomfortable alliance with the Reform movement on Israeli "Who Is a Jew?" matters. This has inclined the Orthodox to lump the two by the single term "Reform."

A case initiated in 1985 brought the issue into strikingly clear focus. An American Reform convert, Shoshana Miller, applied for Israeli citizenship under the Law of Return, asking that her identity card label her a Jew. The prevailing politics enabled the government registrars to refuse her request. She appealed to the High Court. The government, under pressure from Diaspora Jews, announced that all converts, from any form of Judaism, would be listed as Jews. The Orthodox sent out an alarm. Miller won her case in 1988, but the Interior Ministry registrar refused to accept it as a precedent, insisting that other non-Orthodox converts need not be accepted.

In 1995, the Israeli Reform movement pressed the issue by submitting a case to the Israeli Supreme Court regarding a woman who had undergone a Reform conversion in Israel. Seven individual opinions were issued by the justices, ranging from complete acceptance of her status as a Jew to complete support of the Orthodox position, which denied her Jewish status. Because Israel does not have a constitution, the Supreme Court can—and is—easily overruled by legislation in the Knesset. The court frequently does not push its issues, not wanting what power it has to be usurped by politicians. Such was the result in this case, though the court's attention did push the government to set up a series of committees to study the matter.

Late in 1996, I called the Israeli consulate in New York to inquire about making *aliyah,* about exercising a right to return to the homeland as an Israeli citizen and a Jew. I asked the young woman who answered the phone to define a Jew. She said, "If you have a Jewish mother."

I said, "My mother isn't Jewish, but my father is. I am a Jew."

She said, "No, you are not a Jew," and hung up the phone. I was dismissed by the first person I called.

In March of 1997, the religious parties submitted the conversion bill in the Knesset, hoping to put a stop to the discussion and make Orthodox control of conversion the binding law of the land. That same week, with shops closing all around me for a Jerusalem Shabbat and rocks being thrown in Me'a She'arim, I wondered where I stood with the Agudath rabbi who had agreed, with some regret, to tell me why I wasn't a Jew.

ISRAEL

2

"The law is stronger than us. Israel will not cease to be. We can be diluted, we can be watered down, we can lose a lot of blood, we can lose six million physically and six million spiritually in almost the same generation. We will not vanish. A tenth will remain, and from that tenth everything will be rebuilt."
—*Rabbi Nachman Bulman*

I ONCE SPENT a summer at a Jesuit college in Cleveland. It was 1970. I was twenty and bursting with confidence in a short red dress and high platform sandals, my hair gathered in a red ribbon down my back. Redrawing the makeup around my eyes, I encountered in the bathroom one of the nuns of an order that had been newly freed of a habit. She wore a light gray jacket and a skirt that covered her knees, and her gray hair was uncovered and cut close to her hard face. She briefly glared at me and shook her head as she left. The door swung back as a nun in full regalia entered, a mighty cross on her chest, her neck and shoulders tight in stiff starched white, yards of black draped from the crown of her head to her long heavy skirts. Her sweet old face opened into an easy huge smile, and she said, "How wonderful in red and high shoes!"

The lesson was clear. The first nun, willing or forced to forego isolation and identity, unsure of how others saw her and how she must now see herself, was threatened by another's extreme choice. The nun who had no doubts, confident of her place and pleased with the burden she freely chose, could celebrate God's creation of a human whose joy was found in another way.

I remembered these nuns on the cold Jerusalem day I put on a long dress, removed my makeup, and covered my head to prepare to meet an ultra-Orthodox rabbi at the Ohr Somayach Yeshiva near Mount Herzl. I was traveling with family these first two weeks in Israel, and my brother was furious that I should "wear a costume to please a lunatic." I said it was a sign of respect, insurance that the rabbi would not instantly dislike me, a practical, professional approach to meeting someone from another culture. The closer truth was that I knew that this rabbi, with whom I had already spoken several times by phone, would accept me as a creature different from him, but that was not what I wanted him to see. I wanted him to look at me and see his own daughter, to recognize me immediately as family, before he told me I was not a Jew.

Rabbi Nachman Bulman said this first meeting was "personal," and I saw it is a test, and as a gift. He would save the hard words for another time, divulge them only if he saw that I was able to handle them personally and professionally. We met in his simple office at the Yeshiva, and I dared not move lest a rustle muffle the old man's soft voice.

"Even though you don't have the status of a Jew, there would not be a rejection of you," he said, his old eyes cloudy as any sage's who has trained his vision inward. He told me of a folk saying, "'A Jew does not become a non-Jew, and a non-Jew does not become a Jew.' It is deeply ingrained in us."

"We believe that when the Jewish people was constituted, there was an experience which touched and penetrated the psyche of being of all the souls of our people who then lived and whoever afterward were going to live," he said.

"Maimonides, our greatest rationalist, wrote very irrationally. In one of his letters, not in his formal legal code, he wrote that all of the Jewish souls that were going to come into existence for all time would never leave our people or our village and would not become a past tense. They may be forcibly converted. They may rebel against the Jewish tradition. There could have been crusades.

There could have been rapes. There could be thousands or tens of thousands who fell out of our people. They will come back—great-grandchildren; great-great-great grandchildren. They will find their way to conversions.

"There could have been the opposite—people who, for a variety of historical and religious reasons, fell into this people. They could become converts. When we see a genuine convert, it is a turning back home.

"It's not something that can be argued. It's not something for which a brief could be presented. It's a gut instinct."

Rabbi Bulman wore Old World clothes. He was comfortable beneath his hat and inside his warm wool coat. He told me he knew "something about journalism," and it was clear he knew more about the world and its writings than I expected. He spoke of science, and of Kant and Hegel; in asides, he did his best to integrate his mysticism into the hard-edged science I could understand and accept more easily than I could accept his faith.

"Moses taught us Torah as a heritage, not an inheritance. The difference is that an inheritance one does with as one pleases. A heritage one is not master over. He passes it on or he tries to get rid of it but he can't. It's not his to decide what to do with.

"We are taught, 'There should be no other Gods to you other than me.' That further, 'He's a zealous God.' That word 'zealous' in Hebrew is only used where idolatry is spoken of. Idolatry is akin to bringing a third party in between husband and wife. These passages are figurative, of course. We don't ascribe anthropomorphisms to a God who is not physical in any way.

"The sins of the fathers are the sins of the children, the children of children, and the children of children of children. There are two lines of reasoning. One is that idolatry becomes so endemic, it becomes embodied in the person or the group, it takes some out of the Jewish people. He waits before a final judgment for up to the fourth generation. The other way is He excludes in the first generation, second, third, up to the fourth, and then at that cut-off point he no longer visits the sins of the parents on the children because they're held to be already not accountable.

"This fourth generation tells an account of four stages to which people are of the Jewish religion. They get up to a certain point where either they leave with finality . . . or, they don't leave with finality, but then they no longer take halfway courses. They don't go anymore for a third or a fourth or a half of Judaism. They leave—or return home all the way.

"The tradition was consistent, [all the way] back to Moses. It was not man-made. In certain areas it was adumbrated, expanded, flushed out by man. But in its origins and its fundamental principles, it's a product of communication between the God who made heaven and earth and . . . our people."

Rabbi Bulman offered me a cookie. We joked about age and weight. He asked me questions about my life, beliefs, and family, and I told him as gently as I could that he was hurting and even frightening me by not recognizing me as a Jew. He took a deep breath, bowed his head, collected his thoughts and continued, softly, so very softly.

"Tradition goes back to its divine origins and it goes ahead from generation to generation. In our tradition, one who is not born to a Jewish mother seems to be departing [from the Jewish people]. And one who is not born to a Jewish mother can enter [Judaism] if he or she chooses.

"The pragmatic historical record of intermarriage does not justify our bending the law. We have found that it doesn't work in the long run. We have found that those who are [halakhically] Jews, who became Jews though they were not born to Jews, are regarded as direct children to Abraham and to Sarah of Israel.

"You will need to find your way here," he told me. "Or you will find your way out. My gut instinct is, you will find your way in. Take a while. Nobody is disenfranchising you. Nobody is delegitimizing you. We're only saying, 'You'll kill us. We are not going to falsify the law.'

"As a matter of fact, we haven't even given up on the pagans either. If not for us there would still be cannibals. The pagan world needed a god with a body. So they were determined that they'll take monotheism. But they'll take it with a holy ghost and a father and a virgin and a son. They couldn't handle it any other way. But we changed the face of the world in that moment. The broken remnants of [the Jewish] people ended up dispersed all over the world. At crucial junctures, sparks from our fire changed the face of mankind. We're not going to change now, because we can't."

I felt more comfortable now. He was starting to talk to me a little less carefully, and my scarf had loosened enough that I could hear him more clearly. He hadn't used the argument my old boyfriend used when I asked him why a child of a Jewish mother was a Jew, but the child of a Jewish father wasn't. "Because," said the boyfriend, "you know who the mother is." I had prepared a spectacular answer to that one: "Now we *do* know who the father is! God taught us to read DNA!" I never got a chance to use that line because no one in Israel used that argument. Instead, they spoke as this rabbi did of a compassionate tradition. A gentile should not marry a Jew. An unmarried mother most often went back to her own people. The child was of her, and of her people, unless the child made a conscious and public declaration of Judaism, and left its mother's people to join the Jews. I had made such a decision, though in this rabbi's mind, and in the minds of many others, my declaration had not taken the right form.

By the same humanistic reasoning, a Jewish woman raped by a Roman soldier could return to her Jewish family. The child that came out of the rape was not forced out of the community because of the vicious act of its own father. For the first time in my life, conversion began to make some kind of sense. But what still made no sense were all those ultra-Orthodox men throwing rocks. I asked the rabbi why, if Israel was for all Jews, the ultra-Orthodox could justify violence to make the land theirs alone?

He maintained his humor, though there was some tension now. I had failed to understand all he had said: He was not taking the country. The country was being taken from him.

"We are a little akin to the Indians at Wounded Knee," Bulman said. "Does anybody expect those last free Indians to play by Robert's Rules of Order? They're not going to walk away from it. They are going to be violent. They are going to throw stones because they say, 'You took away a continent from us, and now you expect us to play by your rules? We're older than you so you put us on reservations?'

"There are moments when one part of our tradition has to work through a rabbinate. And the other part of our tradition has to work through the children of the last Indians, from whom the land of Israel was taken away.

"And we are to change the law so that it is amenable to the poor Reform rabbis? They are children. They play with marbles."

They are children? Of course! To him they must be! Children belittle a parent's beliefs; they rebel and dismiss a parent's understanding of life and history. If Reform rabbis are children, they may come to their senses when they grow up.

"It is not your choice to make the *halakha* bend to your personal anguish," Bulman said. ". . . I am a disciple and a child of Jews who once knew a Chasidic rabbi, generations ago, who said that if he really knew he was a real Jew, he would do a dance every morning. And he was more angel than human.

"Ach, I miss my teacher. He left a lot that was confusing, a lot that didn't end up the way he would have wanted. He ended up himself in a later generation rejected by many of the Orthodox community. But I remember him standing on his feet, five hours in a row, and delivering Talmudic discourse. And then a non-halakhic discourse on Jewish religious philosophy. Five hours. And thousands sat there with their mouths open, without being able to move or to breathe in those five hours. He and his disciples are going to be taught by those . . . children? The Torah is bigger. And it's not going to be played with."

We were finished for the day. He told me that we must meet again, and that then I should ask him all the questions I had been saving. Next time would be different, he said.

I returned to Rabbi Bulman several days later, after I had attempted to speak his truths to Reform Jews, and to the members of my family with whom I was traveling. They were angry with him—and angry with me for seeing his side, for allowing him to "spew."

At our second meeting, in the office in his home, I wanted Rabbi Bulman to respond to this. But now *he* was angry. The voice that was low and quavering before was clear and firm now. The overburdened gentle man who sought not to break my heart would now take me on my own terms, and that might mean a fight. He drew himself up in his chair and challenged me.

I said, "They say you are a fanatic."

He said, "So what?"

"They say that the Orthodox pick and choose among the commandments in their own way. That many of them do not serve in the Army and therefore . . ."

"Therefore—therefore, a non-Jew is a Jew. Right?"

"Well, yes."

"Damn them. A non-Jew is a non-Jew and a Jew is a Jew and some do not serve in the army and some do. It's garbage! It's garbage and it comes from a stubbornist mentality which they find it very hard to shake off."

I said, "Talk to me about patrilineal descent."

"Patrilineal descent is not the normative principle to define Jewish identity. It hasn't been ever since we were a people. We are bound by a law. There never was a time in the history of our people until twenty years ago when in order to bring in non-Jews in the millions, patrilineal descent was made a decisive principle.

"Reform didn't do [this] for the first two hundred years of its existence. Conservatives didn't do it. It still doesn't do it. So, ask them . . . ask them! All of a sudden patrilineal descent? The Jewish world never knew such a thing. Now, the contrary is true. Matters of family definition, family status, go after the father. A certain part of an inheritance goes with father. But national religious identity always went with mother.

"Who is splitting up the Jewish people? Who is forcing whom?" he asked. He told me that Ben-Gurion and his generation understood that if we were to remain one people, certain threads would have to be maintained so that Orthodox and non-Orthodox could still, if they wished, marry each other. It was, said Bulman, something of a trade-off. But if now the non-Orthodox "take a stand that forces us to accept their standards, then they're forcing us out of what they want to make the Jewish people. We will not vanish. They will vanish.

"It's possible for a non-Jew of whatever race—man, woman, anybody—to become a Jew. This is not a racial issue. It's not possible for a non-Jew to become a Jew, from our point of view, other than by halakhic standards. And halakhic standards don't mean due process. It means the willingness to become a Jew in Torah terms. Those who don't want to do so, let them not seek our kind of conversion. Let them do whatever they please. But let them know that they're cutting their children off from ours. This is the issue here: Shall we remain one people or not?

"This is the last thread! If they ate ham in front of an open ark on Yom Kippur—any Reform Jew, any assimilated Jew—they do not stop being Jews. But if they want us to accept conversion without halakhic conversion, and they want us to accept patrilineal descent, something which they never thought of until just a few years ago, we know exactly why. Because they were overwhelmed by such a massive torrent of intermarriage that they tried to maintain their institutionalism somehow. We should all drop dead because of that? We've been around a long time. We know what happened to every single dissident movement, every branch which cut certain connections with the Torah. They withered. They vanished. Where are the Sadducees today? In another few years, heaven forbid, where will Reform be if it continues this way? That will save anything or anybody? They must drag us with them?

"We can set up registries and marry only with our own. We don't want to do that. We want to make it possible for our children and theirs to continue to be one people. We don't want them to decide for us that we must stop being the Torah people for which our fathers lived and died for thousands of years. They're saying to us, 'You want to show you're democratic? Stop being who you are.' So they catch that we are not angels and we're selective. But there are certain things for which we die. And we don't give them up. They're trying to force us to stop existing.

"We should surrender because they have a democratic vote? That means we give up our Torah. We fold. We close the house. We're not going to close the house. If we closed it, the last ten Jews—or the last one Jew—will reopen it again. It will not be closed. We're an eternal people. We've lived through a lot more than that."

But Rabbi, I said, "you *are* closing the doors. There is no civil marriage in Israel, and no Reform or Conservative rabbi can perform legal marriages in Israel. Why must only you perform legal marriages?"

"Torah marriages. Because in this one country, Ben-Gurion understood that if he wants the religious [Orthodox] community to be part of the national consensus, then he can say to [us], 'You have to accept private violation of everything that you regard as holy. But there are a few things that we're not insisting on.'"

I asked how it was decided if someone qualified for a religious marriage.

"I have performed marriages of non-religious Jews hundreds of times!" he said.

"Then who," I asked, "is going to Cyprus to get married?"

"Those whom the law, the *halakha*, does not allow to get married," he said. Non-religious Jews may marry each other so long as they are both, by *halakha*, Jewish, which is to say they have Jewish mothers. But those who are not Jewish by halakhic standards, and Gentiles, may not marry Jews and so must leave the country to do so. Israel will accept those marriages as legal, but children of those marriages will not be accepted as Jews, unless the mother is Jewish.

I asked, "What do they have to do to prove to you that they're Jews?"

"You find out [were they in any way registered as Jews] earlier? Do you have parents? Grandparents? Like you do in any country in the world when you want to find out who's a citizen. That's how we do it with identity here, too. The question has come about because thousands have come from Russia who are just not Jews. Or the thousands who have come from American Reform. So we'll ask questions. Who's your father? Who's your grandfather? I can tell you that everybody bends backwards up to here to enable such identity to come through as enabling marriage.

"But what the *halakha* does not permit, then the Israeli rabbinate cannot permit because it's a halakhic-functioning organization.

"Everything has come apart. If everything unravels in a system, so those who are part of the unraveling want the system to go along with them. But that's the same story in every country in the world. That has nothing to do with *halakha*. That has to do with the fact that it was understood that the survival of this people—given the fact that we're not French"—he was now pounding the desk—"we're not Scandinavians, we're Jews! We're not Catholics. We're not Muslim. We're Jews! Given that fact, that we have a unique past, a unique present, a unique character, you don't cut the last threads of possible unity for the future. You want to make sure that this Torah should not live another generation? Force us. And then scream at us that we're forcing you.

"Why in hell do they have to go around saying that we don't

want to preside over marriages of non-religious Jews and the non-religious Jews can't get married here? That's tripe! That's vicious lies. Most of the marriages of this country to this day under this halakhic rabbinate are marriages of non-religious Jews. And the overwhelming majority of Israelis want that. [Only the minority] cannot get married according to Jewish law. So it has to be defined [whether] we are saying that Reform Jews are not Jews. That's not what we're saying at all. We're saying that Reform Jews are Jews [if their mothers are Jewish]. But a non-Jew can't become a Jew unless he goes the halakhic way. I'm not interested, you'll forgive me, in debating with them. I'll do that privately. But . . . I want to distinguish between your own existential dilemma and that of Jewish law.

"The issue of Jewish law has to be taken in terms of the large picture and the whole. Whatever ways are findable should be found within that system to ease your anguish. That's something entirely different than what these demagogues are arguing.

"Israeli secularists arguing this case are not arguing because they have any respect for Reform or Conservatism. You should hear how they speak about those Reform when they come back from visits [to America]. They are a lot more cynical about them than I am. A lot.

"And this Reform in America, what are they looking for here? You don't see that they see the handwriting on the wall over there? Their history is a record of so much blazing success at holding back the tide of assimilation and intermarriage? You don't see the hypocrisy in it? It's laughable if it weren't so tragic. Israeli secularism starts from a deeply, deeply prejudiced vantage point. They're not heirs to the American tradition of partial respect for religion, and partial insistence on non-establishment religion. The locals are heirs to the principle that any kind of theistic religion is a threat to mankind, is stupid, is primitive, is anti-rational. There is a profound axiology in all this.

"Could the local religious establishment counter that axiology by more intelligent discourse? It could be. And for that I would almost be desirous, not just willing, at faulting my own. But in order that there should be this kind of discourse, you and I have to ask ourselves another question. Is intelligent discourse capable of making Arab intransigence a little softer?

"Tell me, who is winning the debate for the non-affiliated in America? Is it the Black Hats [ultra-Orthodox]? Or the others? Where is there a new core and a new army of hundreds of thousands of Jews? They and their children who keep mitzvahs? Or the Reform [who make] an effort to make everything kosher. The Reform rabbinate says that patrilineal is kosher. 'That will save us! And then when the non-Jew or non-Jewess comes in, we'll just fall all over them and we'll love them to bits.'

"The law is stronger than us. Israel will not cease to be. We can be diluted, we can be watered down, we can lose a lot of blood, we can lose six million physically and six million spiritually in almost the same generation. We will not vanish. A tenth will remain, and from that tenth everything will be rebuilt.

"This pressure is not coming from Israel. This pressure is coming from the U.S. Why is it coming from there? Because all of [their] stuff is just not working. Their children [and] their grandchildren are just not Jews. So, what's being accomplished? Nothing! And how will they become Jews if the *halakha* stops being?

"Let's first admit that the whole [Reform] program over there is a fraud and is bankrupt. Let's admit that. It's bankrupt from its own perspective. You're all finished! The thing is a blatant lie.

"Who is forcing me to stop being me? You want me to drop dead as a Jew the way my fathers were? I'm not going to.

"Some of us bear in ourselves memories—conscious, unconscious—of a Jewish life, greatness, nobility, martyrdom. We are going to surrender the life of an eternal people because of an individual situation? Are we to be condemned? We're not about to let clowns play with our Torah like little bubble games. The want us to step aside! It's outrageous! It's beyond words!"

He was tired. He had kept his promise to me and I would keep my promise to him. We were to part as we came together, discussing my personal frustration, my need to be accepted.

"The question isn't do we want to lose you to the Jewish people and to the Jewish tradition. There was a cruel, cruel series of events which tore you out," he said. "There are ways for you to return. All the doors are open. The choice is yours."

3

"God never wanted it to be this way."
—*Rabbi Benjamin Segal*

IN TRYING TO EXPLAIN Judaism to children, I make the mistake of trying to make the complicated simple. Orthodoxy is a relatively easy concept, as is Reform. But Conservative, I mistakenly say, is "somewhere in between." It isn't. Its differences from the other two movements are vast. Yet so long as the Orthodox consider the Conservative movement heretical, Conservative and Reform are, after years of tension, bound together, at least politically, as I heard in the words of Rabbi Benjamin Segal. Segal, born in America, the president of the Seminary of Jewish Studies, a Conservative institution in Jerusalem, responded to what I told him about my interview with Rabbi Bulman.

"It is mind-boggling to me," Segal said. "First of all, his worldview is not from history. I can show him a book from the fourteenth century before there were Reform Jews and before there were Conservative Jews, and all the rabbis were complaining that none of the Jews put a mezuzah on the house. All the generations were fighting against things. There are millions of examples. The commentaries are full of 'This is what the law is, but we don't teach it because people won't do it anyway and it would be an embarrassment.'"

Bulman "is the Sadducee, the people who would not change. It was the Pharisees who said something as radical as, 'Torah is not just what is written in the Bible.' He is unable to change. He will disappear just like the Sadducees. There is always this sort of left

37

and right. I don't want him to be a pluralist. I don't require him ever, ever, ever to perform a marriage ceremony for someone [whose conversion I took part in]. I refused, as a Conservative rabbi, to perform a marriage for a woman who had converted Reform. But [Bulman] can't let the State of Israel not let my converts get married with me. That's all. I'm not asking him to recognize me.

"So it doesn't matter that he thinks I'm wrong. The matter is power. The matter is use of power. It's not good for him. It's not good for me. It's certainly not good for me that the Jewish people are suffering. People who could be attracted to Judaism are rejected [by him]. In his terms I would tell him, 'You are forcing people into models and forcing them away from Judaism.' It's not good for him. It's certainly not good for the Jews. And that is not the march of history. . . . At the moment, politics being what they are, a small minority that holds his opinion has been able to control legislation, but not forever.

"If he thinks he is winning, he should explain to me, for example, why more and more people in Israel do not get married by the rabbinate at all. They go to Cyprus, they live together, they go to a lawyer to make a contract, and they go to Reform and Conservative rabbis and don't get registered. There are less people being married now than there were ten years ago. And our population has grown at least fifty percent. . . .

"I mean, these [ultra-Orthodox] people are the pits. They think they have a direct line to God. They are destroying the Jewish people! They are tearing us apart for no good reason. It's going to take us thirty years to get back some of the Jews and [some of the] loyalty to Israel that they have chased away in a single year. They are being immoral toward individuals who are good, wonderful Jews who have every right to pursue their lives as Jews. They are using power and forcing other people to use power where religion should be God's will. God never wanted it to be this way. God talked about receiving the Torah. God talked about expecting the Torah. God said lines in his own Torah like, 'If you observe My laws and if you don't observe My laws,' knowing full well He doesn't want to force you. But that's your choice and you better have the ability to do it one way or another. And the [ultra-Orthodox] simply don't understand Jewish tradition, modernity or anything else.

"In theory, Conservative Jews could say, 'I welcome a law that says conversion only according to *halakha*.' We observe *halakha*. But, because the secular law of Israel determines who decides what *halakha* is, it rules out all [Conservative] converts. Another concern is: Who can function as a Jew? And here you have the question of marriage, burial, and other things. And in these cases, the rabbinate is given a monopoly. Civil marriage is mentioned every once in a while. It was mentioned about a year and a half ago publicly, and I presume still privately, as a solution for the many Russian immigrants who are not Jewish. It has never taken off. I don't know if it will or not. The Conservative movement is on record as favoring civil marriage. It's not that we don't want people to get married under a *huppa* [marriage canopy], but we feel that the only way that these things would develop is in terms of people choosing religious things rather than be forced to them.

"Right now, from all three movements, let alone outside the movements, there are different definitions of 'Who is a Jew.' The rabbi who is Orthodox may not deal with someone who thinks they are a good Conservative Jew. Similarly, a rabbi who is Conservative may not deal with someone who thinks they are a Reform Jew. And it's not just across movements, it's even within movements. I don't think we'll get together on that. Not in my lifetime. Unless the Messiah, he or she, shows up. But the question as to whether the state is involved in that definition is a critical one for Israel that will be resolved one way or another. . . . Because of the march of history, we will move through the painful process that the Church moved through. It might be beyond my lifetime. But I think that process is inevitable. . . .

"So once I have a Jewish state, I don't want religion in the state, OK? [This is] a Western principle. You shouldn't compel anybody to do what they don't want to do. Where do we [Conservative Jews] fall? Well, we probably fall to the right of that scale. . . . We will always have the menorah, which is a religious symbol of the Temple as our national emblem. I don't want to cancel out the Law of Return. But this new state hasn't worked this one out yet in a political system that's ass backwards in everything. So, I have some sympathy for the place. In the meantime, I'm in pain. I'm in pain if I see a convert who won't be accepted; I think it's wrong.

"Israel is for the Jewish people in a wider sense. I think Israel is for Jews whom I don't accept as Jewish. Israel, at the moment, has defined Jews for the purposes of immigration. I don't know that I would change that very much. There has to be some logical definition. That one was taken from the world of anti-Semitism and Nazism. It's unfortunate, but that's how they got it. There may be some better logical definition, but with all the other issues that we have, I don't think we can come to an agreement.

"What do you do when there are three definitions going: nationality, religion on the [identity] card, religion from the [government]? What is that doing to Israel and the Jewish people? You know, we bring all these people here and then say, 'You can't get married.' What a wild, stupid statement. Probably the only country in the world who could pull something like that. It's a time bomb—or a formula for change.

"This [conversion] law will probably, in a very cynical way, result in more Conservative and Reform funding and activities in Israel. Where will that go ultimately? I wouldn't be surprised if within two years we've got a computer system separate from the government computer system of 'Who is a Jew.' [It will tell us] who got married, who converted. It will be ours, it won't be theirs. . . .

"The unity of the Jewish people is going to suffer because Jews around the world are going to feel cut off. This state is supposed to be for everybody. Every time you make a bold statement that [someone] is not part of it—well, at a point the people say, the hell with it. . . . There will be a painful realignment of some money . . . to Conservative and Reform causes. In the meantime . . . there is going to be more division, more tension around the question of religion. . . . I'm not sure this is bad for the Jews. You know, growing pains aren't bad. Every child has to grow up.

"We have to fight as hard as we can. We are going to lose a lot of battles, but we're going to fight on every corner until we win our battles."

4

"Moses was an assimilated Jew."
—*Rabbi Richard G. Hirsch*

RABBI RICHARD G. HIRSCH was the only person I spoke with in Israel who saw me unquestionably as a Jew. He is an American Reform rabbi and, since he belongs to the only Jewish movement that sees me as a Jew, he would not attempt to talk me into conversion. He emigrated to Jerusalem from Cleveland in 1973. We shared background, accent, cadences, and worldview. He reminded me a bit of my father perhaps because he expressed anger much as my father did. He is the executive director of the World Union for Progressive Judaism, an organization that years ago helped shape my own Judaism at a conference it held for its Youth Section in England, at which I learned how much I had to learn about Judaism. He is also head of the World Reform Movement, and as far to his side on the theological spectrum as Bulman is to his.

"Something is becoming clearer than ever before," Hirsch told me. "Partially as a result of technology, and partially as a result of the one world," he said. "There's no such thing as borders anymore. There are no geographical borders. There are basically no ideological barriers which separate one Jew from another. We have one destiny. And because we have one destiny, and because we proclaim to the world that we are one people with one Jewish State, therefore everything that affects a Jew in one part of the world affects a Jew in another part of the world, particularly in the State of Israel. The State of Israel is the only state which was

43

ever created in the history of humankind . . . to paraphrase Lincoln, 'by, of, and for a people,' who live outside of its borders. . . . What makes Israel distinct from any other state in the world is its relationship to a people living outside of it—to world Jewry. And what makes world Jewry distinct from any other people in the world is its relationship to the land in the State of Israel. So, therefore, there are no borders, there are no boundaries.

"The State of Israel was created for the Jewish people to pre-serve the Jewish people. The Jewish people weren't created to have a state. The State was created to keep the Jewish people alive. [Theodor Herzl, founder of political Zionism] basically was an assimilated Jew. It's interesting, if one looks at history, all the revolutionary people in Jewish life were assimilated Jews. That is, Herzl was an assimilated Jew. Moses was an assimilated Jew. The Herzl revolution was that the Jewish people were in danger of disappearing. There were twin forces at work at end of the nine-teenth century. One was anti-Semitism. . . . And the second was assimilation, voluntary assimilation.

"Now, jump over a hundred years. It's exactly a hundred years since the convening of the World Zionist Congress. . . . We've demonstrated that we can keep the Jewish people alive physically, at least in the State of Israel. The state is not really in danger of extinction. But the question is, what is the character of the state? What is Jewish about the Jewish state? How is this state different from all other states? And that's why in America, and in England, they've gone from the question of Jewish survival to Jewish con-tinuity. The emphasis now is how do we stay alive spiritually and culturally? How do we keep Jewish values alive? And that's the question that affects not only life in the Diaspora, but also life in Israel. Because the reality is that there are people in Israel who are also assimilating. . . .

"Think of what's going to happen when there's peace and you've got young, Jewish entrepreneurs working in Amman and in Beirut and Cairo. . . . They're going to marry non-Jewish girls like their counterparts [in the Diaspora] have done all the time. In fact, if one takes a look at what's happening to the Israelis who leave this country . . . and who are living in Los Angeles, Chicago, New York, London, Amsterdam, there's probably a higher degree of intermarriage among those Israelis than there is among the native Jewish populations of those places. Why? Because most of them have nothing to do with the local Jewish community. . . . What's happening is that in Israel, Jewish identity is becoming nationalized, without religious roots . . . [even while] American identity is becoming religionized. . . . [One of my grandfathers] came from Russia, the other came from Hungary. When they asked them at Ellis Island, [as] they were coming into America, 'What are you?,' did they say 'Hungarian?' Did they say 'Russian?' No. They said, 'Jew.' They were standing alongside Greek, Italian, German, Frenchmen, but they said, 'Jew.' Today you ask my grandfather's great-great-grandchildren, 'What are you?,' a high percentage would not say 'Jew.' I've got one aunt, for example, who has eight grandchildren, and only one of them married a Jew, and he and his wife are assimilated and don't go to a synagogue. But if they say, 'Jew,' they mean they're on a par with Protestants and Catholics, which means that Jewish identity has been transformed from an ethnic identity, a peoplehood identity. That represents a great danger to the totality of Jewish peoplehood. Because we're not a religion. And the only thing which today keeps us from becoming a religion is our identity.

"The main factor which keeps us from becoming just a religion is our identity with the State of Israel. What is a religion? A religion is beliefs and religious practices. . . . If you ask the average Conservative or Reform Jew, 'What do you believe?' the Reform Jew might say, 'We don't necessarily have to keep kosher.' Or, 'We believe it's okay to ride on Shabbat.' In other words, they would identify themselves, not positively, but by what they don't do.

"There's been a contraction of the comprehensive character of Jewishness in the American environment. And the only factor, the primary factor which enables us to retain our Jewishness is the relationship to the State of Israel. But what if it doesn't mean anything to you anymore? You're repelled. You're alienated. You say,

'I'll be damned if they don't consider me a Jew, so what do I need them for?'

"The issue is not rights for Reform. The issue is: What is this society going to do about the many hundreds of thousands of people who are living here who aren't Jewish and who want to be Jewish? If you, for example, were to come here . . . and supposing you were to marry another Jew here. You might feel compelled to convert. The Orthodox wouldn't accept you for conversion. Last year alone, ten thousand Russian immigrants wanted to apply for conversion. The rabbinate accepted four hundred. Why did the rabbinate only accept four hundred? There have got to be a quarter of a million people here who aren't Jewish, but who would like to be Jewish. Why isn't [the rabbinate] accepting them? They include, incidentally, not only immigrants, [but] children who have been adopted by childless Israeli families. They include righteous gentiles who are living here who want to identify as Jews. Why [doesn't the Israeli rabbinate] even consider converting them? Because they will not commit themselves to live an ultra-Orthodox life.

"Now, this society can't long continue being exclusive instead of inclusive. What has been demonstrated? That you can't keep the Jewish people alive with Orthodoxy. Where do all of us come from? We all come from Orthodox backgrounds. If Orthodoxy were the panacea of the Jewish problem, you wouldn't have a Reform movement. You wouldn't have a Conservative movement. You wouldn't have secular Jews who are the majority today. Where did they all come from? They come because they've been alienated by, are repelled by, or are indifferent to, Orthodoxy. The Council of Jewish Federations put out a census that demonstrated that 52 percent of American Jews are out-marrying. The reality is it's much higher, because when two Jews marry, they establish one Jewish home. When two Jews marry non-Jews, they establish two non-Jewish homes. When two Jews marry each other, it doesn't mean that they necessarily will have established a Jewish home, like these cousins of mine. One out of eight of my cousin's children married a Jew, and they're not Jewish. Their kids won't be Jewish. Why? Because they're not giving the kids a Jewish education. So, what does that mean? It means two-thirds are not even going to establish Jewish homes.

"According to this 1990 study [from the Council of Jewish Federations], six percent of American Jews are Orthodox. Just one aspect [of Orthodox Judaism] concerns me, and that is that the majority of Jews are not going to be Orthodox. And certainly the majority are not going to be right-wing Orthodox, meaning that they reject the secular world. They live in a ghetto mentality. It means that you're so concerned about preserving the Jewish people that you don't want to let the outside world in. They don't have television. They don't serve in the army, and they don't believe in a Jewish state, and they don't sing the national anthem, and they don't observe the national independence day, and some of them don't even speak Hebrew [believing that using the holy language for everyday matters is a desecration]. Not only all that, but they don't want to let the outside world in, because they're afraid of the outside culture. Now, how many Jews are going to live that kind of a life? Secularism has been found wanting. And so the only way to keep them alive is through some kind of liberalized Judaism, whether you call it Conservative or Reform or Reconstructionist.

"If I had my way, I would merge [all three movements]. But there's no justification whatsoever in Israel for separate Conservative and Reform movements. The real struggle is for the soul of the Jewish people. And it's a struggle between ultra-Orthodoxy and modern Judaism, between the right-wing traditionalists and the modernists. It's just because of certain vested institutional interests that we're not really together. But basically we're one movement. Why? Because we believe that in order to live as Jews and to keep the Jewish people alive, you have to respond positively to modernity. You can't reject modernity. You have to learn how to adapt.

"When the State of Israel was established, Ben-Gurion wanted to have unity. How many ultra-Orthodox Jews were there? A very small percentage. But he made a deal with them. Ben-Gurion honestly thought that we had to create this new Jewish society, and that sooner or later Judaism would adapt to this new Jewish society. And [just as] you would have a new society for Jews, you would have a new Judaism for this Jewish society. But what's happened? It's worked the other way. And that's why Ben-Gurion permitted them to be exempt from the army, and why he set up a separate educational system which, in retrospect, was a terrible thing, because it divided the Jewish population. The minute a kid is born, he already is divided from the rest of the Jews because of the separate educational systems. But what Ben-Gurion aspired to didn't transpire. Instead of the Orthodox adjusting to the needs of a modern society, they have demanded that the modern society adjust to *halakha*.

"Now, you can't have modern society ruled by *halakha*. . . . Never will the ultra-Orthodox accept the equality of women. Never will they permit women to serve as witnesses in a court. Never will they permit women to entertain cases of divorce. Never will they permit women to be rabbis or to get called to the Torah. A [modern] state can't be ruled by halakhic principles.

"*Halakha* was not a product of a modern society. It was a product of a society where Jews lived a separate and separated existence. But it's impossible to adjust [*halakha*]. Therefore, in order to keep the majority of the Jews alive, you have to have a modernized, liberalized, progressive kind of Judaism. If the state only recognizes one form of Judaism because of coalition politics . . . the state becomes an instrument in the hands of the Orthodox. It won't hold up over a long period of time. And it will also antagonize the Diaspora, which is what you see happening now. The result will be that you will have a total separation, a schism, between the Jews in Israel and the Jews of the Diaspora, which is the danger here.

"It's not the issue of conversion. Conversion is one little symbolic thing. The real issue is what kind of a Jewish people do we want to have. Is it a modern people? Do we have a modern state? Do we relate to the rest of the world? Are we open? Democratic?

Or are we a state which is only composed of right-wing religious and secular [Jews]? The tragedy of Israel is that religious coercion has resulted in the rejection of Judaism. Sometimes I'll get introduced [by Israelis] as 'the non-religious rabbi,' because their definition of religion is Orthodoxy. In other words, if you're religious, you're Orthodox.

"It's going to be resolved. It may take a generation. It may take two generations. This people cannot endure half pluralistic and half monopolistic. And, unfortunately, Judaism is not held in high esteem by everybody in Israel. The status of the rabbi is much more respected in America . . . a rabbi is nothing here."

Hirsch was the first of many who told me that in recent months it had been reported that some ultra-Orthodox rabbis charge $10,000 to $15,000 for "a quickie conversion." Finger-pointing is an Israeli sport. Both sides charged that the other was corrupt. I knew enough about politics and money to believe them both, for the reason Hirsch himself gave:

"Power leads to corruption. Right? And, therefore, religion has a terrible name here.

"So, the real issue is not 'Who is a Jew?' It's 'Who is a rabbi?' But basically, it's even more than 'Who is a rabbi.' It is 'What is a Jewish state?' Or 'What is the Jewish people?' This is not a political issue. It's an ideological question: Is there only one form of Judaism? Are there different expressions of Judaism? My answer is yes. There are different forms [even] among Orthodoxy.

"We'll have to work it out. If all Jews are going to consider Israel their spiritual home, then all Jews have to feel at home in this state. The 'Who is a Jew?' issue is repellent to the Jews in the Diaspora. We're putting up a $15 million building. We're here to stay. We're not going to let anybody read us out. We're not asking the rabbinate to read us in. We're not here by privilege. We're here by right."

5

"Sometimes in the dead of night I feel that if we were not in the government and didn't have religious blocks we might do better just presenting Judaism with the beauty that it has and the persuasive powers that our people have."

—*Rabbi Emanuel Feldman*

RACHEL GOLDBERG is the daughter I didn't have, but you may have. She laughed about her name, said that when she was a student at Brandeis Rachel Goldberg and Danny Cohen were the equivalent of Jane and John Doe, so she always has to explain, "That is my real name."

She lives in a religious neighborhood in Jerusalem and goes to an Orthodox synagogue. The child of a Jewish mother and father in America, she went to a Jewish day school in Chicago and studied at a co-ed yeshiva. She spent a year on an Orthodox kibbutz in Israel. Her major at Brandeis was Jewish studies, and she studied at Pardes, an institute devoted to traditional texts. She is a searcher who by upbringing, intellectual ardor, and personal decision is a deeply committed modern Orthodox Jew. She is well-spoken, funny, polished, accomplished, and deeply Semitic in appearance: shining deep brown hair and eyes, olive skin, delicate but well-defined features, high cheekbones, and a lithe body perfected in the gym where she teaches aerobics. If she is not your daughter, she is the wife you designed for your son.

The ultra-Orthodox rabbis in Israel see her another way. She has recently married a young Orthodox man, who also is from Chicago, but her credentials were questioned, and the process soured what should have been one of the happiest times of her life. Because Goldberg's parents had been married by a Reform rabbi, her Jewishness was put to the test.

Both Goldberg and her fiancé had lived in Israel for four years when they went to the *bet din*, a Jewish court of law, to apply for permission to marry in Israel. They were required to show their parents' *ketubbah,* the Jewish marriage contract, and to bring pictures of themselves as children with their parents, and letters from rabbis who knew them to be Jewish and could testify that they had learned the laws of "family purity."

"First, you go in to the rabbi and open a file. That's when you pay 400 shekels [approximately $50]," said Goldberg. "The woman has to go in and meet the *rabbinit*, a woman who asks you when you last got your period.

The *rabbinit* does some arithmetic and determines a date on which "the marriage can take place"—seven "clean" days after a menstrual cycle has ended. "The truth is, tons of people lie," said Goldberg. These women have already planned their wedding, or they don't know precisely when they might menstruate, so they give an answer that will force the *rabbinit* to produce a wedding date of their own choosing.

A *ketubbah* is drawn up, including a date and time during which the marriage will be performed. Among other things, this tells the court when the *Yihud* (seclusion period) will take place. Goldberg explained, "Right after you break the glass you have to be together for the time it takes to cook an egg." *Yihud* is a symbolic consummation of the marriage, requiring a witness who, in modern times, is frequently a child who merely stays with the bride and groom in a secluded place for a few minutes. The ultra-Orthodox rabbis sometimes send witnesses to strangers' weddings to certify that all is carried out properly.

From there, the young couple went to another office to complete another file and answer more questions with "scores of people and everybody waiting to prove something to them," said Goldberg. "I was there in the room when a pregnant girl and a man came in. He had to swear he was the father. It's a giant bureaucracy. Here, a rabbi looks up the name of the rabbi who gave us this letter confirming that we had studied with him, but the rabbi who gave us our letter wasn't in the book. We are talking about an Orthodox rabbi in Jerusalem, and even he just wasn't good enough!

"So they sent us back to the first rabbi we had seen, who kept us sitting there in his office while he talked on the phone about purchasing a VCR. And time was running out. They are only open four hours a day. So I said, 'I don't want to support these people's children, I want my shekels back!' So we left the rabbi's office and went back down and told this woman we want our check back and she yelled about how we wasted this important rabbi's time. But we got it back. We decided we would go to the U.S. and get a civil marriage and then we would come back here and have a 'wedding' at a hotel."

The Israeli Conservative Movement estimates that 20 percent of Israeli couples are not married by the official Orthodox rabbinate. They have a legal wedding performed outside of Israel, which is then recognized in Israel. A second wedding may be performed in Israel by a Reform or Conservative rabbi. The Israeli wedding is not legal, but symbolic. Some have only a wedding performed by a Reform or Conservative rabbi in Israel, though this does not make them legally husband and wife. Some sign palimony contracts to make their partnerships legally binding. Others simply live together, have families, and take advantage of Israel's benefits to single parents.

"My husband's uncle is an Orthodox rabbi," Goldberg said. "And when he heard our plan he told us they would screw us forever, treat our children like *mamzers*. So he wrote a letter to someone he knew in Jerusalem and told us to go see that person, a 'Big Rabbi.' We went back to the first rabbi and told him about the letter and he said, 'So go upstairs to the "Big Rabbi" and get the letter.' The 'Big Rabbi' was really nice and shocked that all this was happening. At this point, I was so upset I couldn't deal with the Hebrew!" said Goldberg, who speaks the language fluently.

"If I didn't have this kind of commitment, I would absolutely leave this country," she said. "I understand there have to be some rules. I may not agree, but I understand why to them this is important and for that reason I was willing to do it. But the whole time I was thinking, 'What if I were Reform?' And I felt this even the more so because I have seen the good in the Orthodox community. But what if this was all I knew of that community?

"Well, anyway, the 'Big Rabbi' upstairs wrote, 'She is okay,' or something like that, and said I had to bring in two witnesses. The downstairs rabbi looks at the letter and the note and says, 'okay. You're okay.' And I say something about still needing two witnesses and my fiancé sort of hits me in the arm, like, 'What's the matter with you?' So I said something about how I had misunderstood and we left." They had their Orthodox wedding in Israel, but Goldberg still worries about the two witnesses she didn't get. "So maybe even now our marriage isn't okay," she said.

Willingly and lovingly living an Orthodox life in the homeland, this young bride and future mother worries that, because of her, her children will be subjected to harsh scrutiny. "That was my whole problem in New York," she said. "My friends couldn't understand why I would be a part of this Israeli life."

Six months later, Goldberg said she no longer wanted to be a part of Israeli life. At the least, she said, she needed "a break."

"I am not a 100 percent Zionist martyr," Goldberg told me on the phone from Jerusalem. "I am just not happy here and it's not because of the politics or the Arabs. It's the Israelis. I know that in America everybody is sick of everything being Politically Correct. But in Israel, people here are so abusive to anything alternative you can't even have a gay friend."

She and her husband now live in California.

My young friend Kim describes what it is to be an American: "When I was in junior high, I saw that 'In God We Trust' was printed on the money, and I went berserk. Church and state are supposed to be separate! I refused to pledge allegiance to the flag because of that line 'one nation, under God,' and the teachers said we didn't have to pledge if we didn't want to."

At eleven, then, she walked smack into the great American dichotomy and learned the deeper truth: the United States is not a land without religion; it is, at the heart of its history, the Puritan homeland, the place Christians built to worship free from persecution by fellow Christians. To ensure their own survival, they dedicated their government to religious freedom for all, a practical necessity they never suspected would entice so many Jews to the neighborhood. In the U.S., church and state are separate in really only one important regard: The state may not force a particular form of religion on its inhabitants. Citizens may practice religions that are different from those practiced by the majority. From the notion that all forms of Christianity are protected came the notion that no religion may benefit under law to a greater degree than another. Children reared in the public school system and trained in the principle of absolute freedom learn to see government and God as separate entities: Government as universal, God as personal. Where one begins, the other must end.

A citizen cannot be forced to pledge her allegiance to that government; if she was born to it, her allegiance is assumed. But just as Jewish converts are required to declare their faith, new U.S. citizens are required to take a loyalty oath. This is not required of those who, by birthright, may take the country for granted. All are equal in the eyes of the law, but "converts" to America may not lead it; it is unconstitutional for an immigrant to be president.

The United States was not founded for Rachel Goldberg's comfort and protection, but it gave her both. Israel was founded for her, but there she found no comfort or protection. In America it is expected that all sides of an issue speak to each other and seek common ground. Such is not the case in Israel. When in 1997 a broad-based commission was at last formed in Israel to attempt to break the conversion deadlock, the participants agreed to keep its proceedings secret.

"It is a different mentality here," said Rabbi Emanuel Feldman, for forty years a rabbi in Atlanta, and now the editor of *Tradition: A Journal of Orthodox Jewish Thought.*

"Everything in Israel is intensified. The United States is a much more relaxed place. Here a controversy reaches a fever pitch immediately. Everything is volcanic. It's not only the heat or the Mediterranean or the Middle East sun that drives people bananas. It could also be, and sometimes I think it's true, that this is a seat of everything spiritual in the world. Something seems to emanate from that religious or spiritual volcano that still hits us in our souls."

"Maybe there ought to be civil marriages," said Feldman, to my surprise. Though not a member of the Agudath party, he is in every way as staunchly Orthodox as Rabbi Bulman. The difference may be that he is perhaps twenty years younger, has more recently come from America, and is still in the throes of culture shock. He has no problem telling me that I am not a Jew, though.

"It's too bad because you certainly could 'pass' for a Jew . . . I'd love to bring you in because you have all the qualities to be an outstanding Jewess. It just took me a few minutes to see that. I would love to bring anybody in, but that's not how to save Judaism. You bring converts in, but meanwhile you lose your own Jews?! It makes no sense.

"It would take nothing for you to become converted. But that's not my job. I never converted anyone into Judaism in forty years as a rabbi. I would never turn anyone down who says they want to talk to me about conversion. Even those who were legitimate candidates I did not personally convert—it's a scenario which repeated itself in my life hundreds of times. Of a woman coming to me who wanted to be Jewish, primarily wanted to be Jewish because they wanted to paper-over an intermarriage and they wanted the in-laws to feel that their son was marrying a nice Jewish girl, when he was in fact marrying out of the faith . . . I use the woman as an example because in most cases it was the woman coming into Judaism, not the man.

"Jewish law requires me to ask her to meet certain standards. Right? [As], say, a Frenchman who wants to become a citizen of the United States has to meet certain standards before he can become a citizen. . . . Jewish law tells us clearly what those standards are: An acceptance without reservation of Jewish belief; belief in one God, belief in the eternity of the Jewish people.

"I've had some converts come in who were shocked to hear that they can no longer observe Christmas. They thought that being Jewish was, oh, you know, you light candles on Friday night but you can really do what you want. Your whole life has to change if you're going to be Jewish from another faith. You can't be Jewish and believe in Jesus. You can't be Jewish and believe in Mohammed. You can't be Jewish and be an atheist. You can be born a Jew and become an atheist if no one throws you out of the faith, but [you can't] come into Judaism from outside and say, 'I don't believe in God.'

"Equally as important: they would need to take upon themselves the obligation to observe and practice Judaism, which entails more than Friday night candles or having gefilte fish or having a Passover Seder. All of which (except the gefilte fish) are very important but they have to accept upon themselves observance of the Sabbath, prayer, some knowledge of Hebrew in order to be fluent, some knowledge of Jewish history: a subservience of the self to the discipline and the belief and the faith system of Israel, the Jewish people, and of the Torah. It can't be done overnight. Once they accept the beliefs, the obligation, the commitment to practice, then they have to go through a course of study to learn what it is that we believe in, to learn what it is that we practice and how we practice it.

"The third step is they have to be taken to the *mikvah* in the presence of a duly constituted, properly authorized, observing rabbi. He has to be an observant Jew, also. It is the height of hypocrisy for me as a rabbi to tell you you have to believe in A, B, C, if I myself don't believe it.

"I was a rabbi in America for forty years. No one can tell Rabbi Emanuel Feldman that the Reform and Conservative are doing it according to *halakha*! They're not doing it according to *halakha*! . . . So it's all a pretty circus. . . .

"I'm interested in trying, through Jewish law, to preserve the Jewish people. Anything that's going to attack and challenge and weaken the Jewish people, I'm going to fight. I think that the Reform approach to Jewish life weakens the Jewish people. . . . Maybe we'd be better off without religion in the government. Maybe we ought to have a separation of church and state here. I'm not convinced that what we're doing is the right thing.

"I don't think I'm unusual. I may be unusual in being honest here. My mind is open about whether we ought to have religious parties or not. We certainly gain a lot by having religious parties. We do have the Sabbath, the official day of rest, we have *kashrut* in the Army and the hospitals, we have marriage according to Jewish law, conversions according to Jewish law. . . . But sometimes I wonder if we haven't lost a great deal as well. I mean, we've certainly lost the secular public opinion. And we've gained enemies—Jewish enemies—by forcing them to abide by certain things that they don't believe in. I have confidence in Judaism as a way of life, but sometimes in the dead of night I feel that if we were not in the government and didn't have religious blocs we might do better just presenting Judaism with the beauty that it has and the persuasive powers that our people have. We would do just as well if not better. And we wouldn't make enemies along the way. "Of course," he said, by way of explaining his willingness to explore these issues, "I'm an American."

6

"It is a genocide of Judaism."
—*Rabbi Raffi Frank*

IF THE NOTION of a chief rabbi is puzzling to an American, the notion of two chief rabbis in one country is astounding. Yet Israel has two, one Ashkenazi, representing eastern European tradition, and one Sephardi, representing southern European custom. A former Chief Rabbi of Ireland, David Rosen, calls this two-rabbi chief rabbinate a "hydra-headed monster." A holdover of the British mandate, they are paid by the government—another remarkable notion—for their services as exclusive jurists over matters of marriage, divorce, and conversion. They are both, of course, ultra-Orthodox.

I called the office of Chief Rabbi Yisrael Meir Lau because, among other things, his Sephardi counterpart does not speak English, and because I, too, am Ashkenazi. I had heard that Lau was a fascinating and congenial man, charming. And I knew he had a frightful story of survival in Buchenwald. I very much wanted to meet him. His assistant, sergeant-at-arms, and interference-runner, Rabbi Raffi Frank, took my call. I told him I was writing about the "Who Is a Jew?" issue and asked for an appointment with Lau.

Frank said, "It is only one way, you know. It's sitting in the Bible. Halakhically, historically, one kind of a Jew . . . to survive as Jews. We will not participate in anything like this. It is a genocide of Judaism."

If Israel is my home, my symbolic "father" was not speaking to me.

Some weeks later, Rabbi Lau came to Columbus, Ohio ("For me," he said, "the other side of the world") for the dedication of the Columbus Torah Academy. I learned that he is a consummate storyteller—engaging, warm, dramatic. He spun his anecdotes, spoke in passing of matrilineal descent, and made his point:

"There are 160 nations' flags in front of the United Nations building in New York. In 150 of them, you will find Jews, even in North Korea. Only in two countries the Jewish population in the last ten years is increasing: Canada, and I have to say I am a little ashamed of having to say it, Germany. In the 148, the numbers are getting down and down. . . . What happened in those 148 countries for their Jewry? Since 1945, you have six million Jews in the United States. . . . The Jews in America should now be 70 million, you have only 10 percent of that today. Where are the Jews in the United States of America? Not a flood of water . . . not a flood of fire, but a flood of assimilation . . . confusion, loss of the way, being cut off from roots. So we are today in a real war for Jewish existence, for Jewish survival and Jewish immortality. We must promise that the chain will be an unbroken one."

The rabbi ended with a tale of a woman whose father, a great rabbi, was killed at the hands of the Nazis. She attempted to leave Judaism, to see her son raised as a Catholic, and was told by one of her father's students, "If you leave your child in their hands, you help them complete the 'final solution.'"

My father would have agreed with this, which is one of the reasons he worked to make me a Jew. I don't think I could have explained that to this chief rabbi of Israel.

7

"It is a horrible sickness that is going on."
—David Hartman

RABBI DAVID HARTMAN often appears to be the most disillusioned American in Jerusalem. I see him as a scientist, because he appears to believe that if he—and we—study and think hard enough and learn the innovative powers of *halakha*, we will find the formula to share a common tradition of learning. A former leader of a congregation in Canada, he emigrated to Israel from the United States in 1971. Since then he has gained the trust—and the support—of many Jews who have built him an extraordinary laboratory: The Shalom Hartman Institute, where, with its stunning libraries, offices, and technology, scholars break Judaism into its components in the hope of understanding its whole.

An Orthodox rabbi, father, husband, and a preeminent scholar of the works of Maimonides, Hartman settled in Israel with the idea of living more completely as a Jew. He found a society deeply divided by beliefs and politics. I hear a sigh between the lines of his writings, in the pauses of his spoken conversation. Within the daily rhythms of Jewish expression and custom in Israel, he found not a simpler life but a far more complicated one, where the enemies of unity are Jews.

Conservative and Reform Jews regard this Orthodox thinker highly and would see him as a conduit between them and the Orthodox community, as I believe he sees himself. But the Orthodox, particularly the ultra-Orthodox, find him troublesome and something of an agitator because, in his attempt to give

unswerving intellectual honesty to his study of *halakha* and the
modern world, he will not toe their line.

"I asked David to speak [at a] dedication of one of our synagogues," said Reform Rabbi Richard G. Hirsch of the World Reform Movement. "I said, 'David, there are two historic aspects to
the invitation I'm extending to you. One is, you're the only Orthodox rabbi we would have invited to address us. And the second is, you're the only Orthodox rabbi who would have accepted
the invitation.'"

Hartman is, indeed, one of the very few Orthodox rabbis in Israel who engage in public discussion with Conservative and Reform colleagues. In "An Open Letter to a Reform Rabbi" in
1989, he wrote,

> Israel must be a place where diverse Jewish groups, with their
> own perceptions and values, can engage in serious discussion
> . . . . Respect for religious pluralism is a vital necessity if Israel
> is to serve as the spiritual and physical home of the entire
> Jewish people. One cannot embrace Zionism and the Law of
> Return, yet delegitimize Reform and Conservative rabbis
> throughout the world. One cannot say, "All are welcome
> because we share a common destiny," yet deny them reli-
> gious freedom and dignity because of their nontraditional
> belief systems.

In response to the political "Who Is a Jew?" flare-up in 1988,
he wrote in *Conflicting Visions: Spiritual Possibilities of Modern
Israel*:

> The issue of who joins the community is fundamentally re-
> lated to what the community believes is essential for being a
> Jew in the modern world. There are many different ap-
> proaches that people have to what they believe constitutes
> Jewish identity. In asking ourselves "Who is a Jew?" we are
> beginning a process in which Jewish identity is defined by
> choice and conviction rather than the accident of birth or the
> demonic intentions of the Hitlers of history.

I believe we must always keep on the agenda the Who is a Jew? issue, but we must never resolve that question with legislation in the Knesset. Israel has engendered this concern and conflict. In so doing, it has potentially done a great service to the Jewish people. . . . Israel must be the center that invites Jews to talk, to disagree, to argue passionately for their conviction but yet to realize deeply that Israel will say "Welcome" with love and respect for all Jews who want to participate in the genuine discussion. . . .

Nine years later, as the question again flared up, Hartman's philosophy was mixed with depression. Israel, he said, had not shown "love and respect for all Jews who want to participate. They don't talk to each other."

"It is a horrible sickness that is going on . . . people are hysterical over a large rate of assimilation. They're hysterical over . . . [whether there] will be a future. Therefore, the Reform and the Conservative are the ones who are identified as leading us to assimilation. They [are seen as having] knuckled under to modernity: 'We have to reject them, do battle with them.' That is what is being said in a serious way. In other words, the Orthodox identify the Conservative and Reform as in some way saying 'yes' to a new Torah, which is modernism and secularism and liberalism. That is why you hear . . . [the Orthodox] talking about liberalism and democracy, saying, 'I have to go to old-time religion otherwise we are not going to remain.' That's what the Institute here is about: We accept the challenge of modernity."

The challenge Hartman spoke of is, for him, not breaking with Jewish law, but finding clues in *halakha* to living in the modern world. Yet, he is not a proponent of patrilineal descent.

In doing that, he said, American Reform "broke the consensus. You don't invent traditions, you see. You don't invent your people. I could understand the person who feels that they are Jewish because their father is Jewish. The question is, how did this community reflect upon this identity? Not a simple question. It said that we are going to give greater weight to the mother than we are going to give to the father because the mother had the greater influence in the child. There is a biological tie deeply throughout the mother and child, a lot deeper than the biological tie between a father and child. A father is more of an educational process. With the mother and the child it is an elemental primitive love connection. And here comes a movement that says, 'We're breaking that.' Now, that wasn't too wise. Because that breaks . . . any bridge that you have with the rest of the community.

"To what degree does the Reform movement seek to build bridges with the rest of Jewry on issues of personal status? They have not answered that question, or . . . some [other] very important questions: What are your conditions for entering? What do you demand of the convert? Do you believe conversion is necessary? The Reform movement has to ask itself to what degree did they demonstrate a desire to be part of the larger community? Are they prepared to admit certain demands? . . . Is there something that you think Jews must do which gives a content to their Jewishness? Are there any 'musts'? Are there any 'ors'? This is not a question of how you feel; this is fundamental, essential. They have spoken with great clarity on theological issues. They have spoken with great clarity on ethical issues. But they have not spoken with great clarity on ritual issues which have always characterized the Jewish people.

"I want their voice to be heard. Reform has a major contribution to make to the people who are standing on the margins of Jewishness. [It can] provide a way of entry, a way of connecting. I think [that Reform is] deeply involved in the struggle to keep the Jewish people alive. Because of that, they are my brothers. They are members of the family. Members of the family have to be accepted—and then disagreed with as members of the family.

"I don't accept the Reform approach. But I accept them as persons that I take seriously. And I have respect for the things that they have done. I think that they have restored ethics—the Jewish spiritual consciousness—in a very serious way. I think they have a very deep sense of God, which is very important.

"People who feel that they are part of the Jewish people, I take them seriously. They share the destiny of the Jews. They share the burdens of the Jews. They share the common commitment to care for Jews. They, fundamentally, are Jews. They are in the family."

Am I part of the family?
"You're part of the family."
Are my children?

"If you brought them up as Jews, they would be. Formally, from a halakhic perspective, you need to do a symbolic act of conversion. So you solve that problem. And that is not to make you Jewish. You feel you're Jewish. You know you're Jewish. You feel and you know and you are. But you need a passport. Where do you get that passport? I believe that we have to have a unified world which accepts standards upon entry, [including] all groups.

"Jewish leaders should provide a compelling understanding of Judaism which would keep people Jewish, so that the issue is not Reform and Conservative. I told people, 'Let the Orthodox become better. Let the Orthodox become stronger.' People are not going away from Judaism because of the Conservative/Reform movement[s]. On the contrary, Conservative/Reform has been an enormous barrier against the loss of the Jewish people. Look, yourself. You see.

"The issue is, how do you keep alive the tradition in a modern secular society, where the options of being Jewish are few and the options of just assimilating into the wallpaper are many? And the excitement of living a Jewish life is not felt to be very alive. You need educated leaders.

"Let the Reform movement become strong. Let the Conservative movement become strong. Let the Orthodox movement become strong. We'll see who has the power to sustain this people. We'll see what it will become. The future will tell us who will have the power to create commitment, who has the power to generate loyalty.

"Who keeps you Jewish? Did you fall in love with Moses as a dream, or are you terrified by Hitler's evil? I don't want Hitler to be the definer of Jewishness. Have we gone to such a point that we can't hear the music anymore? Listen to the music wherever you hear it. I'm not telling you where to go hear that music. If you hear what's beautiful in the Reform temple, go there. And let that music invade your soul. That's my hope."

8

"It's clear, once you think about it, and strange, that being Jewish, according to halakhic sources, has nothing to do with how you behave, and it has only to do with kinship."
— Dr. Zvi Zohar

ONE OF HARTMAN'S senior scholars, Dr. Zvi Zohar brings to his work an Israeli concept of Judaism that is fundamentally opposed to the notion that Judaism can or should be split into movements. "I personally feel that whole split into Reform and Orthodox and Conservative was a big mistake," he told me when we met at The Shalom Hartman Institute.

"People should be able to disagree without splitting. The main contribution that this makes is that people know who they don't even have to listen to. If that person is not of the right denomination, they know that it's wrong. It really precludes the possibility of real discussion. In pre-modern Judaism, wide degrees were possible without announcing that they were setting up new religious movements."

Zohar is a Jew who cannot be easily labeled. He volunteers that he was brought up Orthodox, but to him and to many Israelis, Judaism is Judaism. Period. There are a few things all Jews must do to be Jewish, but on the whole there is a wide range of valid interpretation of the law. Like Hartman and others with whom he works, he seeks common ground mapped by history, religion, sociology, and culture on which all denominations may walk. He studies questions of current concern, most recently the conversion issue, to learn what he can about what it means to be a Jew.

He is inclined to tell you what his research into the "Who Is a Jew?" issue has shown, and to dismiss any questions of personal belief—his or anybody else's—as irrelevant.

"I don't see myself in the position of telling anything to Americans—or to Israelis, for that matter. But I will happily tell you about the research that I did for several years together with my friend, Professor Avi Sagi of Bar-Ilan University. [We wrote] an intellectual history of the various positions and writings of rabbis on the laws of conversion, beginning with the late second temple down to our times. We set out to [determine] ideal conditions and necessary conditions. In other words, the ideal convert should be somebody who's going to be an ideal Jew. But, as a matter of fact, is it necessary for a person to fill that bill in order to become a convert? Along the same lines, which parts of the conversion ceremony, as described in the sources, are essential [for a conversion] to be valid according to *halakha*? And which parts, if they *did not* happen, the conversion is still valid according to *halakha*. After we did this, tracing these issues through the centuries, we then asked ourselves, 'Well, what does this indicate to us about how halakhic sources viewed or view what conversion is all about? What's happening when somebody converts?'

"What we found is that from Talmudic times onwards, there is virtual unanimity within *halakha* that, for a male, the [conversion] procedure is valid if the person was circumcised and then immersed in a body of water which has certain specificity, either a natural pool or a *mikvah*. And that this immersion took place under the auspices of a *bet din* [a Jewish court of law]. For this purpose, the *bet din* does not have to consist of rabbis. It has to consist of three people, classically three males in good standing. What 'good standing' means is an interesting question in itself, but let's leave it at that for this moment. And, at a certain time, around the twelfth century, there emerges a suggestion that there's another component which is necessary: dialogue between [the candidate for conversion] and the people who are accepting him as a convert; what they tell him and what he answers them. In the twelfth century, there emerges a claim or suggestion that there's another component which is necessary: to accept or to receive commandments. Once this suggestion emerges, then there are two, more or less, trails, as it were. One group of people continues to hold that this is not a necessary requirement, and another group of scholars who hold that this is a necessary component, but there's a wide diversity of opinion on what it means.

"So there are about six different opinions of what this means, ranging from the least—that somebody commits themselves to the procedure at the ceremony. Then there are other people who say, this means that somebody has to accept and be part of the Jewish religion, and not of a different religion. Then there are some people who say that it means that the person has to acknowledge that Jews, in general, are subject to commandments and that [the convert] knows this, and, nevertheless, wishes to become Jewish. In other words, it's a sort of informed consent, that they wouldn't be able to later on say, 'Oh, we just made a big mistake because nobody told us that Jews were expected to fulfill commandments.' In a sense, acceptance of the commandments means recognizing the commandments as a sort of fact 'out there' without committing yourself to actually following them. Other people say acceptance of commandments means that you accept that according to Jewish belief, God is going to reward those who accept commandments and punish those who don't follow them. And that, in knowledge of this, you nevertheless want to become a Jew. Once again, this doesn't necessarily mean that you are going, in all cases, to follow the commandment. But you know that you might be getting into trouble if you didn't, or that it would be a good thing for you if you did.

"Another explanation is that accepting the commandments means to follow commandments according to your own best knowledge. That would depend on what the rabbi tells you, and you sincerely commit yourself to that. At the other end of the scale we find another opinion: that it means committing yourself to actually follow a life style according to the commandments as understood by Orthodox rabbis. The first halakhic authority that we found who actually stated that this was in 1876, in eastern Europe.

"Over the course of the twentieth century, within eastern European rabbinical circles and others influenced by them, this last opinion has become more and more prevalent. So that it could be said that today, many Orthodox rabbis believe that this is the true eternal one and only meaning of the requirement that a convert accept *mitzvot*. However, many Orthodox rabbis did not, during the twentieth century, accept this view."

I asked him, "May we simplify this greatly? If you were to write a conversion law today, based on what you found. . . ?"

"First of all," he said, "why should the state make a decision on matters which are part of religion, in general, and so subject to variety within the religious halakhic tradition itself? So, it's not clear why there should be such a bill, in general. But, certainly, in fact, if the bill being written would only say that conversion in the State of Israel has to be according to *halakha*, this would still leave a very wide range of latitude for rabbis. The crux of the matter here is not that conversion has to be according to *halakha*, but that a certain person within the official Chief Rabbinate is going to be the one who will make the decision whether specific conversions are according to *halakha*. That's the real problem. Because, in Israel, as a matter of fact, all conversions done by Reform or Conservative rabbis fill the bill of being according to *halakha*, because they require circumcision for men, immersion, some require immersion in the sea or whatever. Halakhically, that's a valid body of water. And they require, also, in fact, acceptance of *mitzvot*, which certainly fits the whole range of these opinions, except the last one."

That took us back to the matter of witnesses, and who exactly fits the description of "a Jew in good standing."

"That depends, of course, who you're asking," said Zohar. "The classic move on the part of Orthodox rabbis was initiated in the United States. The most outright proponent of this was a Rabbi Mosheh Feinstein."

Feinstein, who died at the age of ninety in 1985, was president of the Union of Orthodox Rabbis and chairman of the American branch of the Agudath Israel Council of Torah Sages. His renown halakhic interpretations took into consideration scientific and medical advancements of the twentieth century, as well as issues of personal status.

Feinstein's suggestion, said Zohar, "was to make exactly plain that, by virtue of being a rabbi in a non-Orthodox movement, the person [serving as witness] totally lost any hope for 'good standing.' Rabbi Feinstein did this for two reasons, one of which may be commendable, the other of which is more highly problematic. The more highly problematic is that he wanted to totally discredit non-Orthodox varieties of Judaism. He wanted to save the American Jewish community from [certain halakhic problems]. For example, could Reform marriages [be] valid while at the same time Reform rabbis do not require a [Jewish] bill of divorce [a *get*]? I understand that Reform ruled that a civil divorce is valid also Jewishly. Under this constellation, if a Jewish woman married a Jewish man by a Reform rabbi, and they later divorced, and this woman remarried a Jewish man, her children from the second union would be considered *mamzerim* according to *halakha* because she had not had a bill of divorce from the first husband. Rabbi Feinstein was trying to avoid this by claiming that Reform marriages themselves are halakhically invalid, and therefore, there's no problem, because the child born from unmarried parents is no problem at all. Halakhically, 'illegitimate' is kosher, but *mamzerim* is not. I think he succeeded, as far as Orthodox halakhics are concerned, by indicating that Reform rabbis are simply not in good standing and therefore they can't perform a halakhically valid ceremony. Under this reading, they can't perform a valid ceremony of conversion, or anything else for which you have to be in good standing in halakhic eyes.

"I feel it probably would be more elegant to achieve this same end by a different move, by saying that it's not an issue of whether Reform rabbis and their congregants are in good standing or not, but whether the ceremony that they intend to perform is, in fact, the same ceremony which *halakha* calls *kiddushin* [sanctification]. Probably, most Reform rabbis would agree that they don't intend for this to be *kiddushin* in the strict sense because, for example, they would not be happy [with the stipulation of *kiddushin*] that a married woman who later has sex with another person is subject to stoning in the Biblical law, whereas the husband is not. So they want to carry out a Jewish form of marriage, but they would probably agree that this Jewish form of marriage, as they understand it, is only outwardly similar to the ceremony known as *kiddushin* because they don't intend it to entail all the consequences that Orthodox *halakha* intends it to entail. If halakhic Orthodox rabbis would [agree] to this evaluation of what it is the Reform rabbis are doing, they wouldn't have to invalidate the rabbis personally, but only to agree that this ceremony does not halakhically qualify as *kiddushin*, even if carried out by friendly, nice, and well-intentioned people, because it's not what these people are intending to do.

"The second stage of our research was very surprising to us. Having been brought up in Israel and in Orthodox schools and families, we were inclined to accept that the position that's now advocated as the true halakhic position was the dominant position all along. But we found the whole issue of commitment on the part of the convert to follow a religious Jewish life style was, according to the vast majority of halakhic sources, not essential. Then we asked ourselves, 'What did halakhic sources think they were doing if the notion of commitment to Jewish religion was not essential?' The question is, according to the classic Jewish position, how do we know if somebody's Jewish? And the one way we don't know about this is whether they behave Jewishly.

There's no connection absolutely between how the person behaves and whether or not they're Jewish. Never was.

"To take an extreme two cases, let's say somebody who was born in India became convinced that Judaism was the true faith, that the Torah had been revealed by God to the Jews and that it was something which people should follow because it was the divine truth. And that person began to absolutely follow the Torah and observe all of its commandments and to behave as the most devout, pious Jewish person. No single halakhic writer would ever claim that this person is now Jewish. This person was now a fine, devout, gentile who recognizes the truth of Torah. Conversely, if a woman was born to two Jewish parents and converted to Catholicism, and she found a fine Catholic husband who's not at all of Jewish descent, and she had children, those children would be unquestionably Jewish according to all halakhic sources. It's clear, once you think about it, and strange, that being Jewish, according to halakhic sources, has nothing at all to do with how you behave, and it has only to do with kinship.

"How this kinship is defined is a matter under discussion. There's a good case to be made that in Biblical times, only the father mattered. The mother didn't matter at all. In Biblical times, you find everything patrilineal. Only patrilineal. And that's why non-Jewish women married to Jewish men in Biblical times never had to convert at all, including Ruth."

Sooner or later, somebody had to mention Ruth, the non-Jew who married a Jew. When she was widowed and there was famine in the land, she chose to stay with her husband's people rather than return to the land of her birth. She said to her mother-in-law: "Whither thou goest, I will go; and where thou lodgest, I will lodge; thy people shall be my people, and thy God my God; where thou diest, will I die, and there will I be buried."

Ruth, the quintessential Jew and convert, did not undergo conversion. I might have struck oil here. Was Zohar going to say that I am a Jew?

"I'm not involved in trying to single-handedly reverse a trend," he said. "In the matter of history of culture, that's a very long time ago. For the past nineteen hundred years, it has been agreed that matrilineal descent is what determines the Jewish kinship group."

Oh, well, so much for Ruth.

"What *halakha* is saying, which generally fits the general picture which emerges from the Bible, is that Jews preceded Judaism. Jews are a group of people who trace some type of common ancestry. Ultimately, they see themselves as some kind of big family. And birth is a necessary and sufficient criterion for belonging to this group. Over and above this, once somebody belongs to this group, then this group also has a certain religion which this person is supposed to follow. But it's not vice versa; the religion doesn't have the group. The group has the religion. And the way of identifying who belongs to the group has nothing to do with the religion. And the way of identifying who should be observing this religion is totally contingent upon that person being a member of the group. So that the logical progression is from kinship to religion, and not vice versa. You can talk about somebody who is or is not Jewish, and you're not talking about how they act. The second order is that people who are Jewish should see themselves as part of the Jewish religion, and behave in accordance with that. But if they don't, they're still Jewish.

"If some person believes and follows the Jewish religion, but is not part of the Jewish kinship group, they're not Jewish. Now, I'm not saying that this is a fact of nature. Kinship is a socially or culturally constructed fact. Who is a family? What is a family? What are the boundaries of the family? This varies greatly from culture to culture, matrilineal, patrilineal. . . .

"Obviously somebody who comes from a Jewish father or from a Jewish mother has half their genes from one family who's Jewish. So, they're not more or less Jewish genetically than somebody who comes from a Jewish mother. But that's not what's at stake here. It's accepted by anthropologists that kinship is a cultural construct. And this varies from group to group. From the year zero [people] didn't think [of themselves as] a specific religion. But they certainly saw themselves as a kinship group. That the Jews were a kinship group goes way back. What apparently switched, at some point, was whether this is a patrilineal or a matrilineal kinship group. And when, exactly, it happened, it's not clear. Sometime during second temple times, apparently."

That late? I asked, still hoping to find justification for patrilineal descent in here somewhere.

"Certainly not during first temple time," he said.

"Good," I say, but I don't think he really understands, or cares, what I'm hoping to get from him. He apparently doesn't have it to give anyway.

"It wasn't an either/or position. It wasn't [that] you could be either this or that and still be Jewish. If you had a Jewish father in Biblical times, then you were Jewish. . . . This is in dispute between Judaism and Islam. According to Islam, descent is patrilineal only. According to Islam, in fact, a Moslem man can marry a non-Moslem woman who continues to be a non-Moslem and live a non-Moslem religion, as long as she agrees that their children will be brought up as Moslems and the children are Moslems by virtue of their father. So that, today, if a Jewish woman marries a Moslem man, their children are Moslem according to Islam, but Jewish according to Judaism. I don't know what the statistics are, but it certainly happens. Jewish women, over and above their inherent attractiveness, also have the advantage as far as many Moslem men are concerned that they don't require a bride price.

"To return to the issue of Jews, according to this notion, Jews could never accept [as Jewish] anybody else. Because either you were Jewish or weren't Jewish. And since Jews should only marry other Jews, nobody non-Jewish could ever become a Jew, just like, according to the Jews, nobody who was born Jewish could ever become a non-Jew. You could become a Jew who believed in

Buddha, or a Jew who believed in Jesus, but you couldn't become a non-Jew.

"According to this trail, if you weren't born Jewish . . . there is [only one] possibility [for joining the Jewish people]. And that's what the conversion ceremony is. It's a ceremony of birth. The person who converted is, according to *halakha*, considered to have no biological relationship with their original family. That's one reason why they get a new name. And, to return to the issue of kinship as culturally constructed, should a brother and sister both convert according to *halakha*, they would be able to marry each other because they now have no biological connection with each other whatsoever. This is one of the things which the rabbis said is true, but it's so shocking, that actually we won't enable people to do this. The circumcision is seen as a symbolic cutting away . . . of a physical aspect of gentiles. Circumcision, in the context of a conversion ceremony, is different from circumcision of somebody who is born Jewish. Circumcision of somebody who is born Jewish doesn't make them Jewish. They were Jewish before that. Circumcision [of a convert] is the symbolic casting off of some physical part of you that represents separating yourself from being a gentile. At this point, according to *halakha*, you're neither gentile nor Jew. Immersion is [a] rebirth into being Jewish. It's like coming out of the womb. Once this ceremony or ritual has been performed, that person is now considered once and for all Jewish to the extent that if they now should decide that it was all a big mistake and they want to go back to being a Catholic or whatever they were previously, *halakha* will consider them to be in the same category as someone born Jewish who made that decision. Just as somebody who was born Jewish cannot be anything else than a Jew, so too this person. And that's why this conversion ritual is appropriate for the understanding of Jewishness. If being Jewish is a matter of birth, then it has nothing to do with what you believe. Now, hopefully, the people who are on this 'admissions committee' won't want to accept into the Jewish kinship people who are inappropriate. Because they are part of the club forever, you might want to have certain standards as to who and why and what to admit.

"Is a Reform conversion valid according to this construction? This can be dependent on various things. First of all, it could be that the informed [convert] thinks that what they're doing is joining the Jewish religion, rather that joining the Jewish people. It could be that this person thinks that matters of ritual are basically irrelevant to Judaism. Therefore, they would have some other type of ceremony which they think was especially appropriate. Since it's not a matter of what the person sincerely does or does not feel about this, the ceremony simply would not have happened in a way that worked.

"It's like somebody saying, 'Well, I came to America. And I live here. And I really feel part of the American nation. And I celebrate the Fourth of July. And therefore, I should be able to vote in the elections.' And you say, 'Well, no. You have to be a citizen of the United States in order to vote in the elections.' 'Well, I don't see why I'm different from all the other citizens. I live here. I pay taxes.' In order to become a citizen, you have to apply to a certain department, and fill out certain forms and only then—and if they accept you—will you be a United States citizen. You say, 'Why these technicalities? The main thing is my sincerity of heart and my belief in the values of the American democracy.' Which are certainly very noble sentiments, but they wouldn't be able to get an American passport.

"All of this is a separate issue from the question of whether or not Reform rabbis . . . are in 'good standing' so that they could form this [acceptance] committee. They could be in the best possible 'standing,' but not follow these minimal procedural definitions of what this symbolic birth is, and it wouldn't work. Rabbi Mosheh Feinstein notwithstanding, it's not so simple to disqualify people who are acting in good faith. The typical [Orthodox] move is to portray Reform and Conservative as acting in bad faith, that they know that the Torah requires Orthodoxy, but they are deliberately doing something else, so this disqualifies them completely from being in good standing. But since this is a caricature of what Reform and Conservative rabbis think that they're doing . . . it's not so simple to disqualify them from good standing. In my understanding, the more crucial issue is whether this was or was not a valid ceremony in the light of Jewish culture and history.

"On the basis of all this, are [Conservative and Reform] conversion ceremonies [valid] for people who are not intending to follow an Orthodox lifestyle? What the person at the time of conversion intended is not the necessary component of a valid conversion. It's on the basis of this that many rabbinic authorities have argued in modern times that if there are people whose father was Jewish and mother wasn't, or an intermarried couple, everything should be done to facilitate their conversion without regard to how they're going to afterwards behave. Because, it's much more important to have everybody we want in the kinship group than to have everybody behave exactly as we Orthodox would like them to. There could be various degrees of behavior tolerance, diversity, but the group boundaries [are] blurred if you don't know who is or who isn't [a member]. Which is one of the reasons that intermarriage . . . was considered traditionally very problematic.

"Since Jewishness is not a matter of personal belief, but rather a matter of kinship, then it should be a simple technical matter to come in and get your papers signed."

9

"Everything is possible. That is the beauty of *halakha;* that is the whole concept. Part of the problem is that there are too many people who do not have the guts to expropriate the halakhic monopoly from the hands of these people."
                                                              —*Avraham Burg*

IT IS A MISTAKE to think that the "Who Is a Jew?" issue in Israel is about money. It is also a mistake to think that money plays no part in it. Israel is now a player in world economics in a kind of loose partnership with the U.S. More than $1 billion a year is raised in the Diaspora for Israel. Most of this goes to education, health, and resettlement of Jews from other countries.

Lately, a number of Jews, especially in the U.S., say they would prefer to give to specific causes rather than to a general fund, such as the United Jewish Appeal. UJA and the federations aligned with it are perhaps the most successful money-raising machine in the world. Jews are expected to give by virtue of *mitzvot* to help the poor and to ensure that the homeland will be a safe haven for all Jews in time of need. As "Who Is a Jew?" becomes widely asked throughout the world, more Jews are wondering why their contributions have, in some way, been used disproportionately to benefit Orthodox institutions in Israel.

Conservative and Reform Jews simply do not have much influence in a state that officially recognizes the Orthodox as chief rabbis and official decision-makers. Of a world Jewish population of approximately 13.5 million, about 4.5 million live in Israel, according to the American Jewish Committee. While only 10 percent of Israelis are ultra-Orthodox, virtually all the remainder, those whom rabbis call "secular," are in fact "Ortho-dox" when they need to be. Only 20,000 consider themselves Conservative, a mere 5,000 to 10,000 consider themselves Re-form, according to a spokesperson of the Masorti movement, as the Conservative movement is called in Israel. In 1997, there were 49 Masorti congregations, and 22 Reform in Israel.

Most Israelis cannot see the point in what appears to them to be a watered-down version of the one true religion.

"The temple they don't go to is Orthodox," said Avraham Burg, chairman of the Jewish Agency, which has an annual bud-get of a half billion dollars collected by UJA and federations in the United Sates. Burg, who also chairs the World Zionist Orga-nization, speaks to and for the Diaspora as the man who takes, and disseminates, its money.

"From my point of view, what is important is the people behind the money," he said. "It's the men and the women beyond the dollar. I'm not interested in money, I'm interested in you. The money itself is just a detour. Okay? If I want to find the money, I'll find the money some other place and I won't have you. It's a loss."

I will hear this argument many times in Israel, from a wide spectrum of people who say they would rather have $1 from many Jews than millions from a few. What they want, they say, is connection to Israel from Jews throughout the world. Each dollar is a promise, a kiss, a pledge of faith and devotion to the land and its people. It is also a token of power. He who gives most often wins. If the average Jew is to have a say in where the money goes, he must combine his dollar with others' as a show of force.

Burg does not oppose giving to specific institutions, to the Conservative and the Reform movements for building institutions in Israel, promoting tolerance and understanding through public education. But he does not intend to diminish the existing money machine in the process.

"I don't believe that in order to do something you have to negate something else. Ninety percent of my time overseas is for fundraising. I never speak about UJA, God forbid . . . I say, let's have a larger pie rather than just a larger slice."

The first thing people tell you about Burg is that he's a good guy. The second is that he is the son of a great Israeli political leader, Yoseph, who was, among other things, minister of religious affairs. Avraham, then, is the royal Orthodox son, acceptable as few are across the spectrum. Though he sends his four children to Conservative schools, known as Tali schools, he is careful never to define himself as one kind of Jew or another.

On the day after the first vote on the new conversion bill in the Knesset, I asked Burg why a surprising number of generally noisy politicians have abstained, allowing the bill to pass without having to put their names on it.

The answer, he said, "has so many layers. The first, the simple one, is a lack of leadership. The other layer is that people think, 'If I vote this or another way, what does it do to my future ?' I do not believe in leadership which is built on lack of positions. The third layer, which is the only layer which is important . . . says there are some people within the Labour Party and some other parties who are really not persuaded that alternative Judaism, which is not their understanding of what Judaism is all about, should have any rights in Israel. It's not an issue of right or left. It is an issue which divides many of the Israelis [and is] mainly based on lack of knowledge and on ignorance [about the Reform and Conservative movements]."

I told him I do not understand why Conservative and Reform are seen as a threat.

"It's a good question," he said. "I'll give you an example, but I don't want anybody to believe this is an analogy, God forbid.

It's like people were so frightened from the demon of the Palestinians, because we didn't know them. Once we knew them, all of a sudden it was a different ball game. The same with the Reform and the Conservative movements. Here is actually the issue: [You can] look at Reform as the last gateway before somebody leaves the Jewish people, or the first gateway when somebody walks in.

"It's a local problem," he said, "because the issue of 'Who Is a Jew?' in the '80s and '70s [did not occur in] the same social environment as today. Now, the Jewish people have families [in the Diaspora] who are coming from heterogeneous home regions, and not homogeneous Jewish regions. Communications, and the fact that American Jewry is going back to synagogue, and that synagogues are more important and more effective in the life for religion [means that] identity is more important to the individual than it was twenty years ago. I'm concerned—and I'm still very optimistic [about the outcome].

"I'll tell you why I'm optimistic: Israel is one of the most important pillars of identity for a common American Jew. Take Israel out of people's lives and it isn't a Jewish life, right? And therefore I hear more and more American Jews saying, 'Israel is too important to us to leave it in the hands of the Israelis only.' And I see a way for the movements to say, 'You know what? Let's change our patterns. Instead of having a kind of mutual involvement, let's invest differently in Israel.'

"The conversion problem is the problem of our country. Let's say I'm a rabbi. I have a community in Tulsa. I have 200 families. They come to me and say, 'Rabbi, what does it mean, "Our Beloved State of Israel"? Are we Jews or aren't we Jews? Will our state have us? What's going on in our homeland over there?' This is the problem."

I told him what I know of the view that assimilation will devour Judaism, because it will cause too many Jews to disappear.

"Many things disappeared," he said. "The roles of conversion have changed so much that I've got to look at a generation with so many opinions. I promise this is not the problem. The problem is the state of mind.

"Everything is possible. That is the beauty of *halakha*; that is the whole concept. Part of the problem is that there are too many people who do not have the guts to expropriate the halakhic monopoly from the hands of these people. The secular nation has surrendered the monopoly over the interpretation of our identity to a group of people which denies the right of these people to even exist spiritually. That's the problem. And part of the pressure put now by the ultra-Orthodox will create, by the end of the day, a counter-pressure. People will say, 'You know what? There is a limit.'

"If I read correctly my Israeli reality, people are looking for alternatives in the schools, universities, in courses. I see the kind of lectures I'm invited to give. [They are] not about the Bible and *halakha*. The only thing they want to talk to me about is church and state. . . . I look at the current situation and I can give you some readings. If we understand these readings, maybe it will lead to a different future because the future is not just out of the blue. It is something that is developed. There [will be] a kind of an evolution. The [political] parties will not exist the way they are. The [recent] direct election of the prime minister reduces the force of the big parties. The big parties will disappear. Once this happens, another thing will happen: the more advanced we are, the less [we will] need the religious parties to make a majority. Their power will be diminished tremendously, dramatically. And there will be a reappearance of Jewish expression on the secular side of Israel."

10

"When there is no anti-Semitism, it's much harder
to maintain your Judaism."
—*Menachem Revivi*

MENACHEM REVIVI is director general of the United Israel Office,
which dispenses money in Israel from the UJA and the Council
of Jewish Federations. It also distributes about $25 million per
year from the U. S. government earmarked for the settlement of
Soviet immigrants in Israel. Revivi's past several years have been
dominated by the settling of these immigrants, but his present is
consumed by the conversion issue and how it may affect his
clients.

"The beauty of the federation system, the beauty of the UJA is
that the old woman from New York and the old woman in Kiev
and the old woman in Jerusalem are my problem," he said. "I
can't say, 'I'll take care of her and I will not take care of the others.' That's my understanding of Jewish responsibility . . . it
means that you have to get more involved in how the money is
being spent."

It is easy, said Revivi, to raise money in an emergency, when
there is "big drama": a Holocaust; a war; 20,000 Ethiopians who
need to flee their country; the Russian Jews. . . . But Jews must
stay together now on a "normal basis," he said. They must look
for "common denominators," discuss the issues, exchange ideas,
and decide where their money will go.

"There are no shortcuts," he said. "It's a very complicated club we belong to. We believe the issue of the conversion law is just the tip of the iceberg of something much deeper and much wider. It's a question of how the Israelis define their Judaism, and how they practice it, and whether they are sensitive to what's happening to Jews outside of Israel. Americans look for meaningful expressions of their Judaism in a very creative way. Reform, Conservative, Reconstructionism, creative services—these things are meaningless to the Israelis. So if you put it all into the extremes, here we are and here you are and it's almost like talking about two different things unless we will come and say [that] each of us has something to add. We have to educate the Israelis about what it means to be a Jew.

"We know from your [American] experience that when there is no anti-Semitism, when there is no threat to the existence of Jews, it's much harder to maintain your Judaism. You have to look for the positive, you have to look for things that you have to do within yourself. No one else can do it for you.

"We are very good when it comes to Jews who are in danger [and who are] oppressed. We have to rescue Jews? We'll sacrifice everything. We have to go to Addis Ababa and load 20,000 Ethiopians in twenty-four hours and bring them over? We are great! But [if we're] talking about [whether] you care about the Jews in Cleveland and how sensitive you are to the fact that they do not feel at ease with the way we treat them, we didn't reach this point yet."

I told him I hear that life is not easy for Ethiopians and Russians in Israel. Their Judaism is questioned. They have been persecuted as Jews all their lives, and now they are told they are not Jews and that their children cannot marry Jews.

"The Ethiopians were welcomed very nicely in Israel," he said. "And the same for the Russians . . . generally speaking. A country that has social problems in the volume that we face these days, [that is] still absorbing the influx from North Africa, from

Morocco, is [still] ready to take in, in five years, almost 20 percent of its population. That's something that you would not hear
of [even] in the only superpower in the world—the United States.

"So we took them. . . . But the burden on the everyday life of
the Israelis is something you would not understand. For example,
I live in a neighborhood where there is a bus [whose route] starts
there and goes to the end of the city. And the people from the old
neighborhood in Jerusalem got used to getting on the bus on the
rush hour and it would be half empty and they'd find seats. Now
they have a major absorption center for immigrants there. When
they get on, [the older neighborhood residents] don't have a seat
anymore.

"So we have to enlarge by 20 percent the number of children
in your classroom and you as a parent say, 'I had a better education.' So we compromise. Since 1991, 700,000 Jews came here.
[That is possible] because the Law of Return doesn't go by the *halakha*. The Law of Return talks about everyone that had a Jewish
grandfather or grandmother three generations back is entitled
automatically to be a citizen of the State of Israel.

"We are opening our arms to everyone who had something to
do with Judaism," Revivi said. He is right only in the sense that
U.S. citizens are right when they say that 'America will take you
in whatever your color or creed.' We do not know or bother to
add the caveats: America will take you if we don't have too many
of your kind, if you can afford to live here, if someone will spon-
sor you. We do not bother to tell people that during World War
II this country, under Franklin D. Roosevelt, who was so popular
with American Jews, turned away thousands of Jews fleeing
Hitler, most of whom were returned to the Reich and murdered.

Israel, a democracy, will take in "anyone" who is persecuted as
a Jew. But unlike the U.S., Israel will deny you some basic rights
if you are not a certain kind of Jew.

"I was very much involved with the absorption of the Russians
on a personal level and a professional level," said Revivi. "Most
of them, especially those who came in the last waves, did not
practice anything Jewish. Some of them did not know that they

were Jews. Judaism to them was something negative. They did not have anything positive to balance it. [In Russia] because you are a Jew there are certain jobs you can't get, there are certain schools you can't get into, there are certain positions in the army you can't get. That's what it means to be a Jew for them. People reminded them they are Jews, but they did not know what does it mean to be a Jew meaningfully.

"Now, they had an opportunity the first time in their life . . . they belong to a country which is much more advanced than the country that you are in. They were given an apartment, Hebrew classes, loans, social security, health care—everything. So they came! Most of them did not come for any Jewish, Zionist motivation. They came for a good financial opportunity. We had to tell them what it means to be a Jew in a positive way. If they are halakhically Jewish or not, no one is asking until it comes to certain parts [of their lives]. If their daughter wants to marry, then the rabbinical authorities are checking who they are. That's part of the reality of Israel.

"We have reached the point now that people say, 'Let's kill the status quo.' Both sides are saying it. There is a funny coalition now between the far left and the far right Orthodox who are saying, 'Let's change the Law of Return.' There are all kinds of weird rabbis who are looking in India and China and say, 'We found the lost ten tribes. How do we know that they are Jews? Because we saw Friday one old woman light the candles. So they are Jews.' [This has] nothing to do with Judaism, but they started to work on them, prepare to convert them, and get them to settle in Israel where it's cheaper [to live] than in their territories. [If we don't have rules], our country will be an open basket for everyone who doesn't have anywhere else to go."

Revivi is sincere, but to my mind the people who had no rights because they were Jews in the Soviet Union are denied rights because they are not perceived as Jewish in Israel. Their identity cards are said to be a security precaution, but they serve other functions as well. At job interviews, for example, it is not illegal to ask a person's religion, as it is in the United States, and it is legal to deny non-Jews jobs for security reasons. Non-Jews are denied certain stipends given to Jews. And it is well known that jobs, military promotions, and housing are refused to those who pose a threat not to security, but to unity.

"You know, in this 'club' there are some expectations for membership," said Revivi. "And how do you go about it? It's really by dealing with the issues on a national level and on a personal level.

We worked very, very closely with Natan Sharansky, who is taking a lot of stuff because people got used to seeing Natan Sharansky as Anatoly Sharansky, the famous refusenik who was ready to fight the establishment in order to convey his values. Now when he has responsibility and he takes some pragmatic steps, people say, 'Hey!'"

Ah, Sharansky. If you do not recognize the first name it is because he has changed it from Anatoly to Natan. Now a member of the Knesset for the Russian immigrant party as well as Industry and Trade Minister, Sharansky managed to be out of the country rather than vote to legitimize his constituency during the conversion law vote in the Knesset. I asked Revivi to help me reach Sharansky, and he immediately called Sharansky's secretary, as I called her nearly every day for weeks. Sharansky never said no. He just managed to be away, not only from reporters who sought an explanation for his absence during the vote, but from the Jerusalem Book Fair where for some time he had been scheduled to speak.

Revivi told me that Sharansky had told him, "He's trying to put everything back under the carpet." I've heard this before, but generally the phrase is "put the genie back in the bottle," to make the issue go away and save it for another time.

"We know it's not a solution," said Revivi. "Sharansky talked to Israelis five years ago about civil burials. Because there were

[only] three types of burials: Jewish, Christian, and Muslim. But then suddenly we realized there were—no one knows exactly the number—a hundred thousand Russian Jews who are not Jewish. You know, someone who is married to a Jewish woman and he is Christian. He said, 'I have a cross in my home and I lived all my life as a Christian. I followed my wife to Israel, but I don't claim that I am a Jew. I don't want to be buried in a Christian cemetery because now I'm part of the Jewish state, and my family and my children are Jewish.' So now they introduce the civil burials. People would be able to be buried respectfully without defining themselves religiously.

"For fifty years, we kept this status quo and people got used to living with it. They say there are some areas in life that should be vague until you can open it up. And that was the genius idea of Ben-Gurion. But now everyone is trying to say, 'Let's continue to live in this ambiguity.' I hope the law will not pass. It will be very hard to change. I don't want to go through this process. On one hand, you can say it's healthy because it's forcing the Israelis to deal with the issue. But it will lead into something that will be seen in the eyes of the Israelis differently than in the eyes of the Americans. That's what my worry is. My concern is, how will we bridge the gap, get the Jewish communities to understand each other better? And this law would escalate the rift. I think the only way to bring the two communities together is to get to know each other better.

"Americans who have [visited] Israeli families say, 'We saw the wife lighting candles on Friday, and then they went shopping, and the following day they went to the beach on Shabbat, and they had a bar mitzvah for their son and on Yom Kippur they fast, and they might even go to *shul* on Yom Kippur. So you Israelis are like us [who are] Reform and Conservative.'

"Ahh, it's an insult to us! You tell us we are Conservative?! We are Jews! And if we have a bar mitzvah for our son, it will be in an Orthodox place and we can go to Orthodox synagogue in the morning and then take a taxi and go to the soccer game. It's hard for Americans to understand. The cultural gap is huge.

"My first exposure to American Jewry was when I was twenty-five, the first time I went out of the country. I went to Englewood, New Jersey. I got to know what it means to be a Jew abroad, that as a minority you have to spend energy. That is when I came to know that you [Americans] take your Judaism seriously. You have to swim against the main tide in order to stay Jewish. To be a Jew [in America] you have to ask yourself, 'Where do I send my kids to the nursery school, and where do they swim, and where do they play basketball, and what neighborhood do I go to, and where do I give my charity money?'"

I asked him about the people who now speak of giving their money directly to the organizations they believe in, rather than let Revivi and others decide to whom it should go. Some go even further, and say Israel is a wealthy country and Jewish charity money should now stay in the Diaspora to help the needy there.

"The minute they'll disconnect themselves [from Israel] they'll punish Israel because then they will be 100 percent meaningless [to us], and not relevant to Israeli life," said Revivi. "I don't believe Jews can be conditional in their love. If you are right or left or Orthodox, or Reform, you always can find something to be unhappy with. I love my son if he brings me 'A' or 'F.' I'm happier if he brings an 'A.' But I don't condition my love for him according to his performance."

A few months after I spoke with Revivi, the United Jewish Appeal committed itself to pursuing a supplemental campaign to raise $10 million for Israel's Reform movement and $10 million for its Conservative movement in Israel. "We shall embark on a Reform building campaign the likes of which have never been seen before in Israel," said President Rabbi Eric H. Yoffie of the Union of American Hebrew Congregations, the Reform organization in the U.S.

11

"'We're talking about a red-herring issue."
—*Bobby Brown*

THE SECOND OF Prime Minister Binyamin Netanyahu's wives was a convert—a non-Orthodox convert. That may be my favorite fact about him, because the Orthodox who gave him power do not accept her as a Jew. I'd have loved to have spoken to him about this, but the closest I got to him was Bobby Brown, his Diaspora Affairs Advisor, and he chased away my questions about this by saying he doesn't talk about the Prime Minister's private life. He did tell me that the Prime Minister would like to get this whole conversion business, this "Who Is a Jew?" genie, "back in the bottle," and his explanations were elaborate and philosophical. I consider him a wonderful source on the current practicalities of change in Israel: He has reason to know what is possible, and he has reason to want all sides to come as close together as possible.

"First of all," he said, "there are two issues here which blend together. One is the immediate issue of the laws dealing with immigration. The other one is the greater issue of the status of various strains of Judaism in the State of Israel.

"I'll just give you an example. We have about 200,000 non-Jews who are living in Israeli society today whose spouses [are Jewish] or who are part Jewish. Something in the neighborhood of 2,000 have come forth wanting to convert. So what do we do? We're ignoring the effects of 198,000 non-Jews in an Israeli and Jewish society, who speak Hebrew, who work in the same places, go to the army, go to schools, go to social occasions—and who

93

have intermarriage. Are we encouraging them to convert? Are we giving them the path to convert? Are we giving them a reason to convert? Or are we accepting them as they are? We're ignoring a very large social question for a very minor one that deals with people's egos and people's positions.

"Going one step further, we're not even talking about whether these Conservative and Reform converts are Jews or are not Jews! We're talking about how they're listed in the population registry. Let's say that they're listed as Reform converts. [Then] they are listed as Jews! So, we're talking about a red-herring issue because it's symbolic.

"There's an enormous amount of misunderstanding about exactly what this law covers. I think, in general, Israeli leaders don't understand the emotionalism and the sensitivity and the pain that this law would symbolize, which goes far beyond the boundaries of the law itself.

"Societal norms in America are not necessarily identical [to those] here. I'll give you an example. My daughter is an Orthodox woman, [who] serves in the army. Her job is taking kids around the country and teaching underprivileged kids—like a soldier/teacher. [While I was on a trip in America,] all of a sudden I heard that such a group was on the border in Jordan, and a Jordanian solider opened fire killing seven girls. Okay, it turns out that my daughter was supposed to be on that [trip], but . . . she went on another one by chance. When we in Israel make exceptions [about] who can go in the army and who can't, we're not only talking about feelings, we're actually making decisions that might be the difference between life and death—who dies and who lives. That's a very serious distinction to make. Yet in our society, my daughter, who is an Orthodox girl, is serving in the army; someone else who is an Orthodox girl or an Orthodox boy may not serve in the army on religious principles. Christians, Muslims [who are citizens] don't have to—or they can volunteer. Only non-Orthodox Jews have to [serve]. . . . Certain people have advantages and certain people don't. And that's tolerated within our society.

"Another example is a new immigrant who comes here from the Soviet Union, and gets certain privileges as a new immigrant [such as a special mortgage]. An Israeli who went to the army, served all his life, may not get the same privileges. So it's not an even keel. . . . It's not a question of everything is equal.

"I have a 'Geiger counter.' It's letters we get here. I've gotten about 1,500 to 2,000 letters from Conservative and Reform Jews in the States [about the conversion bill]. I've gotten about three letters from the Israelis. And it's more natural for an Israeli to write to his own government than someone from a foreign country to write to the Israeli government.

"Americans do have rights [in Israel] and Jews have rights. Over the years, [Israel has] asked the Jewish communities around the world to stand with us. They stood by us politically, economically, spiritually. And . . . that does give them a right to have a say within our society. So we have to take them into consideration. We are symbolically and historically and ideologically the sense of the Jewish people. And that gives us certain responsibilities because the world also recognizes the connection between the Jewish people and the State of Israel.

"I don't think the government has a right to decide [the conversion issue]. I don't think the court has a right to decide it. This particular issue is a societal issue. It has to be tried in the court of Israeli society. If the Conservative movement develops a large following here, that's the decision of the [Israeli] society. If the society, the average Israeli, rejects it, that's also a decision. . . . [The Knesset] should not be interpreting *halakha*. I'm not sure the Arab parties [in the Knesset] should be the ones deciding on who of the rabbis is able to do conversions in the State of Israel and who isn't.

"By the way, they talk about the 'average Israel' . . . that's a second 'Geiger counter.' The fact that one side [in the Knesset] voted heavily [for the conversion bill] and the other side had all sorts of appointments with dentists that day shows that they're worried about the effect on the electorate, the effect on the political party system. Many, many people in Israel don't know the

difference between Conservative Judaism and Satanism. They
have no idea what it is they're talking about.

"In America, it would be abhorrent for the government to
build a church. Here, when we start a new community, we have
to put in offices, and we have to put in a shopping center, and we
also put in a synagogue. We put two synagogues! One for the
Sephardi and one for the Ashkenazi. We are a Jewish state, so
there is a government involvement in religion. Even the Christian
Right in America—it would be abhorrent for them to start a
Christian Right Party! America as a society would find that abhorrent. In Israel, we have now twenty-three Knesset members
representing religious parties.

"What essentially is happening is the Conservative and Reform
movements are looking for a toehold in the State of Israel. And
there are many ways of gaining a toehold. One way is [to do]
some of the things the Conservative movement is doing—meeting
needs. So they started schools which are very well received, which
teach a certain amount of tradition which [is not taught] in secular schools. They're not really religious schools, but somewhere
in the middle. . . . The other way is to go to the courts and say
'We have certain rights' and demand them. The court of public
opinion here doesn't like the idea that a strange group they don't
know is going to court to overturn their world.

"Israel, as does any democratic country, works on the basis of
legislation. American Jews are very politically aware and very politically involved, and they use that political involvement to bring
about the kind of legislative goals that they believe are in the interest of America and Jewish people. And here nobody, nobody
has made the effort to sit down with members of the Knesset.
[This is] basic lobbying! . . . Lobbying around the world is not an
illegitimate thing!

"I'll tell you something else: Programs of religious pluralism in
Israel, in my opinion, have been ill-defined. What does religious
pluralism [mean]? It means you give money to the Conservative
movement or you give money to the Reform movement so they
can build something? If you were trying to convince a white

Southern neighborhood [in the U.S.]—I'm not making a comparison—to be tolerant, [do] you do it by moving in black people?

"Don't impose, but do create a certain amount of education. You get Israelis here who are not deeply involved in this particular crisis of probing or understand what the Conservative or Reform movement is. I'm not talking about guys who have spent time in America. Stop an Israeli on the street . . . and ask him what is the Conservative Movement? What do they believe in? What does it do? How is it different from Reform? How is Reform different from Orthodox? Have they ever heard of Reconstructionist? 'Yeah,' they say, 'they believe in Judaism without God.' The backbone of understanding is education.

"If you [look at] the history of Israel in the 1880s—a bunch of berserkos started small communities. And they were really the beginning of the modern return to the State of Israel. Fifty people in the middle of nowhere starting a community under the oppressive Turkish rule would not have appeared to be the strong foundations of the future State of Israel. But [if you] have a certain amount of belief in what you are doing, others will follow you."

In April 1997, Prime Minister Binyamin Netanyahu, Bobby Brown's boss, said of the conversion bill issue: "It is easier to resolve the problem with the Palestinians than to resolve this."

Six months later, he said that if a compromise could not be found, he would back the conversion bill.

12

"This is a battle about the legitimacy of their [American Jews'] identity, not just a battle about their children being able to find a safe haven."
—*Rabbi Einat Ramon*

JUST BACK FROM A dawn radio appearance in Tel Aviv, her long black hair flying, the circles under her dark eyes deepening, Rabbi Einat Ramon received seven phone calls in the course of our conversation, some from Israel, some from the U.S. She tended to each of them because there was no one to do it for her. She was the director of the information bureau of Masorti, the Conservative movement in Israel. That meant she was its official spokesperson. It is to this rabbi that the media, other rabbis, and the public had to turn for information on all things Conservative in Israel, and she had been deluged with calls since the conversion bill was brought before the Knesset. She carried a beeper, listed her home phone number on her business card, and traveled on a moment's notice to speak for Israel's 20,000 Masorti Jews. She had had very little sleep for days.

It was a part-time job. She would resign some months later, but would remain an effective spokesperson for the movement, though no longer its official one.

Some Israelis saw the appointment of a woman to the post as a gimmick, but once you met Ramon you understood she was the right person for the job. A sabra who spent years in the U.S. and served as a rabbi there, she is earnest, well-spoken, deeply committed. In the apartment in Jerusalem she shares with her husband, a Reform rabbi from America, I settled into a comfortable chair with a cup of tea and watched her happen.

"The situation's impossible," she said. The Russian Jews are not going to become Orthodox, "so we have to find some kind of a solution for the problem, for the benefit of the state if it wants them to remain culturally Jewish."

She spoke of a proposed compromise in which all converts who want to can immigrate to Israel and be registered as Jews on their identity cards, as the current law provides. Under the compromise, the origin of their conversion would be registered with the Interior Ministry so that the Orthodox will know "exactly whether someone is a Reform or a Conservative convert, and therefore they can't marry them. We can live with that so long as the convert won't be subject to any discrimination in the work place, in the military, in society."

I asked her about the need for identity cards listing ethnic group, telling her that in America such a thing would be seen as the first step away from democracy.

"I think as long as there are security problems, we will have identity cards," she said "It's like having a driving license in America." The difference is that the card "traces your religion, but it's really not a registration of religion. It's a registration of nationality. Citizenship of the state is not a proof of nationality. That's partly because in Judaism there is a kind of an overlap of religion and nationality, and it's very difficult to separate."

The conversation turned again to my inability to understand completely the need for demarcations of this kind. Rabbi Ramon looked for a way to explain it to me through her experience as a rabbi who traveled weekly to a small congregation in Montana. She was once asked to conduct a Yom Kippur service on a Friday night, rather than on the actual Holy Day, which that year began on Saturday night. One December, the congregation asked her not to conduct Shabbat services, and it was some time before she understood that they did not want her to see that they had decorated their homes for Christmas. She realized then, she said, that some of the directors of the congregation were not "officially" Jews.

"One day they decided that they were Jewish," she said, and their presence "influenced several decisions." Some were embarrassed about their non-Judaism, she said, and about "whether they were really Jewish at all. They traced themselves to their great-great grandmother who was Jewish, and then, when a rabbi was on the scene, they up and left the community," because with no Jewish background or education they began to feel isolated.

"The community cannot operate if there are no boundaries, and there are no definitions of who is in and who is out," she said. "When it comes to making decisions about when your rabbi comes, and about various behaviors and various customs in the community, you have to base it on some kind of Jewish lineage, Jewish education, Jewish knowledge. That Montana thing was the epitome of American unwillingness to define any boundaries of community."

However, she said, when it came to her becoming a naturalized American citizen, the process was rigorous.

"I had to say ten times that I had no connection with anything 'communist' ever in my life. I had to prove that I can provide for myself financially, and undergo all these tests [about American history and government]. . . . And all that time that I was a resident, but not a citizen, I could not vote. I enjoyed the wealth of the country; I enjoyed the work opportunities. I also had to pay taxes. Believe me, it was definitely harder to become an American citizen than it is for an American to become Jewish. Ten times harder. Because if you came from the wrong class, or the wrong race, or you have some kind of an ideological background that America objects to . . . basically, America doesn't want more citizens. That's why Israeli immigration laws, as strange as they are, are the most liberal in the world."

I asked her if I can be a citizen of Israel.

"Absolutely," she said.

Without converting?

"Yes, but they won't register you as a Jew. I had patrilineal descent children in the community. And they were raised as Jewish. I think under these circumstances, people should just do the ritual of conversion and not have to study anything. It should be a really easy conversion process for a person who has been educated as Jewish."

She spoke of the legislation that requires Diaspora Conservative and Reform converts be registered as Jews, eligible to receive all the benefits of a Jew and have all the obligations. "That's the law as it stands now," she said. "Based on that court decision, the Reform movement, and later the Conservative movement, appealed to the court so that Conservative and Reform conversions done here would be recognized." The Masorti movement filed a case on behalf of adopted non-Jewish children converted by non-Orthodox Israeli rabbis.

The court has not ordered the Interior Ministry to register them as Jews. "They have left the whole issue in a very gray area. They have not acted bravely," she told me. Brave acts in Israel are sometimes not enough, however. A 1985 ruling that cemeteries be provided for those not Jewish by *halakha*, and for non-Jewish spouses, has not been obeyed, she told me, because the Religious Affairs Ministry is controlled by an Orthodox bureaucrat. No land has been provided for such cemeteries, she said.

Adoption is an even trickier business, she said. Previously, the law required that Jews could only adopt children of Jewish mothers. Because most of the children available for adoption are not Jewish, "no one really paid attention to that kind of anomaly in the law," she said. Many of the children received Orthodox conversions, but the Orthodox became more strict in demanding that families of such children lead an Orthodox life.

"That was impossible for them," she said. "The children were left non-Jewish. But in practicality, they grew up as Jews in a Jewish society. They're not registered as Jews, and they often are subject to discrimination when they grow up. We hear here and there that they are not permitted in some courses in the military that are prestigious. This is an impossible situation."

Ramon said that her movement hoped that the plight of the children would touch Israeli hearts and that a court case on their behalf would break the conversion deadlock. Masorti performed a public conversion for twelve adopted children, who were then denied status as Jews. Masorti appealed on behalf of the five families who were willing to appeal. Two were accepted as Jews by virtue of certificates provided by the Conservative movement in the U.S. Two others, who had the same American certificates, were not. Another was provided what Ramon calls a "quickie" conversion by the Orthodox to put an end to the court cases.

"We had other cases of people studying toward conversions here. They went abroad for a few days, finished the conversion process there, and came back with conversion certificates" which, according to Israeli law, must be accepted in Israel. However, though the conversion was technically done outside Israel, the course of study had been performed in Israel and on that basis some applicants were rejected—but only some. Again, no precedent was set.

"The Orthodox would like to drop that opportunity for Israelis," said Ramon. "But the truth of the matter is, of the maybe 160 people that we convert a year, maybe three are concerned about their registration. Most of these people are patrilineal Jews, and married to Jews. . . . Symbolically, it's about the legitimacy of other movements. Practically speaking, it's about the recognition of Conservative and Reform converts in this country. The status quo is becoming nearly impossible. There is a feeling that the Orthodox cannot deal with many of the religious problems and they don't have the spiritual and intellectual tools to do that."

Netanyahu has said that Americans don't understand the issue and cannot be harmed by it. Ramon said that Netanyahu is not giving Americans enough credit, that their rabbis certainly understand that a change in the conversion law would delegitimize them. But, she said, she doesn't know to what extent mainstream American Jews "understand the harsh reality that this is a battle about the legitimacy of their identity, not just a battle about their children being able to find a safe haven."

Israelis themselves are just beginning to understand what this fight is all about, she said. "For the last two days, the radio has been talking about this endlessly. Not so much about conversion, but about the Conservative and Reform and whether there is room in this society for us or not. . . . I think that the conversion bill really brought Israeli attention to that issue."

There has not been a huge outcry in Israel on the "Who Is a Jew?" issue, she said, because "Israelis are basically apathetic to any issue that's not war and peace." Those are the only issues for which large numbers can be brought in for demonstrations and protests.

I saw this for myself when an organization called Hemdat organized a demonstration outside the Knesset in opposition to the proposed conversion law. It didn't look like much to me. But Israeli television covered the gathering as a serious outburst of public sentiment.

"We didn't publish [advance] information about the demonstration," said Zamira Segev, executive director of Hemdat. "I got a permit for fifty people. There were about 150–200 people there. We organized it in two days and a half. We didn't know till the last minute when it was going to be. If we had published it in the papers, I don't know if thousands or tens of thousands would come, but it would have been a couple of thousands, for sure."

I'm not so sure. But there were outraged people on the line, some of them Americans, some of them students. Until the demonstration, I hadn't heard of Hemdat, whose name is an acronym that in Hebrew means the Council for Freedom of Science, Religion and Culture in Israel. It was founded in 1983 by a Supreme Court Judge and an archeologist because of Orthodox opposition to archeological digs in Israel on the ground that they disturb ancient Jewish graves. Hemdat has branched out as a proponent for pluralism, by way of opposing religious coercion, and lobbies specifically against change in the Law of Return and the definition of "Who Is a Jew." The organization is sponsored by liberal organizations in Israel, including the Reform and Masorti movements. Abba Eban is chairman of the advisory board.

"I want Americans to be involved," Segev said, to have the power to "influence our government towards pluralism, toward different alternatives of Jewish life. [American Jews] should have a strong lobby here. Jews all over the world on Pesach say, 'Next year in Jerusalem!' So there is this contact between being Jewish and this land."

13

"Israel today is the only country in the free democratic world which . . . denies Jews religious freedom."
—*Rabbi Uri Regev*

WHEN "WHO IS A JEW?" is asked, Reform Jews the world over look to Rabbi Uri Regev for an answer because he is a modern Macabbee: rabbi, lawyer, sabra. Regev, who is nearly fifty years old, is the man behind the Israel Religious Action Center, the Reform organization that daily battles "Who Is a Jew?" issues in Israel. It is Regev's organization that files strategic lawsuits to encourage lawmaking or, in the case of the conversion bill, to prevent it. It is Regev who represented Reform Jewry on the Israeli committee that wrestled with a compromise to the conversion bill. And it was Regev to whom I turned when I set out on this journey, and Regev to whom I returned at journey's end. Both meetings took place in the U.S., to which he is a frequent visitor. Our first meeting was in New York, five months before the conversion bill was read in the Knesset. I left that conversation with lists of names of people to interview and lists of books. That was before even Regev knew that his issue was about to take the Jewish world by the throat.

Shortly after I arrived in Israel, Regev left for the U.S. to explain the conversion bill to American Jews. A year later I met with him again, at the Union of American Hebrew Congregations' Biennial Convention in Dallas, where he was an honored speaker, a hero in the halls, and a modest celebrity. Over coffee and danish too early in the morning, he measured the past year, speaking patiently into my tape recorder as he graciously

accepted the handshakes and kisses of many who stopped by the
table to greet him. Before I met him, he had been described to me
as a man of great appeal; and, when a woman in her sixties
caught my eye as I was speaking with him, she put her hand over
her heart and motioned to him in exaggerated longing—a girl-to-
girl signal as much as a Jew-to-Jew one. The Orthodox Jews in Israel see him as a scourge to be reckoned with, but I have yet to
meet an acquaintance of his—man, woman, rabbi, or reporter—
who doesn't say he's "a terrific guy." And I suppose he could be
terrific to me—if he would say I am a Jew. I hope someday he
will.

We began speaking about his work on the Neeman Commission, which had recently postponed making recommendations for
a compromise to the conversion bill to the Israeli government,
and thus stalled the bill—and more of Regev's lawsuits—a while
longer. The commission was run by Israeli Finance Minister
Yaakov Neeman in a notable, unique, public attempt to bring Orthodox, Conservative, and Reform Jews to the table to seek a
compromise. While the actual proceedings of the committee had
not been made public, newspapers had carried stories about the
real (and symbolic) participation of the various groups—and
about the Chief Rabbinate's unwillingness to participate openly.
Neeman himself was said to be a well-meaning man in a singular
position. He had no political base and no constituents to please.
A successful tax and corporate lawyer, he was appointed to the
Ministry when the previous finance minister resigned. While Neeman had been vociferously attacked by the far left and the far
right for his various stands on such issues as the Orthodox being
required to serve in the Israeli army, he was widely seen as a serious person, perhaps the one man in Israel who had nothing personal to gain or to lose however the "Who Is a Jew?" issue was
decided.

Neeman stated publicly that his hope was for a "uniform standard" of conversion, marriage, and divorce that all denominations could agree on. At the time, it had not been made public that
Neeman's further hope was for mass conversion of the Russian

immigrants, a notion that would apparently never be acceptable to the Orthodox, and so was likely to scuttle the entire compromise process.

Despite all this, Regev spoke of the committee with some hope. "There is a chance that we will sometime come together. I think the more concrete questions that I'm battling with are: What kind of an accommodation can there be that would enable us to come together; and, what will it take to get there? Not having a crystal ball, I have certain insights based on my experience. But I realize that they may have no bearing in reality. And that the natural and political turn of things may be very different.

"One thing is clear to me. We are facing an unbridgeable gap in terms of our interpretations of the Jewish tradition. . . . I have a difficult time seeing . . . some overarching interpretation that will bring it all under one roof that will be harmonious and acceptable by all. If that is the initial premise, then the question is: What can be done?

"I compare Israel with the United States. And I say that with all the problems of Judaism in an open society and assimilation, and everything else that we know is plaguing the Jewish people and Judaism in places like the United States, I prefer the American model. . . . I'm not talking about separation of church and state. I'm not talking about removing Judaism from the State of Israel. I'm not talking about preventing teaching of Bible in state schools. I am talking about introducing the overriding principle that was introduced in the Declaration of Independence, namely, freedom of religion and conscience. And it's not identical to separation of church and state.

"Freedom of religion and conscience, in my book, means *halakha* will not be imposed by the state. [A] Judaism that will take into consideration many additional aspects than the current status quo . . . could, in my view, enhance both Judaism in the State of Israel and democracy in the State of Israel. Because both Judaism and democracy, in my view, are seriously hindered under the current model of this unholy alliance of religion and state.

"There are many European societies where there is no separation of church and state and there is perfect religious freedom; or close to perfect religious freedom. As a matter of fact, in England, for instance, where there is established religion, the Anglican church suffers most by the existence of this established religion, in the sense that it has some token symbols of supremacy. But politicians [in England] are involved with electing officials of the church, which limits the freedom of the church, not the freedom of the public in England. So the different Jewish denominations have the ability to act freely, even though there is an established religion, and England is a Christian state.

"In the U.S., you have a wall of separation, but you have Congressional sessions starting with religious worship. You have a wall of separation, but the coins bear God's name. That is not the case in Israel. And I dare say that, if it was suggested in Israel, there would be quite a public uproar against it. So I'm not interested in the slogans. I'm interested in the essence. And the essence is that Israel is a Jewish state through a number of symbolic and material manifestations, such as the Law of Return, such as the day of rest being Shabbat, such as the official holidays being the Jewish holidays, such as Torah being taught in schools. I would not suggest that we introduce the French system in which all citizens have to marry civilly, and, if they want to undergo a religious ceremony, they do it voluntarily after the civil marriage. But in Israel, clearly, if one wishes to be married religiously, the state should be expected to recognize that. On the other hand, I don't think that Shabbat as the day of rest should be imposed in keeping with the Orthodox halakhic criterion. And I don't think that [closing] public transportation on Shabbat should be maintained in the form that it is now. It does not enhance Shabbat. It only denies people of lower economic abilities from exercising their freedom of movement and freedom of transport. Everyone can drive on Shabbat provided he has the money for it. That is not the criterion for observance of Shabbat. I would not like to see Shabbat turn into any other day of the week. On the other hand, I think it's clear, now more than ever before, that Israelis do want to have recreational activities available to them on Shabbat, such as cinemas and restaurants.

"So what we are talking about is striking a new balance in which *halakha* will not govern the state, in which the individual will be able to enjoy freedom of religion and freedom from religion. I fully endorse not only the right of Reform Jews to be able to pursue our religious faith and practices freely, but the right of secular Jews to be freed from religious coercion. I see civil marriage and divorce introduced side-by-side with the different streams of Judaism.

"What will the Orthodox say to this? Of course, they don't want it. They oppose it vehemently. And it isn't because they take such strong theological exception to us. I think much of the angst is perpetrated because all of a sudden we are perceived, more than ever before, as heralds of change and initiators of change. And the Orthodox establishment, I think, realizes that if they do not find an effective way of reversing the tide, their control is about to end. It's a gradual process, but the writing is on the wall, as far as they're concerned. The majority of the public now more vocally opposes the euphemistically labeled 'status quo.' So they're going to oppose it. That's clear. But if freedom of religion and conscience is implemented in Israel, can [the Orthodox] live with it? Of course they can live with it. Their threats of splitting the Jewish people are but empty words. It's a myth they're spreading in order to try and scare people of change. On the contrary, in many ways, I think that they will find it easier. And some insightful individuals within the Orthodox community realize that. They'll find it easier because the problem that's considered to be most serious in the Orthodox community is the problem, from an Orthodox perspective, of illegitimacy. That's what they wave when they talk about splitting the Jewish people: People won't be able to marry each other.

"Orthodoxy cannot provide solutions to a whole series of categories, whether it's divorces, whether it's Jews by choice, whether it's Russians who are not halakhically Jewish. And because they cannot provide those solutions, and because those solutions are becoming more and more expected, there is pressure building up from the Orthodox rabbinate and a sense of growing dissatisfaction, disenchantment, irrelevance. . . .

"There are ample halakhic grounds to view a marriage celebrated by a Reform rabbi or a civil marriage to be null and void. Symbolically, that may offend us. So what? The children are then not *mamzerim*. So it is by introducing the legal alternatives and civil alternatives that you resolve problems of personal status in Israel rather than exasperating it. More and more within the Orthodox community realize this. Most of them are afraid to speak up. What I'm saying is, it's time that they talk the truth and for politicians to talk the truth, analyze the options seriously.

"If we continue insisting on maintaining Orthodox control of Jewish life, over conversions and over marriages, we are inviting growing crises in a number of areas. Russians . . . study in the same schools [as other Israelis]. They live in the same buildings. They attend the same universities. They share much of the same culture. That will breed social associations and marriages. He who does not open the door for the Russians into the Jewish people and open up alternative options for marriage is bound, ironically, to promote intermarriages. . . .

"The model that I have in mind is, for instance, the peace process—to the extent that it made headway, it was, to a great degree, following external intervention and pressure. It's painful to realize that one needs external intervention and increased pain in order to be able to bring light to people's minds and point them in the direction of peace. . . . The U.S. is the only superpower in the world with a very special relationship with Israel. I think that there are ample external voices of reason that can join hands with like-minded Israelis . . . who feel helpless, victimized, by a political system which has given the Orthodox political establishment power way beyond its proportion in the population, and against the will of most in Israel.

"Looking honestly at the facts, it brings us to the sad realization that Israel today is the only country in the free democratic world which as yet denies Jews religious freedom.

"But please understand, passing of the bill . . . is not going to be the darkest day in my life. It will be a temporary setback which will be a jumping pole for progress."

14

"You have . . . years of blacks and whites in the United States. And you haven't yet settled down. So why do you demand all kinds of things for us in no time?"
—*Theodor Kolleck*

NATAN SHARANSKY did not show up at the Jerusalem International Book Fair, but Teddy Kolleck did. Not in his place, but to promote a book of photos in which his own big face figures prominently.

Kolleck is not merely a former mayor of Jerusalem. Nothing about him is "mere." Whatever Jerusalem might have been thousands of years ago, it is today Kolleck's. It is not quite cosmopolitan, and it is not quite a village, either. It is very nearly suburban in feel because in the strictest sense of the word, most of Jerusalem is in the suburbs beyond the Old City, if you can imagine a suburb all of golden stone, with the great Biblical sites at its core and the Judean Mountains at its periphery. Jerusalem is, in some ways, a backwater to Tel Aviv, just as Washington is a backwater to New York. And for the same reason. It is filled with politicians and lawyers and rabbis, or lawyers who are rabbis, or rabbis who are lawyers, or pols who are rabbis who are lawyers. And if that is an overstatement, I remind you of Golda Meir's declaration that there was one president of the United States, but she was the leader of a country of presidents.

Unlike Washington, Jerusalem as the seat of government remains something of a controversy. Technically, part of it is one of the territories reclaimed by the Israelis in 1967, including the Old City and its Western Wall. The U.S. does not maintain its embassy there, but in Tel Aviv, in an almost laughable attempt to appear neutral to the Arabs, a fact that accomplishes nothing more than a severe inconvenience.

Like Washington or Cleveland or Toledo or Sandusky or Scarsdale, the young people of Jerusalem find it dull, and live for the day they can light out for New York or Tel Aviv. And, like the expatriates of Sandusky and Scarsdale, they spend the rest of their lives trying to get back in.

Kolleck's Jerusalem is filled with flowers, art, plazas, piazzas, and plaques. A patch of land the size of a parking space between a street and a dumpster might be labeled, for example, "The Henry and Sylvia Greenblatt Culture Garden," because the "Greenblatts" paid for the eleven tulips, two evergreens, and bronze Star of David within its stone borders. The plaque will further tell us that the "Greenblatts" hailed from San Diego when they made their donation in 1969. But I have to hand it to them: that little patch is pretty and, because I am a homeowner, I know that those garden-tchotchkes are costly. And I have to hand it to Teddy: Jerusalem contains monumental architecture and homes that look as if they were built thousands of years ago, yet only some of them really were.

Teddy himself was built thousands of years ago, and this is not a comment on his age, eighty-six, but on his character. The man is made of golden Jerusalem stone, chiseled by two thousand desert winters and two thousand desert summers into a great, round, rolling, rock mountain. He came to Palestine from Vienna in 1934. Before he was Jerusalem's mayor, he worked for the Jewish Agency and for the Haganah (the secret armed force of Jews during the British mandate of Palestine), and was Israel's Minister in Washington from 1950 to 1952, after which he was director-general of the Prime Minister's Office.

Behind his great desk at the Jerusalem Foundation, to which he retreated when he was finally defeated, but only politically, there was no sign of the wheelchair and cane that had supported him at the Book Fair. There was, however, a lit cigar as big as a leg of lamb at the center of his face. It was some three weeks after he had recovered from pneumonia. I couldn't help myself. I laughed.

"I won't tell anyone you're smoking," I said.

"Go ahead," he grumbled. "Tell everybody."

The man is gruff, but there is a great good humor in those black eyes.

Or maybe I saw the humor only because I had met his wife, who looked at him with the eyes of a young lover. He offered me a cigar and gave me a hard time.

I asked him about the "Who Is a Jew?" strife in Israel today.

"You just have no patience," he said, pulling a luxurious drag and coughing wetly. "So it will take a hundred years before this will settle down. So what? Why should you find a solution immediately? Take Berlin. You have Christians on both sides. German-speaking on both sides. Plenty of money. They are divided for a short while and can't find a peaceful solution. Here [in Israel] you have Jews from 140 cultural backgrounds, so what can you expect?

"You have . . . years of blacks and whites in the United States. And you haven't yet settled down. So why do you demand all kinds of things for us in no time?"

I asked, "Is Israel supposed to be a place for Jews who aren't Orthodox?"

"Oh, absolutely. I came to a liberal country. I want to live in a liberal country. My children want to live in a liberal country. My children ask me all these same questions."

I told him about the ultra-Orthodox Jews who will not talk to me about this issue. They say I should look in the Bible for my answers.

"So what?" he said. "Speak to several of the Christians in the southern United States and you'll find different expressions for a similar view. We have been waiting for this for two thousand years, so what if it takes a hundred years? You have the advantage of a constitution. We don't have that."

I asked him, "In 1997, is Israel where you thought it would be?"

"I thought it would be much worse," he said. "It's better than I expected. I thought for a generation or two it would be an absolutely impossible situation. But we live quite comfortably here. So you have arguments between Orthodox Jews and Reform Jews and Conservative Jews, but you can be an Orthodox Jew, you can be a Reform Jew, you can be a Conservative Jew, you can be an atheist if you like. It's a free country.

"If you are [all] Jews you learn how to live together and something will come of it. So the world is more complicated than you make it. You want it all very simple. . . . You can't do this by judge and by negotiations. People have to develop a real life. They gave the state a year, they gave the state two years, and now it's fifty years and the state still exists. We went through all kinds of wars, all kinds of difficulties to reeducate the beginning of a culture. I'm convinced it is here to stay."

We talk a little longer about the beginnings of the modern state.

"At the time," he said, "it was absolutely free for Jews to come. If, at that time, a million Jews would have come, the whole history would have been different."

He waves off five more questions, agrees to talk a little about why he and the founders did not write a constitution, and he insists it "was a very liberal decision" because they did not know what the millions who would follow would need. I ask him if it would have been easier if they'd done it, though, gone ahead and made the rules.

"Much easier," he said. "but we weren't prophets. And we did enough."

Fourteen days later, however, Kolleck was no longer sanguine. He wrote to the *New York Times:*

> I am a devoted patriot who does not support the usual general criticism of Israel. However, the situation is such that I cannot remain silent. . . .
>
> I find bitter irony in the fact that it is the ultra-religious communities, who for the greater part of this century fought Zionism bitterly, viewing it as a heresy, who are now trying to shape Israel's civilization.
>
> The founding fathers . . . did not envision this danger. They desired or indeed thought it possible to create a Jewish state in which freedom and civil liberties would not be menaced by any form of dictatorship, least of all a religious one.
>
> But today we see a different reality . . . the recent decision of the Knesset to deny the right of Conservative and Reform rabbis . . . to perform valid conversions. . . . This goes against everything for which the founders of Israel struggled. . . .

15

"I don't want Israel to become another ghetto, something where all the Jews would be here behind a fence and that's it. That's not what I want. One day this country will be a free, ultra-liberal country. That would be so good!"
—*Eli Pelid*

I HEARD A LOT ABOUT "the average Israeli" when I was in Israel, but I never met such a person. Is a cab driver who fought four wars "average"? Is a merchant who wonders when his business will be bombed "average"? Is the down-on-her-luck street woman who asked me to give her a pre-paid phone card "average"? Is the professor in Jerusalem "average"? Or is his father, the concentration camp survivor? Or is his son, the eighteen-year-old machine-gunner?

Is tour guide Eli Pelid "average"? After thirty years in the army, much of it in a special underwater operations unit, Pelid is at sixty-two leading another kind of army. As chief guide for Isram, he marches tourists five and a half days a week through his Israel, with precision, speed, and two quick breaks for fancy cafeteria rations, through the cities and desert, over mountains and past mine fields and Palestinian camps. Pausing at antiquities and gravesites and gunsites, he eulogizes the two thousand years of dead on whose debris the country is built. Do not be late. Do not speak while he is speaking. Do not ask stupid questions. If he tells you something, it is because he has studied it and knows it is true: This is the precise spot, the precise corner of a long-destroyed room at Masada, where two thousand years ago great Jewish heroes drew lots. They killed each other rather than be taken by the enemy.

And this is the precise spot where Jesus did *not* walk on the water. And this is the exact piece of earth in which he could *not* possibly have been buried.

For eighteen years, Pelid has marshaled, bullied, protected, equipped his trainees to withstand the onslaught of those who would destroy them and their faith in the land. Pelid is not "average," but he is the quintessential *sabra*, as native Israelis are called to signal that, like the cactus fruit that bears that same name, they are tough and prickly on the outside, soft on the inside. In two weeks on the road with Pelid, I see no softness, though I can see some tenderness.

On his father's side, he is the tenth generation to live on the land. On his father's side, he is also Sephardic, meaning that his family roots are in medieval Spain—the oldest, wealthiest, most influential of Diaspora Jews for hundreds of years. His mother is Ashkenazi, which means he is also of European descent.

On Pelid's leathery face are traces of the land his family fought and died for and held for generations. At the Ein Gedi spa at the Dead Sea—"I haven't been in that water for twenty years," he said, and I got the feeling the brine was no match for him—he would, finally, talk to me about "Who Is a Jew?," but only for a few minutes. This was not his favorite spot and he would not linger here. He could not give too much of himself to one traveler.

If Israel is lost, it will be to American apathy, he said. "My Israel is a free, liberal country where everybody can live peacefully. And if you say that you are a Jew, and you want to live in this country, and you accept this country, and you're serving in the army, and your children are serving in the army, then you are a Jew."

The Israeli army is seen by many as the model of all that Israel might be. Those who would fight an enemy from without cannot be enemies within. It was necessary to find solutions to the problems of religious and non-religious Jews working and living as a unit, and to the greater problems of protecting a country while maintaining its central ideal: the freedom to live as Jews. If ever there was a Jewish melting pot, it is the Israeli defense force. At the age of eighteen, boys are drafted for three years and girls for two. Men are assigned to reserve units in which they must serve each year well into middle age. Women are exempt from the reserves at a younger age, or when they marry, "because we don't really want our girls to fight. We believe in families," said Pelid. Yeshiva students do not have to serve.

A particularly facile rabbi interpreted *halakha* to make it possible for most Orthodox to serve. Rabbi Shlomo Goren held various high ranks in the army from 1948 until 1971, when he became Chief Rabbi of Israel. Under Goren's guidance and brilliant interpretation of *halakha*, Sabbaths and Holy Days are days of rest for everyone in the military, except those essential for security including military operations. Religious requirements, including kosher and Sabbath laws, are imposed on the whole army. A single prayer book was produced for the military under which all forms of Judaism may worship together. Matters of personal cleanliness are by halakhic standards. A married male soldier must execute a power of attorney so that his wife can get a divorce if he disappears and his death cannot be confirmed by halakhic rules. Pelid spoke highly of the Orthodox soldiers he has known—and he spoke terribly of the ultra-Orthodox who do not serve.

"I'll tell you one," he said, if not warming up to the subject, at least giving in to it. "A soldier was killed. . . . Then, when it came to burying him in a military cemetery, all of a sudden, his mother wasn't a Jew, so he can't be buried in the military cemetery. He was good enough to fight. He was good enough to get killed. But he's not good enough to be buried in their cemetery. He was killed to protect them, to protect me, to protect this country. He was killed to protect my kids. He was killed to protect my wife. And now he cannot be buried in my cemetery? This is not my Israel.

"One of the biggest problems is that you Americans don't do anything about it. And if you don't give a damn . . . then don't blame us."

What should we do? I asked. Should we all come here to live?

"Certainly, come here, but only if you can make it," he said. "Because I prefer a happy Jew in America than a miserable Jew in Israel. I want this country to be good enough to attract Jews from out of Israel. I don't want Israel to become another ghetto, something where all the Jews would be here behind a fence and that's it. That's not what I want. One day this country will be a free, ultra-liberal country. That would be so good!

"So I'm not saying that every Jew should come to Israel. I have no problem with a Jew who is proud to live in America. America was good to its Jewish people. And look at their Jewish minority in the United States. On the top! So America is your home. There is no doubt about it. You should be absolutely loyal to America. But a Jew has a second one. Israel is his home, too. So explain to me why do [most] American Jews never come to visit this country? Okay? That's what I don't like about American Jews. They don't give a damn for this country. They're not coming to look. And it's their home."

But, he said, he understands why my father gave up on Israel. He had an American friend who took the same position for the same reason, and Pelid said he would have done the same.

"Many times people will ask me in this kind of conversation, 'Would you marry a non-Jew?' My answer is, 'Perhaps the person I'll marry here is to be Chinese or black or green. I don't give a damn what kind religion. But I would think of my kids. 'I want you to convert,' I would tell her. For the kids, so they wouldn't have a problem. My children are too good for that. I don't think it's right for me to put my children into such a tight position.

"But eventually," he said, "the only Jews left in the world will be either the Orthodox at Williamsburg and Crown Heights [in Brooklyn] or in Israel. The rest simply won't be Jews. You have to understand it. You happen to be born to a mother who was not Jewish. You are not a Jew, but you've got a Jewish education. But most such children wouldn't even get a Jewish education because mixed couples . . . would make a decision to raise them as Christians. Or to let them grow up to be whatever they want to be. That's what the majority are doing. Which really means that in two generations, there will be no more Jews except the Orthodox.

"So everybody has to make his own decision. And if the decision is this—'I do care for this country, and yes, I want to get involved'—then get involved, politically."

"But . . ." I said.

But, he told me, I had 10 minutes to float on the Dead Sea, and get back on the bus.

The romance of the kibbutz is waning. Children of the original kibbutzniks can't be kept down on the farm once they've seen Tel Aviv and experienced life lived with two incomes. But the diehards prevail in the toughest places. One of these is Joel, an Israeli who was born in New York and now, at fifty-four, is the oldest member of Kibbutz Kfar Haruv on the Golan Heights. His reality does not allow time for non-problems like weddings. His grandchildren attend the kibbutz kindergarten, which, I was told, is in the direct line of fire of the Jordanian cannon perched on the hill above. The idea was that the Arabs would think twice about massacring little children.

Annoyed by my questions, Joel answered them only because I asked them in front of a group of tourists to whom he was showing off his kibbutz. His job is to make Americans love the land, work it, and pay for it, just as he does.

"You live with the reality of where you are," he said. "If you don't want to get married by an Orthodox rabbi, don't live here! Or don't get married, live together. This is not really a problem here because there is no chance to meet a Reform girl anyway,"

he said. Then he fled to the cafeteria to hawk T-shirts to the next
wave of tourists.

With Eli Pelid at Yad Mordechai, I learned the story of how this
little kibbutz, with few people, little ammunition, outdated guns,
virtually no military training, and no hope of success, resisted a
brigade-size force of Arabs during the 1948 War of Liberation. A
few of the great heroes remain on the kibbutz, Pelid told us, and
one of them was there, behind the counter. He spoke no English
and appeared to me to be masquerading as the mythical "average" Israeli. He had no interest in reliving the story beyond sell-
ing souvenirs and history books that bring in a few shekels and
give him a way to pass the time that is left to him.

"Ask him," I said to Pelid. "Ask him 'Who is a Jew?'"

"You ask him," said Pelid, who wanted no part in what he appeared to see as my harassment of a hero. I tried to ask the man
my question in a kind of made-up language I think of as "international." But it did no good. He turned away.

"What do you *want* from this man?" asked Pelid, indignant,
embarrassed, angry.

"I want to know 'Who Is a Jew?'" I said.

The man turned around again and looked at Pelid, who spoke
to him in Hebrew. The hero made a sign to me that he wanted to
answer. His name is Artur Weinman, Pelid translated, and this
was Artur Weinman's answer: "Whoever thinks he is a Jew."

ENGLAND

16

"These things don't have an answer,
they're part of a conversation."
—*Chief Rabbi Dr. Jonathan Sacks*

I MADE MY FIRST TRIP to England in 1967, when I was seventeen years old. I stopped first at Carnaby Street: Beatles, miniskirts, just like home. Or so I thought. I made some Jewish friends and learned what I could of these odd animals, the Liberal Jew and the English Reform, both of whom seemed mighty conservative to me. The best comparison of the movements I heard was from Rabbi Rodney Mariner:

"The Liberals need to have a good reason why the *halakha* should have force; and the Reform tend to have a very good reason as to why a piece of *halakha* should be jettisoned. They often arrive at the same point, but from different directions."

It was years, and many trips to England later, before I understood that while British Jews seem to be British—as American Jews are American—British Jews are, in fact, making do in a country in which they, and all others who are not "upper," are by definition "second-class." When Jews—American and British—point with pride to Benjamin Disraeli, the nineteenth-century prime minister, I think they are buying into the notion that the appointment of this nominal Jew marked the beginning of Jewish acceptance in that country. It was not to be. Disraeli was an anomaly. The man was reared as a Christian, though he professed admiration for Judaism. He was never of the British; he was merely a clever employee of the system. He was created an earl, which is a further source of pride to Jews who live in a profoundly anti-Semitic country that historically permitted Jews in only when they were needed to expedite commerce, hence Shakespeare's Shylock. Of course, the great irony about England now is that so much of its economy is financed by Arabs.

I went to England to speak to its rabbis for these reasons, and also because their world is in another way the direct opposite of the United States, where liberal Jews are the majority of the Jewish population. In England, where Old World sensibilities inform daily life, the Orthodox are the majority of the Jews. Orthodoxy in England "is the religion in which you don't believe—but you respect its authority," said Rabbi Prof. Jonathan Magonet, the principal of Leo Baeck College in London. "You talk to a cab driver in Israel, he will despise the Orthodox, but 'By God,' he will say, 'they have the real thing.' In this sense, Israel and England are curiously parallel."

Yet even here, where Jews have real need of each other, the chief rabbi of The United Hebrew Congregations of the Commonwealth was under attack from his own Orthodox constituency, and from almost every other Jew he is officially said to represent in England, which is to say all of them. And it was all because of a funeral.

Rabbi Hugo Gryn, born in Czechoslovakia, had recently died at the peak of his popularity with British Reform Jews and with the general public that had grown used to his happy erudition, and good-humored common sense. If the chief rabbi represented the Jewish voice in official England, then Hugo Gryn represented the Liberal/Reform voice.

The chief rabbi, Jonathan Sacks, did not go to the funeral because it was held in a synagogue that was not Orthodox, which, in the minds of the Orthodox, is not a synagogue at all. But he did initiate, with the approval of Jackie Gryn, the widow, a memorial meeting—*not* a "service"—under the aegis of the Board of Deputies for British Jews in a public hall—"neutral territory," as Mrs. Gryn defined it. There, Sacks rose to speak of

Gryn as "a friend" and a good man. Sacks never once referred to Gryn as a rabbi, which, of course, to an Orthodox mind makes complete sense because there is no such thing as a Reform rabbi. Thus he slighted non-Orthodox British Jewry, and at the same time enraged the Orthodox Jews because he recognized Gryn at all.

"I was very disappointed that he didn't mention my husband as being a rabbi. It was quite kind of him [to speak of him] as a friend and a human being, but it was annoying to say the least, and to my colleagues, too. I must say, quite honestly, I was too emotional to take it in very much myself at the time. I reacted later. [Sacks] was well-intentioned. I've written to him to say, 'Let's drop this now and let's all get on with our lives.' I don't bear him any malice or any grudge. I respect him and I feel he has a difficult situation."

It was indeed a difficult situation, which grew further complicated when, in attempting to explain himself to his Orthodox colleagues, Sacks wrote to the head of the Union of Orthodox Hebrew Congregations that Gryn was "one of those who destroy the faith." He also wrote that Liberal, Masorti (Conservative), and Reform "have no enemy . . . greater than the chief rabbi," who "is representative of the whole Jewish community."

When the letter was leaked, it provided Liberals, Reform, and more moderate Orthodox Jews with all they needed to undermine whatever legitimate claim the chief rabbi had to represent them, a notion that, to most American minds—and to some British ones as well—was absurd to begin with.

I asked a former chief rabbi of Ireland about the job. David Rosen, who is now the director of interfaith relations of the Anti-Defamation League in Jerusalem, said, "European Jewry, like European society, is essentially Old World, in which there is a dominant ethos within that society. It's not an immigrant society, which by its very nature brings in different elements. There are old schoolboy networks. There are dominant influences within our particular society. And therefore European Jewish communities seek to assimilate or acculturate not into the diversity that happens in American society, but according to a certain particular archetype within that particular society.

"Whereas [in the United States] almost every kind of organization has a variety of different forms of expression by the very nature of the diversity of American society, European societies have a much more centralized ethos, a central address to direct yourself to and central figureheads. As long as those central figureheads will allow them to get on with the business of living, each one in their own diverse way . . . they will be nominally part of it. So within English society, the vast majority of Jews are part of the United Synagogue [whose chief rabbi becomes, officially, the chief rabbi of England]. Not because their lifestyle has been Orthodox, but they still want to be part of it. Certainly its figurehead, namely its chief rabbi, is seen as representing the Jewish community as a whole. . . . To some extent, he's [like] the queen.

"What's happening is that because society at large is polarizing, there's a decentralization. . . . As that diversification takes place, extremes tend to get stronger. Your right wing gets stronger and your left wing gets stronger. And it's much more difficult to hold the center. You need to have a very strong personality who makes it very clear to those extremes that he will not tolerate their sniping and their undermining of his authority to be able to keep that center together.

"When I was chief rabbi of Ireland, one had the burden of responsibility and representation on one's shoulders. And that means you become a more conservative creature, because that's the very nature of authority. So I was the first chief rabbi in Ireland who reached out to Reform congregations. . . . I even spoke there and went into the building to the sanctuary, which horrified many people in the Jewish community. And therefore I suppose, on most issues, I was able to speak for 95 percent of the community. . . . In Ireland, the chief rabbi is a state figure, so he's involved in all state diplomatic cultural rites for the country. You make statements before the Irish Parliament for all kinds of social and moral issues. That's why it's the most fun rabbinic job in the world."

"And the chief rabbi of England?" I asked.
"That's not a fun job at all."
The chief rabbi of England, Jonathan Sacks, was clearly having no fun. In the dining room of his comfortable London home, I was to ask him about this, of course, but first I asked him about his 1993 book, *One People? Tradition, Modernity, and Jewish Unity*, which made a terrifying case against the idea that Jews are unified. Yet, in the book, while he clearly advocated Orthodoxy, he put forth a case that seemed to speak of at least a temporarily pluralistic society in Israel, which would meet the needs of a people in flux. He wrote:

> The most important single step to avoid schismatic confrontation [in Israel] would be . . . to remove the question of "Who Is a Jew?" from Israel's political agenda. This has been advocated by, among others . . . [Rabbi] Jacob Bleich. . . . Jewish status, as a halakhic issue, is beyond the competence of Israel's secular parliament and agencies to determine. It is to be decided by rabbinic courts alone. The Law of Return could then be amended to apply to born Jews only, with the further stipulation that [quoting Bleich], "state officials, without in any way passing judgment on matters of *halakha*," might consider "even technically invalid conversions as evidence of a convert's sincere desire to identify with the aspirations and common destiny of the citizens of the State of Israel." This would not amount to a solution of the problem, but to a decision to let it remain unresolved.

The "born Jew" is not defined in this scenario, but the implication is clearly that such a person is born to a Jewish mother. The concession here is that something other than Orthodox conversion might be considered for purposes of citizenship.

"I think things have not got better," said Sacks when we spoke. "But . . . when I published the book, people wrote to me from America saying, 'We enjoyed the book, but it's too late.' And I got that response both from Orthodox and non-Orthodox Jews in the States. Those who reflected on it quite hard took the view that the Orthodox and non-Orthodox communities in the States had already grown too far apart for the possibility of a serious conversation.

"In a sense, I'm equally disturbed by the fractures in Israeli society. The divisions between the religious and secular in Israel seem to have grown. I had felt that after the tragedy of the assassination of Yitzak Rabin there would be some attempt to come together . . . but there hasn't been. So the . . . fractures between Orthodox and Reform outside of Israel and [between] secular and religious within Israel have grown worse since I wrote the book. And there is, of course, always the possibility of the third fracture which regularly arises when 'Who is a Jew?' is on the agenda: that is, between Israel and much of the Diaspora. So the situation has not grown any better.

"Now one thing that's very striking is this: this particular year . . . is the 100th anniversary of the first Zionist Congress, which was one of the crucial turning points in Jewish history, and which created a vast debate, not on 'Who Is a Jew?' but on 'What Is a Jew?' Is it to live in the Diaspora? Is it to live in Israel? Is it to be different? Is it to be like everyone else?

"One of the most powerful debates in modern Jewish history took place in the 1890s with this huge outpouring of visions as to what it was to be Jewish. Now we're a hundred years on and we've achieved that agenda, tragically and triumphantly— tragically through the Holocaust, triumphantly through Israel. And we answered the basic question: Where can Jews live? Which is fundamentally in Israel and the United States. Europe turned out to be a very inhospitable place for Jews.

"The center of Jewish life was Europe. Today it is no longer the center of Jewish life and many of the European [Jewish] communities are below the threshold of viability. . . . Tensions between the Orthodox and non-Orthodox community [in England] have flared up every so often . . . basically because as chief rabbi I've had to juggle two roles: being the head of the Orthodox community on the one hand, and being, in a certain sense, at least vis-à-vis the outside world, the religious representative of the whole community.

"I started an organization called Jewish Continuity, a big overarching organization for all our identity-strengthening initiatives: education, outreach, community development. . . . And I set up some very complex structures to support the entire community regardless of religious affiliation, but at the same time to protect my own personal beliefs in Orthodoxy as not necessarily something in which everyone believes, but something to which everyone should at least be open. That turned out to be very, very difficult to sustain—even simple things. It is difficult today to stand for a Judaism which affirms the two fundamentals of historic Jewish identity, which are commitment to Jewish faith and a commitment to the Jewish people.

"By Jewish faith, I mean *halakha*, our traditional beliefs and our traditional way of life. . . . If you ask what is the Torah's definition of Jewish identity, the Torah offers two definitions which I call the Pesach [Passover] definition and the Shavuot [festivals of the giving of the Torah] definition. The Torah defines this oddly enough as a word we've come to use for non-Jew—goy. This is goy as a nation. These are the children of Israel who went into exile in Egypt and there they became a nation. And then we have the statement that we read on Shavuot, which is the Almighty appears at Mount Sinai and says to Israel, 'It should be for me a kingdom of priests and a holy nation.' These are the two points in which the Torah talks of us as a nation.

"So where did we become a nation? In Egypt or at Sinai? And the simple answer is that there are two senses of 'nation.' We've been caught throughout all our history between those two senses. On the one hand, a nation becomes a nation by facing a common enemy. The Israelites in Egypt were persecuted, they were enslaved, they were different from everyone else. They became a nation because they were a minority and they were different and they were persecuted. In other words, they became a community of fate.

"But a nation can be built on something else, which is not a common fate, but a common sense of purpose—common destiny. And that was what happened at Sinai and that's where we became a community of faith. So we are a people, but we're also a religious entity.

"Now for much of Jewish history, those things have marched in step, but . . . today they are very much out of sync. . . . And that's our problem."

"I made a decision to pay a tribute to a Reform rabbi who died. . . . This decision created enormous opposition in my own constituency, and therefore I had—through private diplomacy—to communicate with my own constituency, in this case very ultra-Orthodox Jews, and I spoke in classical Hebrew. . . . When somebody chooses to break confidences and make these private conversations public by publishing a private and confidential letter in the press, then that can only be an attempt to destroy the relationships that I have been trying to build.

"So I've suffered a setback, which the rest of the community have too, and the wisest of them do have to understand exactly what was at stake here. I was extending an altogether unprecedented hand, out of friendship, but I had to carry people with me who don't believe in that at all.

"Unless we have some tolerance of the stresses and strains that attach to anyone who tries to bring incompatible extremes together, we are only going to have incompatible extremes. Both in Israel and in the Diaspora in different ways, the Jewish world is seriously divided, and seriously not talking to one another. Not talking to one another is also becoming a point of principle. So when anyone chooses to talk to both sides, and extends the hand of friendship to both sides, they are compromising the integrity of his or her own beliefs. But because you believe in Jews as a total people and various other things that link us—unless there's some tolerance and respect for the hazards of that enterprise—that enterprise is going to fail.

"Look, I was put in a situation as the chief rabbi in which I had to undertake this diplomacy myself. Now I understand that diplomacy has become so hazardous that it ought to be done by people who have a lower profile. In my view, the first thing we have to establish is the principle of peaceful co-existence. It seems to me that those protocols have to take precedence over the substantive issues. Each of us should be asked to recognize that we have a duty to the Jewish people as a whole, which must at times limit the pursuit of sectional objectives. [And] we have to recognize that despite the fact that there are profound differences between us, there's an enormous common heritage: that is a literary heritage, a historical heritage, a moral heritage.

"Here, in my home, we have a Pesach—four children sitting around the table. [Jews] tell the same story, in different ways. . . . And that's how I see the Jewish people. We are sitting around the table, we share a story, we interpret it differently. And what I say to people is 'be open to the story.' Some people will read that story as divine revelation, others will read it as a mix of human interpretation of divine revelation, others will see it as a purely secular heritage of the Jewish people and its own particular character and genius. I am more interested in the fact that we all read the same story even if we don't interpret it the same way.

"Now it's clear that for us to make progress, we need to move away from institutional interests, which are in head-on collision here . . . you have to move away from established categories. Don't forget that the categories which dominate us today are all nineteenth-century categories: Reform, Conservative, Orthodox. They're not very Jewish terms. . . . I think they're radically dysfunctional right now. Don't forget each of them was predicated on an expectation that was not realized. Each felt that it—and it alone—was the route to Jewish survival.

"Zionists thought only in Israel can Jews survive. The first Zionist Congress was held in Basel because all the rabbis in Germany refused to have it held in Germany. They said Jews can't survive as people in their own land, it's too complex, it's too big a leap, we've been out of practice for too long. The Reform community said only progressive Judaism can survive in the modern world. Orthodoxy said Reform is just a staging post on the way to total assimilation. So all of the groups believe that they—and only they—would survive into the future. Now, we're a hundred years on and every one of those groups has survived.

"These things don't have an answer. They're part of a conversation. I think you have to have a conversation out of which something new and unpredictable will emerge.

"Now what do I think will emerge? I don't know, but it is conceivable that at some stage in the future, an entirely unforeseen equivalent of the Chasidic movement in eastern Europe in the second half of the eighteenth century will suddenly appear in Israel. In other words, a movement that breaks away from all religious establishments, goes directly to the people, talks very much in terms of simple piety, values, many of the things that have been undervalued in the heritage in the last little while. A populist movement . . . a new religious movement that will change the profile of Judaism. Then all the relationships will be renegotiated.

"Whether they will renegotiate it constructively or destructively, I've no idea. But I don't believe that the future will simply be an extrapolation from the past."

17

"We are in the process of redefining what constitutes the Jewish identity. I don't know that you can actually go back to a single system. The conflict arising in Israel is due to who has authority to hold this together?"
—*Rabbi Prof. Jonathan Magonet*

RABBI PROF. JONATHAN MAGONET seemed a little surprised that I was riled up on his behalf. I simply could not accept the idea that the principal of Leo Baeck College—which trains virtually all the Progressive rabbis of Europe, both Liberal and Reform—would not be able to officiate at his own child's wedding in the Jewish homeland.

He said, simply, that if his children chose to marry in Israel, "at *that* stage they would have to address that particular problem. But you see, they are no different from anybody else."

Does this not hurt you? I said, wondering if I was facing yet again that great British prohibition against showing emotions. But his explanation was sensible, his emotions intact because he sorted them out long ago.

"It doesn't hurt me," he said. "It's just typical of what happens in the peculiar Jewish world. It's part of the consequences of emancipation . . . where Judaism was put back into the private sphere. *Halakha* was the constitution of the Jewish people . . . when you had autonomous closed Jewish societies. . . . The moment you broke that system, vast areas of Jewish law got moved over to the secular sphere. The only two places where it has power [now] are status and in terms of ritual liturgy: Who is Jewish? Who is married? With the State of Israel—where nationality is in conflict with the religious right—it became a political game where the issue is not only authentic religious belief, but a matter of political power and how you promote your own particular group. I think that the debate of the Reform movement in Israel has long been: Should we enter politics and be a political party, or should we stay out? The fear is that if we become political, we will be corrupt as the rest of them.

"The average Jew in the street is really saying [to all the denominations], 'a plague on all your houses.' In the States, you are in one way ahead of us—in terms of cultural Judaism. In Europe until now, fifty years after the war and because of the war partly, we fell back into defining Judaism in completely religious terms. The idea of a cultural Jewish identity, except on the part of some individuals, you never saw in a positive sense. You are increasingly getting now, at least in the United Kingdom, Jewish book weeks and film festivals, Yiddish groups and women's groups and using your Jewishness in a way to define part of yourself. . . . But the religious aspects are really so peripheral that unless it impinges upon you because it's a seder or you want to get married, it doesn't particularly bother you. I suspect that will increasingly be the case. So that the question of 'Who Is a Jew?, Who Is Not a Jew?' does not arise until . . . it hits you at some moment. The rabbis can rant and rave about it because their bread and butter depends on them defining themselves, but most Jews don't give a damn. . . . It may mean eventually an Orthodox world that is self-contained.

"In England, you are very much aware that you are a minority group. You had to conform . . . and you made sure you didn't make waves. It's only been since '67 that you got this first resurgence of Jewish identity, plus you got the greater ethnicity in the U.K. . . . So it's quite a different history. Here, we just end up in our own little squabbles. Certainly the Orthodox are doing well in terms of their yeshivas and training youth, creating more of an organic community, which is good. And the Reform and Liberal just sort of muddle along and grow."

I asked Magonet about the chief rabbi, in terms of the Gryn incident and what it means for non-Orthodox Jewry in England.

"We talk among ourselves, but then complain no one is listening," he said. "Internal Jewish dialogue in the U.K. virtually does not exist except very privately, off-stage. It's part of the culture here, part of the polarization.

"In this country, historically, the establishment is perceived as being the United Synagogue, which has been nominally Orthodox. Now, it's modeled in a sense on the Church of England. It has a chief rabbi like the Archbishop of Canterbury who is its spokesperson, and for the Jewish community it represents a kind of wall. Anybody who goes against that wall is perceived as being an outsider who should be marginalized as far as possible. So the Reform movements in this country have always been somehow marginalized by the establishment, even though for the last thirty years or so they have grown in size to just under a third of organized Jewry. [For most Jews in England], even though you are a non-practicing Jew, you will retain your membership in an Orthodox synagogue for burial rights and you will give money to them and also to Lubavitch [a Chasidic sect], because the more right-wing you are, the more authority and reality you have.

"That [Gryn] business with Sacks lost a lot of the credibility that the leadership has. It actually clarified where Sacks really is. . . . [We Reform and Liberal] will need to establish our own credentials in a much different way. . . . There are [even] people to the right of [Sacks] who don't accept him as authority. Now we don't accept his authority, not that we ever did. We just went along with the myth. . . . It's not even him, it's the job itself which is the problem. . . . "So you're seeing increasing polarization. It means that issues like 'Who Is a Jew?' become tossed into the pot as good material with which to fight each other.

"There are lots of Jewish peoples, in a sense. Jewish history is full of pseudo-schisms whereby a group of people have not talked to each other for a couple of centuries and they forget what the fight was about, or they figure, all right, so we'll go our separate ways. If that happens, it happens, you know? You can't fight history in that sense.

"At the moment, there is enough room for accommodation if you want it. But, increasingly, the reality of the State of Israel has been a central factor determining where power lies and therefore where authority lies in Jewish law. The 'Who is a Jew?' thing, I think, should be much more scary to the Orthodox community than it is to us. Because you now have a situation whereby the Orthodox authorities in Israel can disenfranchise any *bet din* if they want to by refusing to accept its converts.

"Israel will increasingly become what it already is—a state with its own needs and authorities. The Diaspora will increasingly have less and less significance [for Israelis]. . . . If something has to be done which would be embarrassing to the Diaspora in any way, [Israel] will do it.

"We're just in the transition stage between the dog wagging the tail and the tail wagging the dog. As the Diaspora created the State of Israel, the State is becoming independent, self-regulating, and rules by its own internal crises, problems, organizations, battles. And we take increasingly second place there.

"If you look at the realities, you have 700,000 Russians who have come to Israel. You have the whole of the Eastern European world now in the Jewish market. You have the American situation of intermarriage, mixed marriage, re-marriage, kids. A Jewish man marries one Jewish woman, has two kids, they divorce; he marries a woman who is not Jewish, has two kids and gets divorced. You now have a family with two Jews and four children. Who is Jewish and who is not?

"So if we look at that mess, you've then got the question of who in Israel decides what? Is the Law of Return allowing you to come back as a Jew? And the religious authorities who want a strict *halakha* are probably fighting each other. So the whole thing is now a total shambles. The narrow question about conversions, I think, is really clouding the bigger issue, and I think people are just too scared to look at it.

"We are in the process of redefining what constitutes the Jewish identity. I don't know that you can actually go back to a single system. The conflict arising in Israel is due to who has authority to hold this together."

And how do we solve the problem?

"The only suggestion I can think of is that in the year 2000 at midnight we declare amnesty," he said. "Anybody who thinks they are Jewish at that point would be declared basically Jewish."

We both laughed, but not for long. "But then," he asked, "what happens in two minutes afterwards?

"The Orthodox still believe they are ultimately going to be victors and that the real authority and tradition will be theirs. As long as you have that fantasy, you won't get anywhere. There's no point in compromising because you're always holding out for your future. And the Orthodox, and the Reform, and the Conservatives think they've got the future. And they are probably all right. So in the end, I don't think we are going to resolve it, we'll just have increasingly more fractious groups screaming at each other. And most Jews saying, to hell with it, and just carrying on, using less and less, I suspect, of the more traditional framework for their life cycle. Or rediscovering them in new ways."

18

"It is a bourgeois, nineteenth-century idea
to confine Judaism to being a religion."
—*Rabbi Rodney Mariner*

I MET A PERSON who must almost daily face the question of "Who
Is a Jew?" Rabbi Rodney Mariner is the convenor of the *Bet Din*
of Liberal/Reform Britain, and also of Europe. These Jewish
courts, like Leo Baeck College, are something of a miracle to me
because they are a combined effort of the Liberal and Reform
movements, both of whom identify themselves as "Progressive"
but who are in reality quite different organizations.

"The major difference between the two is matrilineal and patrilineal," said Mariner. "The Liberal movement says quite logically
that the child of a Jewish father who has been brought up as a
Jew should be Jewish, whereas the child of a Jewish mother who
has not been brought up Jewish is not Jewish."

Like Leo Baeck College, which trains the rabbis for both, this
bet din is an example of compromise. Mariner, an Australian who
"didn't manage to get back" to his country of birth after gradu-
ating from Leo Baeck in 1976, considers himself an "independent." He began as a Reform rabbi, subsequently joined the
American Conservative movement, and then became the rabbi of
the Belsize Square Synagogue in London, a congregation formed
by German refugees which is, he said, "quite conservative" in its
style. He is then, in his words,

"an un-Orthodox, independent rabbi . . . so I am in, but not of, the Reform movement. It enables me to have a bit of objectivity. It's been quite useful.

"I can't, from a halakhic position, say that the child of a Jewish father is Jewish, but from a halakhic position I can convert the child in its own right as early as birth. Reform are more demanding than Orthodoxy—the [non-Jewish] mother must undergo a course of no less duration and content than that required for conversion. In other words, she learns everything that she would do for conversion, but without the faith commitment. What often happens is that having learnt it all, [she ultimately undergoes conversion]. That means we solve that problem now very early. . . . That's been a very elegant solution.

"The Liberals used to have a way out of their dilemma which I think is being actually eroded. They used to have confirmation, instead of bar or bat mitzvah, which took place at sixteen. That confirmation was essentially a faith act by an individual. So we had no problem accepting them from the Liberal movement although they are patrilineal and matrilineal.

"As a result of the fall of the Soviet Union, we soon realized that there were Jews coming out of the woodwork all over the place both within the former Soviet Union and the satellites. And many of these people were in fact patrilineal Jews who for several generations had married out, yet maintained the Jewish identity. . . . Our worry was that there would be a whole series of American rabbis—I think that's probably the clearest and truest classification—who would be doing summer programs and arts and crafts in Bulgaria or somewhere like that and say, 'Here. Take this piece of paper, you're Jewish.' We wanted to clarify and codify that. As a result, I set up a European *bet din* with France, Holland, Belgium, and we've now got Germany on board and Great Britain.

"The Liberals were prepared to drop their requirement that patrilineality be recognized because many of them were working in Europe. And so we've established a principle that European rabbis operate on a matrilineal, not a patrilineal line. But we then use a device that we've had within the Reform movement, something called an 'intermediate certificate.' That certificate says, in effect, that this candidate has come before the court to be accepted as a Jew. Now, the requirements [for conversion] are exactly the same, but it recognizes that the journey did not begin outside of Judaism. . . . Until recently, our certificates were acceptable for the purposes of *aliyah*. At the moment, it's dubious.

"[Our] *bet din* operates from the position of being an enabling device. It sees itself in business to solve problems, not to create them. We will bend over backwards . . . to find a way in which someone who sincerely wants to be part of the [the people of Israel] can do so."

I'd been on the road a while now and this was about the twentieth person who was "bending over backward" to find a way to make me a Jew. But their calisthenics, however artful and strenuous, were, for me, disappointing. This rabbi, at least, wanted to give me some kind of a junior license, which is I suppose like a temporary driver's permit entitling me to take the wheel if there is a fully licensed driver in the car. Mariner appeared sincere in his motive, though.

"My position is that anybody who puts their hand out after the Holocaust and says 'I am a Jew' catches my attention. I believe anybody is entitled to say that they are a Jew. To say they are a Jew. And if they want to do something as a consequence of that, in relation to the Jewish community, then they have to expose themselves to some sort of scrutiny and some sort of certification. There is a tension between people who are authentically seeking to regain their roots . . . as opposed to somebody in Poland or the former Soviet Union who sees being Jewish as a means of moving across Europe or even moving to Israel to change their economic circumstances. Now under those circumstances, I've got to look at the issue.

"I'll accept any person who has suffered for being Jewish, whether they were or not, that even suffered for having the label attached to them. But that doesn't mean I'm not going to go ask of them to study.

"My big problem with Israel and its present circumstances is that it has turned Judaism back into a religion. It's part of my argument with the chief rabbi. It comes from too narrow a base in terms of Jewish identity. Because it is a bourgeois, nineteenth-century idea to confine Judaism to being a religion. I glory in pluralism . . . my hope for Israel was always that it would be a superb pluralistic society. It would allow the Black Hats to be Black Hats, as much as it allowed the Ethiopians to be part of its society. Its polarization . . . an absolute anathema. I find myself saying I'm quite happy to give Jerusalem back to the Palestinians. It doesn't belong to me anymore. I lived there for a year and loved it, but I go back there now and I say I prefer to be in Tel Aviv. Because Jerusalem has become a black city—black in the religious sense [ultra-Orthodox]. And it's no longer worth dying for, in my opinion. It has a role in the peace-making process, in the sharing of that site with the Palestinians in order to establish peace for the rest of Israel. I no longer believe that Jerusalem is Israel, and it saddens me greatly. . . . While there may come a time when Jerusalem reattains that sort of celestial idea that it had, it will not take place as long as Orthodoxy, or religion in general, has political power. Judaism has never ever been more in danger of destroying itself in any time in history than when both religion and power come together. Sanctity lies within individuals. Sanctity is about what you do in a place, not what the place is."

19

"But it completely seems to me absurd not to count
into the Jewish people and to Judaism whoever wants
to be, genuinely and sincerely, wants to be counted in."
—*Rabbi Tony Bayfield*

IF THE BRITISH REFORM movement had its own chief rabbi, I suppose it would be Rabbi Tony Bayfield, who is the chief executive of the movement in Britain. At it stands, though, he too is not even able to conduct a wedding in Israel.

"I think my starting point is to say that there is something extraordinary about a group of people who don't want to count in everybody who wants to be counted in," he said. "It's all the more extraordinary if you like Judaism and think it's great; when you look at Jewish demography and the total amount of Jews in the world. [According to the standard definition of Who is a Jew] it is slightly less than the population of Afghanistan, and yet we build the highest walls [around ourselves].

"You have to understand it historically. When the Temple fell, and Rabbinic Judaism developed . . . parts of the rabbinic strategy was to build walls 'round Jews to protect Judaism from the onslaught of the hostile world. There having been periods of Jewish history when there were very significant levels of conversion . . . right up to the sort of closing in of the Middle Ages, the Crusades.

"We, over the centuries, adopted a totally different strategy for survival. Our experiences in Europe in the nineteenth century and the early twentieth century imbued us with a very strong sense of

ethnicity. There is no doubt that some of the things that emerged
from anti-Semitic nineteenth-century German scholarship about
Jews as race we've actually taken on board. I mean, there's the
classic statement in the Talmud that there have been no pure
races since time immemorial. But the nineteenth-century race
stuff certainly reinforced it.

"The world in which we live demands different survival
strategies—radically differently survival strategies . . . I think we
are also dealing with rabbinic power politics. I think that one of
the issues that really threatens the cohesiveness of the Jewish people is, 'Who is a Rabbi?' And the authority of that rabbi's decision. We're also dealing with very, very profound and deep
disagreements about what will work and what will retain the
greatest number of Jews for Judaism, and what will ensure the
survival of Judaism. We have honestly felt different approaches,
different interpretations of the same information.

"I believe that the conversion issue between the British Reform
movement and the central Orthodox bloc in this country could be
solved in fifteen minutes. A formula could be found by which all
of our converts could be recognized. The fact that that doesn't
happen, as I say, has to do with rabbinic power politics.

"I think [the Orthodox have] an enormous amount of fear of
being delegitimized themselves. One of the things that worries the
central Orthodox body in this country is having their Orthodox
credentials questioned by people farther to the right, particularly
in Israel. . . . And I think that we all underestimate the extent to
which the last Israeli general election has implications far beyond
those that we dream of. It has given enormous political power as
never before to a highly politicized right wing whose worldview
is very different than that of the majority of the Jewish world.
And they are a blocking force. I think that it would be possible, if
people wanted it, to solve many of the status problems as far as
moderate Reform and middle-of-the-road Orthodoxy and Conservatives are concerned. Whether that is desirable is another
thing.

"A few weeks ago, I officiated at my daughter's wedding. Now, that was a wedding that could have taken place in any synagogue, anywhere. There were no halakhic impediments to the wedding. The [only] halakhic grounds on which an Orthodox rabbi could raise a doubt . . . could only [have been] on the status of the witnesses. A valid Jewish marriage takes place when [a Jewish man] makes a declaration to which [a Jewish woman] assents, and there is a handing over of something of value, traditionally a plain gold ring. Now, we could find a formula whereby the community employed a panel of witnesses with unimpeachable validity, however far to the right you go. And they could act as, from our point of view, as additional witnesses at every wedding. . . . But I can't for a moment think that the Orthodox authorities in this country would buy it, because it would be acknowledging the Jewish validity of the ceremony that took place in a Reform synagogue with a Reform rabbi officiating.

"The change has got to be well-nigh imposed by the general Jewish population. It will not come from rabbis. The chief rabbi of the United Congregations basically described one of the country's best rabbis [the late Hugo Gryn] as one who has betrayed Judaism. [But] I haven't noticed any galvanizing.

"We're trapped by history. In Victorian times, the United Synagogue was established on the model of the Church of England. It was a broadly based established church with a [chief rabbi who corresponded to the] Archbishop of Canterbury. The Reform, the Liberal, and assorted Masorti [Conservative] movements now account for 25 percent of the synagogue affiliation in this country. It is a different profile from the States.

"The United Synagogue ceased to be a broad church and became a sect—not in the pejorative sense, but in the sociological sense—a much more tightly knit group of people with a much tighter ideology. . . . The chief rabbi of the United Congregations has hung onto the fiction that he's the Archbishop of Canterbury. It manifests itself most absurdly in the situation in which we have a National Council of Christians and Jews with five Christians—the archbishop of Canterbury, the cardinal archbishop of Westminster, the Orthodox archbishop, the moderator of the Free Churches, the moderator of the Free Church in Scotland—and the chief rabbi of the United Hebrew Congregations. Which is a total and complete absurdity. Whilst we maintain that absurdity, it's not a simple matter for us, because enormous power is actually invested in the office [of chief rabbi].

"If we have a genuine and overriding concern for the welfare and unity of the Jewish people, we wouldn't do things as we do. We would overcome ideological sensibilities. We would worry less about rabbinic power and authority. And there are ways of solving some of the halakhic problems. However, I think we are also dealing with radically different worldviews. And radically different senses of what strategies are needed for Jewish survival in a world that is very different from the world which persisted from the fall of the Temple until the beginning of the nineteenth century.

"Logic says that we ought to be claiming for Judaism everybody that we could claim, and counting in everybody who wants to be counted in. But readjusting the psychology of Jews and their responses and feelings takes time. Whether we have all of that time, and who gets lost and hurt on the way, is the major question. Maybe we've run out of time. But it's part of the confusion, which strategies will survive. But it completely seems to me absurd not to count into the Jewish people and to Judaism whoever wants to be, genuinely and sincerely, counted in. I suppose other people would say that you're absolutely right, but in order to be counted in you have to do A-B-C. And ultimately, it's about what hoops that you may have to jump through. I can see every reason for trying to ensure that people have the knowledge and skills to fully enjoy their Judaism. . . . [But] that still isn't the gut reaction, that isn't the face that even most of the Reform community show. I think it's very sad.

"I'm still one of those people who hankers onto talking to all of the Orthodox authorities in this country about finding solutions. . . . I want to continue to try. The hand should always be open. It should always be looking for solutions.

"But it is actually not the most important issue. I'm not prepared to pay [just] any price for Jewish unity, manifestly not. There are values and principles. There is the integrity of Judaism itself. I wouldn't be prepared to sacrifice [a patrilineal Jew] on the altar of Jewish unity. As far as I am concerned, you are Jewish according to the American Reform movement. If you came to one of my synagogues saying that you wanted to get married, you wanted to be a member, we would recognize your Jewish status."

With or without the conversion? I asked.

"If you come with a certificate, some kind of a document from an American Reform rabbi saying that you are Jewish, we would accept it. Well, I would, just as I would accept someone from the British Liberal Movement as a member of my synagogue.

"If an Orthodox rabbi said to me, as they do, 'For the sake of Jewish unity, will you give up making conversions?' The answer is no. 'For the sake of Jewish unity, will you disavow the Jewish status of the people of the Reform movement who the Reform movement have converted in the past?' Absolutely not. And every Reform rabbi would say the same thing.

"What happens in Israel is extremely important. Do we support the worldview? Yes. Do we support the Israel movement? Yes. Do we fundraise for it? Yes. Are some of our rabbis working there? Yes. Is our youth movement a Zionist youth movement? Yes. Do we support and encourage *aliyah*? Yes. Are we proud of the fact that we get more kids to Israel each summer than almost any other Jewish youth movement in Israel? Yes. Have we been lobbying? Have I written letters? Have I sent faxes? Yes. Will I continue to do that? Yes. Will we give up on this round? Never. Never were the Reform and Conservative movements in Israel more needed."

20

**"We do risk becoming separate nations. . . .
There must be courage and sacrifice to
avert this disaster from happening."**
—*Rabbi Shmuley Boteach*

RABBI SHMULEY BOTEACH alarmed me, not because of what he said
but because in his presence I got the feeling he might go up in
flames at any moment, ignited by the perpetual cigar between his
teeth. At the age of thirty years old—living at the top of life and
his lungs—he tries to sit but cannot. He leaps up—ashes flying—
to bark an order at a young staffer of the Oxford University
L'Chaim Society in its London office—a suite whirring with
copy machines and telephones and harried helpers. I do not know
whether they are afraid of their flamboyant boss. None
of them can be much over thirty themselves, and they may
well think that all life and work is lived with such speed and
stress. They no doubt think of it as commitment and, like the university students Boteach inspires, find the work exhilarating and
important.

Boteach serves a purpose whose importance no one can deny:
he excites students and rallies them to Judaism. But some of us
old fogies—distrustful, doubting, or simply exhausted by the
overwhelming energy of the young man—may wonder if this is a
demagogue or a martyr in the making, an American rabbi running for an office in England—or beyond—that does not exist.
When I mentioned to other rabbis that I had spent some time
with Boteach they were curious about him. He is harsh, I told
them. He is insistent. He is sure of his God. He is sure of himself.

He sees the answers, not in the way other ultra-Orthodox rabbis know the answers, but through his own customized lens. He does not merely express ideas, he makes proposals.

"A great calamity awaits the Jewish people with the issue of conversion," he told me in a rush. Time is short. After 5,000 years, time is running out.

"We disagree about each others' Judaism, but not about one's Jewishness. Every Orthodox Jew accepts [that] the Reform Jew born of Jewish parents is a Jew. But we can't agree on a simple standard of conversion. We risk segmenting into two separate people who are unable to marry. What makes it one people—atheist Jews, Reform Jews, Reconstructionist Jews, Orthodox Jews—is that they [can marry each other]. The moment we can not marry one another . . . we cease to be one people. There has to be a single standard of conversion.

"[Because] we no longer have a single Jewish traditional authority, we do risk becoming separate nations. And that can be discouraging. . . . There must be courage and sacrifice. There must be to avert this disaster from happening.

"I think that the Jewish people are not an ethnicity or a race. We are not a culture because my father's Iranian-Jewish culture is extremely different from my mother's Ashkenazi Jewish culture. Also, our religion is Jewish. What we are is a people. We are the children of Abraham, Jacob, and Sarah. And [we are] those who . . . have adopted our people or who have been adopted by our people.

"I advocate an Orthodox-only standard because it is the only standard upon which we can all agree. No Reform [rabbi can deny the authenticity of an Orthodox conversion]. So I think that Reform, if [it] gives up conversion, [can be recognized] as a meaningful expression of Judaism.

"The Orthodox authorities are saying, 'How can you recognize Reform? That's ridiculous.' I'll answer that criticism. I never said the Orthodox should say that Reform is a legitimate or a halakhic organization. They themselves would say that they are a non-traditional Jewish organization. They would say that they have abandoned certain aspects of the tradition because they don't find it compatible with modern-day living. So when I say we should recognize Reform, what I am saying is that we should recognize it as a meaningful expression of Judaism for a large number of Jews who would otherwise not affiliate. For those [Orthodox] who come along and say, 'Oh! This is not Jewish at all and it's a different religion,' that's patently absurd! Reform is not Christianity. And in fact, Reform is becoming far more traditionally Jewish and more halakhically observant as time goes on, much more. And I think Orthodoxy can expedite that process by initiating and continuing dialogue with Reform.

"So is Tony Bayfield a rabbi? He is a spiritual leader of Jews who brings them closer to God. I believe he is, yes. . . . Those Orthodox rabbis who will not refer to Reform rabbis as rabbis, I'm confused by that. Because when we start getting real technical about who are rabbis and who aren't rabbis, even Orthodox rabbis today are not comparing themselves to Maimonides and Rashi. So the whole definition of rabbis has changed anyway. Today, I think 'rabbi' just means, in the vernacular, someone who leads a Jewish congregation. I am perfectly happy to accord that recognition to the head of all Reform congregations. But I think Reform really has to give up conversion because there can be no deal brokered between Orthodox and Reform, ever, for so long as the subject of conversion is not addressed. Because we are ignoring what will ultimately separate us. You can't deny someone else's Jewishness.

"I don't think that 'unity' means that we all share the same kind of worship. I have great respect for Christianity. I have great respect for its law. It's just not the way I serve God. It's the way that they serve God, and that's fine. I respect them and I believe them to be a bona fide monotheistic faith. It's not the way I choose to worship. So [too do] I choose not to attend the Reform. And I think all Reform Jews understand that. . . . There is a very legitimate, very respectable common ground, or middle ground. It does not have to be either/or.

"For example, I can disagree with fundamental tenets of Reform Judaism while still ascribing the highest possible motivation to Reform rabbis. And I can acknowledge them as bona fide spiritual leaders of Jews. People who really, and to the best of their abilities based on their understanding, bring Jews closer to God. I still may disagree with them, but [they are] righteous people. So when we get to question each other's motivation, when I come along to a Reform rabbi and I say, 'You are a destroyer of faith. You are going out of your way to change tradition, you despise the Torah, you despise God, you're an enemy of Judaism!'—that's where animosity comes from.

"If the problem of conversion is allowed to fester, it's going to become a massive problem. If you say to me, your Jewishness is based on how you feel, how you love it, or because your father is Jewish—which one? Let's say you discover that you're father is not your real father. Would you still be Jewish? You still feel Jewish? Should it be enough?

"[Can we say that] anyone who comes to Israel and builds a house [is a Jew]? Would you accept that? Can an Arab come to Israel and build a house?

"[Can] California and New Mexico have two different standards of citizenship, but still [be] one country? There has to be one standard of conversion upon which we all agree. That's just a straightforward observation. . . . Why can't we all agree that, for the sake of the Jewish people, we can have one portal by which people enter the Jewish nation? You want to enter and join something, you have to show a commitment. To me, that's perfectly logical.

"Irrespective of certain affiliation, we all feel good about being part of one people. There is a special feeling that Jews have when they are on a Swiss mountaintop skiing, and suddenly you turn around and there is a stranger from South America, and you're from Britain, but you are both Jewish, and you have something immediately in common.

"Jews are in love with the continuance of the Jewish people. That's why people give money to Israel, why they give money to the Jewish community. . . . Now, I don't believe in unity at any cost by any stretch of the imagination. I will not compromise the Torah and the sense of community, because I think that the Torah is what has insured and guaranteed the survival of the Jewish nation. I will not reduce Orthodox standards of conversion. But I will accord recognition of Reform as a meaningful expression of Jewishness for those who otherwise would not affiliate. The actual discussions must take place between the rabbis. The rabbis are the guardians of the faith. But I'm just saying that lay people should clamor for it."

21

"When you are dealing with faith, no one is right."
—Rabbi Dr. Abraham Levy

RABBI DR. ABRAHAM LEVY is the Sephardi rabbi in London and also the official Sephardi rabbi of Gibraltar, where he was born. I told him an anecdote about the one time the subject of Sephardic Jews came up in my father's house, shortly after a visit from a couple I did not know and would never see again.

My father was in awe. "They are Oriental Jews," he said. "They can trace their lineage back through the generations of wonderful culture." Years later, at the yeshiva in Israel, Rabbi Bulman sounded very much like my father when he told me about a Sephardi wedding he had recently attended, about the beauty of it, and he too described with awe this prince and princess, this royalty of the Jewish people.

"There are two kinds of Sephardic Jews," Rabbi Levy explained. "There are Western Sephardic Jews and there are Oriental Sephardic Jews. Western Sephardi sadly has gone wrong. Western Sephardi, since the expulsion of the Jews from Spain, were living in London, the West Indies, in Amsterdam, and they were highly educated, exceedingly successful in business, believing in beautiful things, prayer books beautifully done, exquisite leather binding—there was a finesse about this religion. . . . It worked for many centuries. . . . You could live as an English gentleman and still live as a committed Jew. It was very nice. There was a synthesis of culture and it worked very well when there was good Jewish education.

161

But when there was assimilation, these were the people who dropped away from Judaism like flies.

"In the eyes of many Ashkenazi Jews, particularly those who had been living in poverty, here were the nobility. We may not have deserved it, but that's how [the Ashkenazi] thought of it. For example, Sir Moses Montefiore [a Sephardi Jew]—you would go to any *shtetl* [Jewish village] in Russia or Poland and you would see his picture because he was a knight and a friend of Queen Victoria's and when the Jews needed help he would go with letters from Queen Victoria to Russia and say, 'You can't persecute my people.' This is beautiful.

"There were two types [of the Oriental Sephardim]. There were those who were indigenous to the lands in which they had been living for hundreds of years. And then there were those who left Spain and were forced to go live in these countries, the Ottoman Empire, Morocco, or Algiers. There what happened was that the Jews who had been living in Spain, thinking themselves far superior to those less educated ones [Jews] . . . kept themselves separate, or very often took [the indigenous Jews] over. So, for example, the first printing press in the Ottoman Empire was not a secular printing press. It was a Jewish printing press. The first book printed in the Ottoman Empire was a Jewish book. That shows you the culture of Jews in the Ottoman Empire.

"Very often, they went back and they raised the standard but not enough to make them like Western Sephardim, which was probably a good thing, because it kept a lot of the sanctity of the religion of the Sephardim.

"The greatest tragedy in Jewish history, in my mind, is the fact that ideological adjectives were given towards Judaism—and that is an entirely Ashkenazi invention. The Sephardic mind never understood ideological adjectives towards Judaism . . . and was always able with a little bit of giving and taking to remain monolithic. And it is for that reason that this subject and this problem is mainly an Ashkenazi problem. It's not a Sephardi problem. The Sephardim have the blessing of being able to remain traditionally Jewish—whether they keep a lot [of the tradition] or they keep a little.

"They do that by a number of ways. First of all, they do it because the Sephardi who does not temporarily observe never mocks what he doesn't observe. The Ashkenazi who doesn't observe often mocks what he doesn't observe.

"Anybody who wishes to come into my synagogue is welcome, whether they are observers or not observers. And I've only got one yardstick: a good Jew is anybody who wishes to be a better Jew. Within that yardstick there is a legalistic yardstick. I can't avoid it. I can't have a situation where somebody who is not halakhically Jewish wants to walk in and say, 'Rabbi, I'm a Jew.' If he is interested in Judaism, I'm interested to be able to help him convert, but I cannot ignore a legal system which has been binding.

"Let's deal with a situation like yours because, coincidentally, I had the identical situation in my office three days ago. A father came to me who is now fairly observant, who had married out and brought me a daughter. And he said, 'What do we do?' I said to him, 'Well you are a Jew and your daughter is your daughter and therefore you have a duty to make her halakhically Jewish and I'm here to help you.' And I will help him. . . . What I do is, if you're Jewish you're very welcome. If you're not Jewish and you want to be Jewish and I can help, you're very welcome. I've got to welcome everyone and nobody has got to feel embarrassed. That is a different thing from wanting a synagogue for homosexuals. That is a perversion. I am not able to change any laws for my people.

"Let me tell you I was the only traditional rabbi that attended [Hugo Gryn's] funeral. I did not go to the Reform temple. I went to the funeral because it was my duty as a Jew to bury another Jew. I was tremendously troubled, but I went. But let me tell you why I would not go to a Reform temple. A church is so distant from Judaism that nobody can conceivably say that Christianity is another form of Judaism. So therefore, I will go to a church to be the official representative, and I have no qualms about it. My going to a Reform religious service is making a statement as to my feelings towards that service—and I can't accept that service. To individual Jews who otherwise would have had nothing, it gives them some Judaism, but to the preservation of Judaism, it can't help.

"When you are dealing with faith, no one is right. No one can be proved scientifically right. So therefore it's only a question of belief.

"The problem of conversion today is the mockery. Judaism only understands one halakhic form of conversion. If what you want is to be converted but to keep very little [tradition], I can't help you.

"[In Israel] there are areas and pockets of Jews who say, 'We want to live with our own tradition and we want Shabbat being Shabbat.' We have to encourage them. For the others, there has got to be some mutual respect. So if, for example, there are hundreds of miles of coastline and some people want to go swimming, why shouldn't there be some sections of beach [open] for them? *Halakha* will still be *halakha*, Purim is still Purim, and you can't take all that away from Jewish life. But there will be religious marriages and there will be civil marriages. And there will be Christian marriages and there will be Reform marriages. I don't accept their marriages. I accept the inevitability of that happening. But if that marriage is against *halakha*, I can't accept [the children] as Jewish. . . .

"My wife says that I look modern but that I am very, very extreme in my views. I don't think I am. It's not a matter of being extreme, you see. I can be as modern as possible. Human law is changeable and divine law, by its very character, is not changeable. . . . Rabbis sometimes go a long way to circumvent it. But they will not discard it.

"I am a passionate believer in Zion. It was the rabbi in my synagogue who brought Theodor Herzl to England. But I am very upset at the way that Zionism has been treated in the Diaspora. The first thing that we've got to do is to do away with [religious] political parties of Israel. It's a bore and we don't need them and that's not the way to put over a love of Israel in this country. The conversion law is a different thing because I think it is not a political issue, it's a religious issue and part of the problem is the mixture of politics and religion. I have no other yardstick, I have no other power to change it.

"My brother sends all of his ten children to the [most traditional] schools. And he's doing it that way because that way he knows it will come all right. And he's right. But he's paying a price which I am not prepared to pay. I'm not prepared to divorce my children from the world, from anything which is a problem, but the proof of the pudding is in the eating. . . the [ultra-Orthodox] succeed! And that's why I get on well with them. And I get along well with the Reform because I respect them and they respect me. And it's for that reason that I can go to Hugo Gryn's funeral and [the Orthodox] don't chop my head off."

UNITED STATES

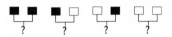

22

"You can't bridge the unbridgable. The issue was, and remains, what will the State of Israel do?"
—*Rabbi Eric H. Yoffie*

IT IS FRIDAY, in Dallas, Texas. At the Union of American Hebrew Congregations' Biennial Convention, over 4,000 of North America's 1.5 million affiliated Reform Jews gather for a Shabbat service of great spirituality and joy. In this big room, to these people, I am a Jew, though, I am to learn, not without the reservation of some Reform rabbis who do not agree with the Movement's decision to accept patrilineal descent. A 1991 study by an American sociologist, Samuel Heilman, found that fully one-third of American Reform rabbis disagree with the decision. Even here, the concept of my existence is a troublesome one. Still, I am home, though it has been some time since I've been to a Shabbat service of the movement I think of as my own. I listen in vain for a melody I know, and can barely recognize the *Sh'ma*—the prayer central to all Jewish worship—which is in the middle of a rousing anthem. The several Conservative Jews, and the one modern Orthodox Jew whom I find in attendance, tell me later they did not feel comfortable in the service. We no longer recognize each other in prayer.

In this same enormous room on the days before and after Shabbat, delegates to this convention had, in sometimes rancorous debate, refused to take up the issue of rabbinic officiation at intermarriages, pledged financial support for Reform Judaism in Israel, and generally played politics with breathtaking passion and savvy. Should they choose to enter Israel's political stream, they would be excellent players.

169

While the U.S. has not yet had a Jewish president (or a woman president, for that matter), it is no longer unusual to find a Jew in a top governmental post. Indeed, for generations Jews have been instrumental in decision-making at all levels of U.S. government. While there are Jewish population centers throughout the country, residential codes discouraging Jews from certain neighborhoods have in my lifetime mostly disappeared. At the turn of the millennium, America's approximately six million Jews are woven into the fabric of the society, free to celebrate their ethnicity, content to practice their faith in any and all ways they see fit. Most—90 percent—are not Orthodox. And of those, the largest number are Reform Jews, and many are second- or third- or fourth-generation Reform Jews; their families left *halakha* behind long ago.

The UAHC's president is Rabbi Eric H. Yoffie. He represents a constituency of Jews whose demands on him are no less than their demands on the governments of the two countries they call home.

He began our conversation "with the premise that we are a single people and that Jews everywhere have a common fate and a common destiny. That means that we care about what happens anywhere in the Jewish world. And it means, in particular, that we care about what happens in the Jewish state. "We have learned that it's a disaster for the Jewish people if we distance ourselves from the land of Israel and the people of Israel. The State of Israel is today the second largest Jewish community in the world. Within twenty years, it'll be the largest Jewish community in the world. The United States will have the second largest Jewish community in the world. Jewish faith is going to be in the hands of these two masses of Jews who, hopefully, will work together to strengthen Judaism and Jewish tradition all around the world. It makes no sense, when you have two major centers of Jewish life, that either center should talk about writing off the other. That's an absurdity.

"The Jews are a tiny people in the world. Our ultimate task, our ultimate challenge is for serious Jews in both places to work together to strengthen the power of Torah in our midst.

"Each community brings some unique strengths and weaknesses to this equation.

"Problems in assimilation and intermarriage are an inevitable consequence of living in an open society. We're facing a demographic decline at the same time that we're facing a religious renewal. We're acquainted with pluralism and tolerance, which is a great strength for us. We have not, at this point, built a substantive network of Jewish schools and so on that will provide the kind of Jewish literacy that [I'd like to see].

"We're quite a remarkable community, in some ways successful beyond our wildest dreams. We've done far more than my grandfather ever would have imagined that we might have done. But we're a paradoxical community. Part of the reason that Israelis don't understand us is that we are simultaneously enormously successful and at the same time very fragile and vulnerable. We're strong. We're powerful. We are thriving among an elite. And there's a tremendous gap between the serious Reform Jew and the non-serious Reform Jew. And that's true for all the streams of Judaism. So ours is a paradoxical community.

"Israel brings a different sort of resource to this mix. You don't have to worry in Israel about reconciling a general culture with a Jewish culture. The calendar, the rhythms of the Jewish year are apparent. Which is both a strength and a weakness for them. Their language is Hebrew. They have certain built-in advantages by virtue of the fact that they come from a majority Jewish culture. We [the Reform movement] bring our own strengths to the equation—a kind of Judaism that is intimately related, but we come at it from a different perspective. What makes sense in this kind of Jewish world is for these two communities to be working together to strengthen Judaism wherever Jews may be found.

"The situation in Israel is very complicated. There's no question that the Orthodox establishment is a corrupt establishment.

I mean, what we know from the history of humankind is that if you put monopolistic religious power in the hands of a government-sponsored religious establishment, the result is disaster. You corrupt the religious tradition which supposedly is being served. That's been the case in every culture in the history of humankind and it's the case today. Why should we think that we are somehow exempt from that process? What has happened in Israel is that Torah and Judaism have been corrupted. That is inherently tragic. Those who are outside of Orthodoxy identify Judaism in Torah with a corrupt political establishment. I don't take any delight in that.

"Why is it that we're not more of a force there? Part of it has to do with the discrimination that exists [in Israel]. Part of it is simply our own fault, because we [don't have a large presence] there. We need to wage a fight for our legal rights, and for separation of synagogue and state. At the same time, we have to build a grass-roots religious presence. And the fact of the matter is, we haven't done it. We weren't in Israel a hundred years ago and we weren't there fifty years ago, either. So we are a new presence on the Israeli scene. We have a great deal to offer. But we have to accept some of the responsibility for our failure to reach out to the masses of Israeli Jews. I don't accept the notion that we're there in small numbers and, therefore, the absence of religious freedom is somehow justified. If religious freedom depended upon one's numbers in the population, Jews would not have religious rights anywhere in the world except in the State of Israel. And if the Jews in any European country were treated the way that foreign Jews are treated [in Israel], the Jewish world would be in an uproar.

"The fact that it happens in Israel doesn't make it any better. These two concerns have to go hand-in-hand. We need to build a grass roots process. We need to fight for our rights and for a better political and constitutional system that will permit Judaism to flourish there. The prime minister talks very eloquently about the need for a free market in the economic realm. We need a free market in the religious realm.

"And where is religion most powerful among Western democracies? In the United States. Why is that? Because of separation of church and state. With the absence of government entanglement in an established religion, and a free market where religious institutions and ideologies are able to compete with each other and appeal to a constituency without government restraint, you find that you have, by far, the highest number of religious institutions, you have the highest church and synagogue attendance.

"We care about Israel because Israel is a sovereign Jewish state. And we know, after the Holocaust, the price of Jewish powerlessness. American Jews have influence. We are a significant part of the American power structure. . . . There wouldn't have been a Holocaust if a Jewish state had existed at that time. We've learned that lesson. In the absence of power, all Jewish values turn to dust.

"I'm a tried and true liberal, but I understand that we have a Jewish army in the world. And that the State of Israel provides that army. It provides a flag and it provides a place of refuge, and it provides protection for Jews everywhere. And for all of our differences, that's exceedingly important.

"There are also the religious underpinnings of our support for Israel. A fundamental commandment is that we look to Israel and we build a community in Israel. The precise meaning of those commandments will vary. My interpretation is quite simple. If you go back to Torah, and you look at the commandments that were directed at the children of Israel as they were marching through the desert, the most important thing was that they were to build the holy community, and Torah would be observed. We have long understood that [Israel] is not the only place where Torah can be observed and where a holy community can be created. That's the very premise of the establishment of a community here. But, having said that, we do recognize that there are certain commandments that relate directly to the land of Israel and can't be observed anywhere else. We yearn for the land of Israel because of the possibilities that exist there to observe Torah and to create holy community. As a religious obligation, while it doesn't call upon us to move there tomorrow, cutting ourselves off from Israel is a disaster and a tragedy that will weaken our community in every sense.

"Israel, for fifty years, has been primarily concerned with issues of physical survival. And when those issues were foremost on their agenda, they had no time and energy for other things. . . . But we live in a different world today. . . . Whatever you think of Arafat and Hamas, neither has the ability to threaten Israel's physical existence. So, for all the political uncertainty, Israel's physical security is far more assured than any time in its history. That means Israelis are turning to other issues. And for us, support for the physical survival of the Jewish state is no longer at the top of our agenda because it no longer needs to be. So all of a sudden, we have new issues to look at. And very high on this list is determining how we build Judaism in [the U.S. and Israel] and how we work together in doing that. We don't have a clue, at this moment, how to proceed.

"We're not a halakhic movement. Either you accept the [halakhic] system or you don't. You can't be a quasi-halakhic Jew. Both the Orthodox movement and the Conservative movement define themselves as halakhic. I would suggest that the foundation of Reform Judaism would be the concept of *mitzvah*, or of an individual commandment. We accept individual *mitzvot*. But we don't accept the halakhic system as binding, and that's a significant difference.

"If you operate on the assumption that Jewish law was given by God to Moses on Mount Sinai, both the written tradition and the oral tradition, then all of your view of Judaism flows from that. We don't begin with that assumption. We say, 'Let's take the *mitzvot* one at a time. And let's analyze the *mitzvot* one at a time.' How do we determine whether a particular *mitzvah* is binding? There are a variety of factors. For any *mitzvah*, you have a command that comes from God. But at the same time, somebody hears that command. And how that person hears the particular command determines ultimately how the command was recorded. And then you have the question of how a community might respond to a particular command. In other words, we look at Torah, and we see a command.

"It's a command that comes from God. Moses, here speaking symbolically for the people as a whole, received those commands. What he wrote down was dependent, first of all, on his own particular characteristics. Moses was a person like anybody else. And his own personal religious predilections and so on, determined, in some measure, what was recorded in Torah. People change from one period to another. And people have a particular set of religious, cultural, and sociological concerns. So the status of the Jewish people at that particular moment had some impact on what was recorded in Torah.

"So when we look at Torah, we don't say, 'We accept it.' What we say is, 'There's an element of divine command.' And then we have to factor in what Moses brought to it and what the Jewish people brought to it, recognizing that, in our particular time, we—as individual Jews, and our Jewish community—are going to view that *mitzvah* in a different light. We have no alternative but to examine the *mitzvot* one at a time, and to decide which ones will be binding for us.

"As a Reform community, we can offer guidance to our congregations and to our broad constituency. We can offer suggestions. Ultimately, we recognize [that observance] will be up to the individual. Ultimately, while he or she can be guided by his rabbi and by his congregation and by his larger movement, ultimately, what he accepts as binding [is] his own personal decision. That is a very complicated, complex, and difficult approach to Jewish life. Because if you take it seriously, it means that you have to study, you have to be very thoughtful, and you have to make a serious judgment in the whole variety of cases. That is the burden of a liberal Jew, and we accept that burden. We urge people to view it seriously and not simply as a matter of convenience, to make a decision that's rooted in knowledge and experience with their own Jewish practice. And to ultimately determine to what extent they feel that they are commanded. Ultimately, that's an individual decision. It's a very different approach than Orthodox and Conservative, and it's really different from Reconstructionist, too.

"'Who Is a Jew?' has all kinds of implications. It means different things to different people. But on the narrowest level, the most immediate level, you know who is a Jew according to Reform tradition. It's somebody who is born to two Jewish parents or somebody who is born to one Jewish parent, where there is a presumption of Jewishness. But you're not considered a Jew under those circumstances unless the child is raised as a Jew and there are various public acts of Jewish commitment, bar mitzvah, confirmation, and so forth. [Patrilineal descent] was a revolutionary approach. There are indeed roots to it in the Bible. In a sense, we have been acting this way for much of the past century. What Rabbi Alex Schindler [UAHC president emeritus, who initiated the patrilineal descent ruling] did was to say, 'If these are our principles, let's declare them openly, and have some integrity in how we view ourselves. And this is what we believe. Let's be prepared to say so.' I thought he was right in doing that. It's not without precedent in our tradition.

"Having said that, there is no denying that for something over 2,000 years, normative Judaism has defined things differently. So this was a break with 2,000 years of normative traditional thinking. But it was done after much thought. And, I think, for good reasons. Part of it had to do with egalitarian concerns. In the world in which we live, what sense did it make for a child born of a Jewish father and a child born of a Jewish mother to be seen as somehow fundamentally different? And that flowing from the firm commitment to egalitarianism, which has been a defining characteristic of Reform Judaism for much of this century and surely for the last quarter century, it followed logically that we had to treat the children of both parents equally.

"I think that there is no question that the increasing rate of intermarriage was a factor here, as well. Our approach was to reach out and to welcome and to embrace intermarried couples, to urge the non-Jew to convert whenever that was possible, whenever there was any interest. And even if there was not, to do everything possible to see to it that the children were raised as Jews and identified as Jews. And the instances where the father was Jewish and was prepared to join the synagogue and raise the child as a Jew, and the mother, for whatever reason, was not interested in converting, it's very important to us to send a message that not only were they welcome in the synagogue, but that we see that child as Jewish."

And now Yoffie considered my case. He said I would be embraced as a Jew if I was *"raised* as a Jew . . . and that's an important element. According to the technical aspects of the patrilineal decision, if you have one parent who's a Jew, father or mother, and you are not raised as a Jew, then you can't make a claim to be a Jew. But beyond that, our movement is very clear: That person is a Jew."

I asked him why, then, I should care about Israel, where I am not considered a Jew.

"The truth is there are a lot of Jews, a lot of people in the United States, who don't consider you Jewish, either. The Conservative movement, which is as large as ours, and certainly the Orthodox movement. So why should you care about the American Jewish community? What we're suggesting is, Jews care about Judaism and other Jews, even if we have fundamental differences with them. But you identify as a Jew. You practice as a Jew. You care about the Jewish people. Therefore, you have to care about Israel, the second largest center of Judaism, both because there are other Jews there and because you care about the health and the vibrancy of Jewish religious tradition. And that depends on strong Jewish people, and on strong Jewish communities everywhere. And Israel is a central segment of that.

"There may be hurt for you and for others [in your position]. Part of the fight that we're fighting in Israel is precisely on this point. What's happening with Russian Jews there? Cultural traditions in Russia were such that if your father was Jewish and your mother wasn't, you were Jewish. The society would look upon you as Jewish if your father was Jewish, and you considered yourself Jewish. You would then come to Israel, and all of a sudden you would discover that Israeli society didn't consider you to be Jewish. Some of those people want to convert. According to our definition, they don't have to convert if they're practicing Jews. The problem that they face is in many ways similar [to yours]. We'll be advocates for our point of view and we'll bring about those changes that we need to bring about. And we are confident that in the long term, the patrilineal decision will be widely accepted among the Jewish people. I strongly suspect that one or two generations from now, it will be far more broadly accepted here. What will happen in Israel, I'm not sure.

"The Orthodox should believe what they want to believe. They don't accept me as a rabbi. They don't accept you as a Jew. Fine. But the State of Israel, that's something else. The State of Israel needs to be a unifying force in Jewish life. Until very recently, it was a unifying force in Jewish life. The State of Israel is the state of the entire Jewish people, not just a segment of the Jewish people. And when the State of Israel, a sovereign state, suggests that only one group stood at Sinai, only one group is legitimate, and chooses to exclude me from its official governmental recognition, that's a very serious matter, indeed. So that's why I have so much of a problem with trying to come up with a joint process [that all the movements can agree to] for conversion. It's a mistake. It won't work. You can't bridge the unbridgable. The issue was, and remains, what will the State of Israel do?"

Yoffie was talking about the notion at play early in 1998 when the Neeman Commission met to find a compromise on the Israeli conversion bill, that one standard could be found to please all the movements. The idea was that a body would be formed of representatives from the Orthodox, Reform, Conservative, and Reconstructionist movements to educate potential converts, with Orthodox rabbis administering the process of conversion itself. Like Yoffie, I cannot imagine such a thing. Many of the people with whom I have spoken over the past year cannot even agree to disagree. None would be willing to compromise their beliefs for the sake of unity, and most of the Orthodox I met do not find a unity rooted in a pluralistic society a desirable end. I wonder, too, if American Reform would be willing to surrender its position on patrilineal descent, as surely it would have to do before Orthodox or Conservative Jews would even consider forming a unified measure of conversion.

Beyond that, many leading rabbis within Reform and without see the question as far larger than the conversion issue. Among them is Rabbi Sheldon Zimmerman, president of the Reform movement's Hebrew Union College–Jewish Institute of Religion, the academic and spiritual center of the Reform movement in the United States. He is also a former president of the Central Conference of American Rabbis, the professional association of American Reform rabbis.

"The real issue is not conversion," Zimmerman said, "because if [another movement] doesn't accept ours, they can always re-convert. The real issue is the issue of divorce—that's really what divides us."

By Jewish tradition, which is strictly adhered to by the Orthodox, women are not freed from a marriage unless their husbands give them a *get,* a Jewish bill of divorce. While that husband may marry another single Jewish woman and with her produce children who are Jewish and in every way qualified to participate in Jewish life, the earlier wife does not have that privilege unless the husband decides to grant it. Jewish children she might have by another "marriage" would be considered the issue of a forbidden union, and would be labeled *mamzerim.* They would be Jewish, but unable to marry most other Jews, nor could any of their future generations for all time. My half-sister—my father's daughter with a formerly married Jewish woman—is such a child. While, according to the Orthodox, I can convert and be considered a full Jew, she cannot.

"The only way around it is to effect something to protect future generations," said Zimmerman, who was a high-profile proponent of Reform's patrilineal descent decision. "If there is anything we have learned, it is that both parents have a claim." Driven by the principle that "both partners [in a marriage] be treated with equality," he and others are now working toward a unified approach to Jewish divorce, as the Neeman Commission looked for a unified approach to conversion.

Though discussions about an agreement on divorce issues have not been made public, it seems to me that the process would have to include dialogue about which rabbis' marriages are acceptable. One part of the solution, as many have pointed out, might be for all movements to accept Reform marriage as halakhically invalid, and therefore not requiring a *get* for termination. Judaism does not stigmatize Jewish children born of an unmarried woman. Because Reform Jews are not bound by *halakha*, they might accept such an understanding because it would not require them to change their Reform ceremonies. Ultimately, though, these matters are seen as problems primarily by the Orthodox, and until the Orthodox can see a need for compromise, there can be none, certainly not within the State of Israel.

But Zimmerman sees in the Jewish homeland an even greater challenge.

"So many Israelis write off Jewish identity," he said, "simply because the only religious identity they witness is one that is literally a struggle, not only for the soil of Israel, but for the soul of Israel. We are really talking about the future of, and the quality of, the spiritual life of the Jewish people in the State of Israel. We [Reform Jews] have something to offer as a way of affirming one's Jewishness and covenant with God, which takes us beyond Orthodox understanding. We have an obligation to reach out to Israelis, to help them affirm their part in the covenant with God and their role in Jewish history, which is more than simply being Israeli, but being Jewish. . . . I believe that a good healthy Jewish environment is Orthodox, Conservative, Reform, Reconstructionist. That's good for the Jews."

Rabbi Ammiel Hirsch is the director of the Association of Reform Zionists of America (ARZA). Hirsch is the son of Rabbi Richard Hirsch, executive director of the World Union for Progressive Judaism. Not quite forty, the younger Rabbi Hirsch is something of a revolutionary, inclined on occasion to go a step past the acceptable, to ply rough waters bravely. It was Hirsch who implied—to the distress of many other Jews—that Natan Sharansky owed Reform and Conservative Jews special allegiance in "Who Is a Jew?" matters. It was Hirsch, at the Reform convention in Dallas, who characteristically surprised his colleagues by asking the members of a seminar audience to donate $100,000 to advertise against the conversion bill in Israel. (Hirsch did, in fact, raise most of that sum, he told me, a move that was countered by the Orthodox who sent out a call for money to advertise in *favor* of the conversion bill.) It was Hirsch who suggested in a radio interview that Reform had "informed members of Congress with whom we have ties, 'Please help us convey [to the Israeli government] that [the Israeli conversion bill and its aftermath] is a very serious matter . . . and one we must stop.'" This provoked the head of Agudath Israel of America, Rabbi Moshe Sherer, to accuse Hirsch of "attempting to undermine the democratic system of a foreign country."

But then, Hirsch is in fact being true to the spirit of the early Zionists, who never used moderate words when speaking of Israel and took all issues to the edge of acceptability. At the moment I met Hirsch, I was puzzled by what an American Reform Zionist was, exactly. That in 1997 there were "American Zionists" not living in Israel seemed to make the term an oxymoron.

"A Zionist is somebody who considers the centrality of Israel at the center of the Jewish people," Hirsch said. "A Reform Zionist is one who considers such matters to be a matter of core religious identity and ideology. An American Reform Zionist is all of the above who happens to live in America. Zionism, when it initially came into being, sought to answer the fundamental question of how to insure Jewish continuity. The answer identified anti-Semitism as the primary problem. The only solution would be a Jewish state. And that hasn't changed. . . . It is possible to be a Zionist outside of Israel. Because the fundamental question is, how to insure Jewish continuity? How to insure the survival of the Jewish people, as a people?

"At the core of Jewish ideology is preparation for Jewish state-hood," he said. "That is the natural state of affairs. That's what is written into God's blueprint for society. The Jews promise a firm loyalty to God, and God provides for Jewish land, Jewish nationhood, and Jewish self-determination. And that covenant has implications from Sinai throughout history and has implications, not only for the relationship between God and the Jewish people, but between the Jewish people and the Jewish people. And that covenant is what generates the responsibility of all Jews. Zionism was, by and large, a secular modern political movement. The reason it succeeded when all of the great social revolutions of the twentieth century failed was it tapped into the core of Jewish identity that even secular Jews could relate to and understood. That there was something grand happening here that went be-yond themselves and beyond a nineteenth- or twentieth-century experience."

But if Israel doesn't want me, I said, and won't let me marry there . . .

"Then the solution is not to say, 'What the heck!' The solution is to join the fight," he said. "That's what you have to do. You sup-ply your political, material, human, and intellectual resources to those who share your values. It's a monumental struggle. The outcome of the struggle will be determined over the next decade. And the winners will determine the future of Judaism over the next century.

"No Jewish community, no group of Jews can compete with the power, prestige, influence, resources of statehood. That's clear, as admirable as American Jewish accomplishment has been. Our problem in the Reform movement is we weren't there when the State of Israel was built. The lesson from that is, if you want an impact on the outcome of the struggle, you have to be there from the beginning of the struggle. [But] we're making a difference."

Indeed, a study by The Louis Guttman Institute of Applied Social Science in 1992 revealed that 45 percent of Israeli respondents were willing to consider Reform or Conservative options to Orthodoxy.

"If you measure where we were in 1973—and I use that as a watershed because that's when my dad moved [my family] with the headquarters of the World Union to Jerusalem—and where we are now, there's no comparison," Hirsch said.

In 1973, "there was one Reform institution in Jerusalem. This then-empty institution called the Hebrew Union College used to have services for Americans on Friday and Saturday morning. There was almost nothing else. Twenty-five years later, there's a movement, active congregations. So we're making tremendous headway. We have a network of kindergartens that wasn't there twenty-five years ago. Our kindergartens are the most popular in the country. Not necessarily because the parents identify as Reform Jews, but they want the best education for their kids, and we supply the best education. But, through that, they have exposure to Reform Judaism. So if you look at the last twenty-five years, there's cause for tremendous optimism. Because all of this was done when the energies of the Reform movement were not devoted almost entirely to Israel. Imagine what could have happened had we devoted the kind of resources that we're just now beginning to see?

"There are [Reform] rabbis who are preparing to run for the Knesset. That, in my opinion, is not a bad thing. I don't foresee us running as a party because we have seen the corrupting influence of religion in politics. We're all engaged in politics here, too. If you're an active member of society, you have to engage the political process in one way or another, because that's how you effect a change in society. . . . But our power is not in politics. Our power is the power of the spirit and the intellect. We're either going to succeed or not succeed based on our ability to inspire groups of people, to create a Jewish society in the land of Israel that is enlightened, tolerant, respectful, a magnet for Jews and for humanity, and fulfills the greatest destiny that was established for the Jews, to be a light to the nations. . . .

"Rabbi Yoffie says we have to return to Torah. We have to return to serious Jewish education. We have to be serious Jews. That's where the ball game is. That's where everybody is struggling, and where the big struggle for Jewish continuity is: to create serious Jews who take Jewish values seriously, who take Jewish study seriously, who try every day to improve him or herself Jewishly, who identify with Jewish institutions, who take Jewish concepts of charity seriously, who take Israel seriously, who lend their resources and support to those who want to advance their own vision of Israel seriously, who raise Jewish families and are insistent that there be continuity in their own family with regard to enshrining Jewish values in their children, and passing them on in their children's children."

23

"When religious problems have to be solved at
the national level the halakhic system rigidifies;
it doesn't function well in the limelight.
It becomes a body of law without soul."
—*Rabbi Dr. Ismar Schorsch*

"I REFUSE TO BE OUT-JEWED," says my friend Gloria Lewit when she
speaks of the Orthodox Jews who would question her religious
practices. She, like other Americans, will not be told what to
do—not even by their own rabbis. And their rabbis won't be told
what to do by *their* rabbis.

In America you can hear, for example, a leading Conservative
rabbi disagreeing with his own movement's hardline against patrilineal descent. "It is too readily dismissed," said Rabbi Harold
Schulweis, who leads 1,700 Conservative families at Valley Beth
Shalom congregation in Encino, California.

"My own subjective feeling is what [the Reform movement has
done in recognizing patrilineal descent] is totally correct. My argument is that the idea of matrilineality is itself a clear case of
compromise. After all, one should say that the sperm is as important as the ovum, therefore both the father and the mother should
be Jewish. But the very fact that the rabbis have reduced [lineage]
to matrilineality, saying they don't care who the father was, was
clearly because they were concerned with spreading the net as
wide as possible to include those who were impregnated possibly
by rape, or whatever the case may be. But clearly, it was a compromise. It seems to me that patrilineality is simply an extension

185

of that idea, to include fathers as well as the mothers as transmitting Jewish status to the child. . . . I think [the Reform movement's position] is simply an extension of that, with very similar motivation: namely, the point of view of *halakha* to see to it that Jews are not lost.

"[Orthodox and Conservative rabbis] use the argument that [patrilineal descent] produces the schism among the movements. My counter to that is that prior to the patrilineality issue the schism was just as profound, and people were just as unhappy with giving women equal rights, and they still are. So it has nothing to do with patrilineality."

But will the Conservative movement ever recognize patrilineality?

"I think history and sociology will make that determination—not *halakha*. The truth of the matter is that increasingly rabbis are going to confront people like yourself who come to them and want to get married and. . . look, I'm not going to be probing. I'll be tickled pink that you regard yourself as being a Jew. . . . From a deeper point of view, Judaism has always gone through stages of change. . . .

"The laity in my own congregation is four-to-one in favor of patrilineality. If you took a poll nationwide, you would find the same thing. The rabbis here [in the U.S.] are simply institutionally stuck.

"Ultimately, I think patrilineality will be accepted" by Conservative Jews.

"I don't think the Conservative movement will ever accept patrilineal descent," said Rabbi Joel H. Meyers, executive vice president of the Rabbinical Assembly, the professional association of Conservative rabbis in the U.S. The Assembly maintains a committee on Jewish Law and Standards, which is the governing halakhic body for the 1.6 million Conservative Jews in the U.S.

"We have rabbis who are on our margin who talk about, 'Well, let's accept patrilineality.' I've heard some of my colleagues say that. But I think if it came to a vote, the vote would be 'absolutely not.' In fact, the discussion was held several years ago and the overwhelming vote among the rabbis was to maintain matrilineality as the definition of Jewishness. So I don't see that changing. I think that's wishful thinking.

"When the Reform movement "redefined 'Who Is a Jew' in 1983, they determined *unilaterally* to go with patrilineality. Sometimes it's a bit disingenuous [for Reform] to scream that the Orthodox want to define 'Who Is a Jew,' when the Reform movement did it in 1983. You have to understand that. I mean, *somebody* has to understand that."

The practical political alliance of Conservative and Reform Jews was forged of necessity. Because the Conservative movement is a halakhic organization, it is somewhat theologically aligned with Orthodoxy. But because Conservative and Reform are, by definition, non-Orthodox, they have over the years learned to work together to advance what both would see as a more modern approach to Judaism. The non-Orthodox movements do, in fact, work well together. In private, though, they can be less than wholehearted in their endorsement of each other. Conservative Jews like to say that the Reform decision on patrilineal descent was a move to fill Reform synagogues. Reform Jews say that for years Conservative Jews thought they would be seen by the Orthodox as close members of the family and would willingly have thrown Reform to the wolves. Because Orthodoxy never came around to that way of thinking—as it probably never will so long as Conservative Judaism ordains women rabbis—Conservative Jews were forced to align in some practical ways with Reform Jews. Meyers said,

"We really pick and choose areas of cooperation and work together in ways we think will enhance Jewish life. And so there are times when we have come together in coalition, and times we have gone our separate ways. . . . We've been asked by many different people, 'Why are you aligned with the Reform movement?' And we have said because we all have a problem together, the right of religious expression in Israel. . . . Currently the question of the religious right in Israel and religious pluralism in Israel is an issue we've been working on together. Both the Orthodox and Conservative movements are halakhically based. The Conservative movement looks at *halakha* as an expansive, evolving *halakha*, and the Orthodox look at *halakha* as maintaining the circle of tradition as it exists. . . . If we could get our Orthodox colleagues and our Conservative colleagues away from [personal] attacks and looking at aberrations, and look at the question of how can someone convert in Jewish life, both we and the Orthodox would be able to define that. We would both agree that somebody converting into Judaism has to observe *mitzvot.* Now, my Orthodox colleagues would have you observe all the *mitzvot.* We [Conservative] would say that's not the litmus test. The litmus test is: How is this convert moving into a deepening Jewish life? We would want [a potential convert] to talk to us about keeping a kosher home. We would like Shabbat observance. What we wouldn't say is, 'We demand the following in your Shabbat.' We understand that there has to be some flexibility. We would have a broader construction of halakhic parameters than our Orthodox colleagues do, but we would require basically at rock bottom the same commitments and certainly the same conversion.

"The question of registering Jews in Israel today is the problem. Under Israeli law, if somebody enters Israel on *aliyah* and proves they are Jewish, the proof being something like letters from rabbis or a marriage *ketubbah* or a conversion certificate, then they should be registered by the Interior Ministry as Jews. Now, what happens over time is, as the Interior Ministry has come under the control of Orthodox religious parties, they have found ways not to register somebody who converts to Judaism in the United States through the Conservative movement. It's become a difficult moment."

And it has become a dangerous moment, according to Rabbi Dr. Ismar Schorsch, chancellor of The Jewish Theological Seminary of America, the academic and spiritual center of the Conservative movement in the United States. Schorsch urges all movements to speak about the issues that divide them, but is distressed by what he terms the "verbal violence" that turns Jew against Jew.

"Verbal violence often becomes physical violence," he said. "I don't think we are immune to that. . . . What dismays me in Israel is the silence of the religious and political leadership when verbal violence occurs. They allow the verbal violence to pass and do not condemn it, do not declare it to be out of bounds, unacceptable in a civil society. That, I think, simply encourages the verbal violence.

"There are conversations taking place in different sectors of the community that are not always visible. I think there's quite a bit of religious terrorism out there. I think the modern Orthodox are intimidated. In some ways, I think the modern Orthodox hold the key to the solution of this problem. They need to emancipate themselves from the religious terrorism of the ultra-Orthodox. I think that they are going to be driven to do that, because the rhetoric of the ultra-Orthodox is simply unrestrained.

"I do see a solution to this problem and that is the disengagement of religion from politics in the State of Israel. The genesis of this problem is the control which one sector of the religious world has over other sectors of the religious world. That situation has to be altered. I think it will require a lot of political pressure. But this is what we have begun to apply from the United States. The Neeman Commission is the first time the government of Israel has sat down to negotiate with Reform and Conservative leadership. That is quite an accomplishment. And I think a compromise is going to come out of that negotiation and that compromise will be accepted by the religious leadership in the State of Israel because they won't have much choice. The [Israeli] government doesn't want to collapse. And that government is going to apply a lot of pressure, I think, to the religious leadership. . . . My own view would be that American Jewish leadership should insist that the vote on the conversion bill [in the Israeli Knesset] should be governed by conscience and not party discipline. I think we [in the United States] have a loud voice. I think American Jewish leadership should say that Judaism is above politics. It should not be subjected to political calculation and, therefore, has to be elevated to the level of conscience, where a person has the right to vote what he believes. And then I think the conversion bill will fail."

But what happens if the bill passed?

"There are few things which are irreversible, but it certainly is going to estrange the Diaspora from Israel for the foreseeable future. You will find increased political activity on the part of Conservative leadership. I think we will redouble our efforts to promote religious pluralism on the ground in the State of Israel. That is why I have been calling for large sums of money from Federations earmarked for religious pluralism. I think that if a conversion bill were to pass, you would see quickly far larger allocations for religious pluralism coming from the Federation world."

I asked him about the unprecedented partnership forged by Conservative and Reform because of the pluralism issue.

"It's a political alliance. Each of us alone could never have successfully raised the issue. It's not a philosophical alliance. There are many differences. Patrilineal descent is clearly a deep division.

And when the Reform movement adopted it in this country it was parochial. It did it in complete indifference to the larger Jewish community. Religious pluralism means you've got to accept and respect people with whom you disagree. If we agreed on everything, we wouldn't need religious pluralism. Religious pluralism works in this country. And if religious differences divide, they can often be overcome. So if a patrilineal Jew falls in love with an Orthodox individual, religious conversion is always an option that can repair the situation.

"In this country, the reason that we can get along is because religious problems are solved at the local level. When religious problems have to be solved at the national level the halakhic system rigidifies; it doesn't function well in the limelight. It becomes a body of law without soul. That's the tragedy of the situation in Israel. We don't have problems with Russian Jews in this country; it's only in Israel where we have problems. We all know that if the Russian Jews could have been converted in Vienna [while en route to Israel], they would have been converted in two days. Suddenly, they come to Israel and there's a sack of halakhic problems. The halakhic system doesn't function very well at a national level.

"Conservative halakhists are loose constructionists. And Orthodox are strict constructionists. But they are both working off a constitution. They read the constitution differently. . . ."

I asked him if it is likely that Conservative and Reform are to come closer together, by Conservative coming to accept, for example, patrilineal descent as it did women rabbis.

"The past is no guarantee of the future. I think that the Reform movement is going to divide in due time. The Reform movement is moving in opposite directions at the same time. You have a considerable dilution of Jewish content in Reform synagogues by virtue of the growing non-Jewish presence. But at the same time you've got the religious leadership that is pushing more and more tradition. I think that in due time you will find that the more traditional Reform Jews will find their way into the Conservative movement because they will look for more rather than less Judaism and that will be hard to find in the Reform synagogues.

"I don't think [Judaism] is going to disappear. I think the question is how many of us will survive and whether that number will be large enough to remain creative and dynamic. I don't think that any form of Judaism alone is going to meet the religious needs of all Jews. The diversity that exists is for good reason. Because we have a very diverse population and a population that is free to choose. So the more synagogues we have, the more Jews we're going to reach, whatever the denomination. The Reform movement exists because there are lots of Jews who are satisfied with that approach to Jewish history and Jewish experience, and with that approach to God. But it's not going to satisfy all Jews and for the Jews that remain unsatisfied we need alternatives. The reason there are so many secular Jews in Israel is because they all have an Orthodox synagogue they don't go to. There would be a lot fewer secular Jews in Israel if there were different religious choices, and if they had non-Orthodox synagogues that they could frequent.

"A lot of Israelis have a traditional bent, but are not necessarily shul-goers because the Orthodox synagogues that are available to them are simply too extreme. The tragedy in Israel is that it is not necessary to be so heavy-handed. The chances are that someone who converts in Israel will live a pretty full Jewish life because they live in a Jewish state. The environment is in Judaism's favor. In Israel, you are living in a Jewish context, so you don't have to force Judaism down anybody's throat. It doesn't work anyway.

"The Jewish state and its support of religion have created a degree of insularity for Orthodox Jews that Judaism has never experienced in all of its history. It is distance from the outside world that creates a vacuum in which religious thinking can run amok. There are no temporizing forces. This was not a problem 2,000 years ago because Palestine was overrun by Greeks. Greek culture was all over the place. The rabbis knew more Greek than the ultra-Orthodox rabbis in Israel know English. Extremism is bred in a cultural vacuum, and the Orthodox in the State of Israel have been allowed to live in total isolation.

"I believe that Israel needs to be a Jewish state. It cannot be an Orthodox state and to make it an Orthodox state will shrink it, and render it insignificant to the Jewish people."

24

"What is ultimately determinative is the effort to try to create a much more visible, vigorous, powerful form of liberal Jewish life in Israel."

—*Rabbi David A. Teutsch*

IT IS NOT UNUSUAL to hear a Reform, or even an Orthodox or Conservative, rabbi refer to the work of Rabbi Mordecai M. Kaplan, the founder of the Reconstructionist movement. An Orthodox man of piety, Kaplan (1881–1983), a Lithuanian who emigrated to the United States, was—and remains—a major contemporary Jewish thinker. Throughout the course of his long life, his ideas changed as he studied biology, history, anthropology, and psychology, and he came to see God as a "cosmic presence" and a "power that makes for righteousness." He ruled out all that was supernatural in traditional thinking.

While Kaplan's belief in the origin of the commandments and *mitzvot* was untraditional, he stressed traditional ritual and developed a movement that saw the synagogue as the central institution of a Jewish life that was rich in study, art, music, dance, song, literature, and virtually all communal activity. Most important, he saw it as the center of a community of Jews who worked as a "religious civilization" to advance social change.

The movement today is not clearly understood by many in liberal movements. In fact, Reconstructionism is, in some ways, more traditional than Reform Judaism, insisting, for example, on kosher kitchens in synagogues. Reconstructionism views itself as a "post-halakhic" movement that is dedicated to Kaplan's insistence that "the past has a vote, not a veto."

195

I heard very little about Reconstructionism in Israel, though in the U.S. liberal rabbis are careful to include it when mentioning the non-Orthodox streams. Founded by Kaplan in 1922, the movement is now based in suburban Philadelphia, where its Federation of Reconstructionist Congregations is located. Estimates are that the movement now embraces more than 100,000 people. By all accounts, that number is growing, and it is easy to see why. In a Jewish world in which rabbis disagree vehemently with one another, and sometimes with the majority of their congregants, the great appeal of the Reconstructionist vision may be its insistence on an unapologetically democratic Judaism, in which rabbis work directly with other members of the community to formulate practice and law in a setting of contemporary culture and ethnicity.

Rabbi David A. Teutsch, president of the Reconstructionist Rabbinical College, began our conversation by quoting the Reconstructionist position on patrilineal descent.

"If one person is Jewish, either mother or father, the offspring is to be regarded as Jewish, and should undergo the rites prescribed by our tradition . . . but no special conversion procedure is required.

"In order to be considered Jewish if you have only one Jewish parent," he said, "you need Jewish life-cycle events and Jewish education. You follow the tradition you were raised in. If you were raised Catholic, you aren't considered Jewish. In an earlier time, when the Jewish community was closed, who was a Jew and who was not a Jew was pretty obvious to everybody because of social associations and religious practices. In the world of the open society and contemporary life in America, the boundaries between Jews and non-Jews are open in unprecedented ways, and reduced so low that you get back and forth across them quite easily. What that means is that it is very easy for a Jew born of two Jewish parents to grow up so assimilated that they have virtually no Jewish identity at all, with no knowledge or practice of Judaism. But there can be a reasonable assumption that, unless that person has taken on another religion, that person is still residually Jewish. However, it means that unlike a world in which you were a Jew and everybody knew you were a Jew and you were raised as a Jew and you observed as a Jew, in this world you can't presume that. The question of how a child is raised, to which culture the child is acculturated, becomes a really key question of the identity in a religious sense and ethnic identity of the child [with one Jewish parent].

"Judaism is, unlike virtually any other Western religion, a profound mixture of peoplehood and religion. And any effort to try to separate the peoplehood element from the religious element in Judaism has resulted in having a form of Judaism that was not survivalist. It was not robust enough to preserve Judaism. Part of what it means—that Judaism is based on Jewish peoplehood—is that the only way a Jew can effectively be part of Judaism is to be part of the Jewish community, where you serve together, eat together, have social linkages. Whereas it's possible that somebody could find Christian books in a trunk somewhere and become a Christian on their own, becoming a Jew in that fashion is almost unimaginable. Because to be Jewish in an effective way, you have to be part of a social association that does Jewish things together, whether that's hearing the Torah read or celebrating Seder. Judaism is gutted by any effort to try to do Judaism entirely on your own.

"Israel is the only country in which Jews are the majority, so it has an impact by virtue of its being our historical homeland, the land where Hebrew is spoken, the land where in some ways it is simplest to live Jewish life intensely. It has a powerful influence on world Jewry. And that's a good thing. It is central to the Jewish consciousness. But as a result of that centrality, policy in Israel is enormously influential by virtue of its numbers as well as its position. Policy made in Israel has a profound effect on the American Jewish community. For example, the rapidly growing strength of Orthodoxy in Israel is one of the reasons why the Orthodox in the United States have taken a much more rejectionist stance on many of these issues than they did forty years ago. The willingness of many Orthodox to break with the rest of the

Jewish community in the United States is reflected in the fact that they are so strongly identified with the Orthodox community in Israel that it's become enormously powerful.

"Most Orthodox rabbis refused to accept conversions under any but Orthodox auspices. Because of that any conversion done at any point in history by a non-Orthodox rabbi was considered by the Orthodox to be non-existent. That means that whether a non-Orthodox rabbi performed a conversion or not made no difference in the eyes of the Orthodox. The only reason why the lineality issue became the kind of issue it is was that it gave Orthodoxy in Israel a convenient handle to do the break that they wanted to do. This fight is really about the legitimacy and authenticity of any form of non-Orthodox Judaism. . . . If we lose that fight, we're creating a greater split around the question of whether there can be one Jewish people and whether we can have a pluralism in which we recognize that, while we think each other are wrong on certain issues, we all are legitimate, authentic, and caring Jews.

"This argument is the one that they picked to fight about. Why this one and not [Jewish divorce], which is more serious in some ways because if you're a patrilineal Jew and you want to marry someone Orthodox, you could always go through a conversion later. But if you [are a woman and] don't get a Jewish *get*, and you remarry and you have a kid, that kid is a *mamzer* in the eyes of the Orthodox forever. And since *mamzerut* is, from the Orthodox point of view, a really horrible situation and a really dangerous situation, you might ask why didn't they make the big fight about that? Because it doesn't have nearly as much of a gut-wrenching turn. And also because in America, if the Orthodox said all you Jews are *mamzerim*, they would so totally lose the support of every kind of middle-of-the-road Jew who is still sending money to Lubavitch or to *yeshivot* in Israel, that it's a bad battleground. They picked this battleground because they thought they could win. They thought they could use the tools of the state government in Israel to enforce their hegemony.

"The only reason why people are [doing those things] in Israel now is because the Orthodox in Israel have turned the official government machine into a Jewish policy agency. Once the Orthodox politicized this issue by trying to change the Law of Return, by doing everything in their power to block Reform and Conservative and Reconstructionist Jews from being recognized as legitimate in Israel, and by choking off government funds from our agencies in Israel, they politicized this to the point where people had no choice but to fight back politically.

"In the long run, the only way it is going to work out is, with the best education in Israel, that we begin to develop changes in liberal religious options for people in Israel in much greater numbers.

"They need us, and here we are getting into my values. Because my values are that democracy opens communities and pluralism strengthens and enhances Judaism. A communitarian form of Judaism could enormously enrich the lives of Israelis, and a pluralistic view toward Judaism will open many more passages to religious life for the huge number of secular Jews in Israel who are not comfortable with Orthodoxy. Those Jews who believe in women's equality in Israel, and who think that that is incompatible with Judaism, must be shown there is a way to combine them. It's critically important on a moral level, because we believe in the moral advancement of Judaism.

"On this particular issue, the Reform and Reconstructionist and Conservatives are not very far apart. There are other issues where the gap is wider. The Reconstructionists talk about being a post-halakhic movement. . . . The *halakha* was designed for Diaspora communities that were self-governing. When the Jewish communities ceased to be self-governing, there had to develop the new approach to how to combine tradition and modernity. The Reconstructionists, in general, are very deeply committed to community learning, community study, and community decision-making. We take a much more communitarian approach to how this should work. But in terms of the actual issue of patrilineality . . . we would stand shoulder-to-shoulder with Reform.

"I don't think that what happens [with the conversion bill] is ultimately determinative. What is ultimately determinative is the effort to try to create a much more visible, vigorous, powerful form of liberal Jewish life in Israel. And in that regard the Reconstructionist movement has started an outreach program just in the last few months, because now in the United States we are strong enough to have the luxury to do that. But also because, in the long run, the issues about the Law of Return and other matters will be determined by the general Jewish population in Israel."

25

"Every Jew is a Jew, but that doesn't mean
that every Judaism is a Judaism."
—*Rabbi Avi Shafran*

ESTIMATES ARE THAT 375,000 Orthodox Jews live in the United
States, though the Orthodox themselves appear to be uninter-
ested in head counts. The cynical view is that it is not in their
best interest to advertise the fact that their numbers are far
smaller than the other denominations. Their argument is that all
such numbers are misleading and inaccurate, because a "non-
observant" Jew may not think of himself or herself as Reform or
Conservative, either. Those on the far right of the spectrum suggest that an accurate count would find Orthodoxy in the lead.

Yet there is little question that of those who are Orthodox in
the United States, most can be accurately described as "modern"
or "moderate" in the style of Rabbi Norman Lamm, the president of Yeshiva University, the training and spiritual center of
mainstream Orthodoxy in the United States, though he, rightly,
does not claim to speak for all the rabbis in his own circle. Yet
"modern" and "moderate" do not translate, even in the U.S., into
a wholesale endorsement of religious pluralism in Israel.

"I'm generally a moderate in most things," Lamm told me.
"However, moderate does not mean you have no firm principles.
And there are some principles that must predominate and must
prevail even if that sometimes has unpleasant consequences. It's
the nature of law, and this goes back not only to Maimonides,
but to Plato. A law is a general rule, and it's impossible that some

individuals should not be disadvantaged by it. You help them the best you can. But the alternative to having that kind of law is to have chaos in society."

Why is pluralism seen as a threat in Israel? I asked.

"I'll tell you why it is seen as a threat. Let's say that we went along with the current buzzword of pluralism. Let's say that the [Israeli] courts overturned all legislation and that whoever wants to be called a Jew, can go to a Reform or Conservative rabbi— especially a Reform rabbi—to convert him or her. Obviously, this is changing the rules by which we've played the game for the last 3,000 years. And it means that the now-accepted norm of what makes a Jew a Jew has been overturned in favor of self-declaration. Which would [make Israel] probably the only country in the world that allows citizenship by self-declaration. I don't want to be accused of being impolite—but, when you get down to it realistically, the Reform have no standards because every rabbi is a law unto himself. That's part of the whole Reform attitude.

"I have grandchildren, may they live and be well, who are coming into marriageable age sooner or later. [Let's say] they're going to want to marry someone who is a self-declared Jew. That immediately presents a problem. The State of Israel is a small country, a small and very volatile country, and a country in which all Jews are connected with each other by many bonds, especially those of shrillness. You want to make sure they can marry everyone. Until now, it is fairly certain if people say they're Jewish you accept that they are Jewish in Israel. Once this rule has been violated—a violation inscribed in law—there no longer is any certainty. Then how do I know whom I can advise my grandchildren to marry?

"The only answer is—this has been done once or twice in Jewish history with devastating results—that we'll declare that the rabbinical courts will have genealogical tables. We'll have to have records of who is who. And that means that if you do not register with the chief rabbinate, then you will not be regarded as marriageable with those who are registered with the chief rabbinate. Which means you will have automatically broken the country into two groups that cannot intermarry with each other. The consequences will be as devastating, or more devastating, than they were when the Jewish kingdom after Solomon broke into two kingdoms of the north and the south, or Israel and Judah—they fought against each other. Now this will be even worse [in Israel] because you can't even separate them geographically. You would have a society torn against itself.

"You can't really compare Israel to America. We Americans sometimes are imperialistic without realizing it. We feel that our brand of democracy is the only one that is legitimate. It's not so. England has an older democracy and they have an established church. I'm not suggesting the same for Israel, but there are various forms democracy can take.

"I know some of my Orthodox colleagues would want to ban Reform from any entrance into Israel. I'm opposed to that. I think that that is a principle of democracy: people can do what they want. However, there are certain principles that are inviolable. In the United States, if someone has given a great deal of money to American charities and helped the government, but he simply was not born in this country nor was he a naturalized citizen, and he simply wanted to declare himself a citizen because he risked his life and his fortune on behalf of the United States—well, you give him an honorary degree. . . . He deserves congratulations and 'thank you.' But that doesn't really make him a citizen. Every society has some rules about who is in and who is out. Those rules should be followed in Israel too, but that's not going to happen if we break down the barriers of 'Who Is a Jew?'"

I told him it's already happened. Jewish officials in Israel *do* demand proof.

"You know why? It's because of the patrilineal thing," he said. "Once they've declared for patrilineal descent, that means that a person like yourself—I hope you understand that what I'm saying is not without compassion—you would be declared a Jew by the Reform group. You would not be accepted by Conservative or Orthodox, by *halakha*. . . . If I have a principle I have to apply it universally. Otherwise, what sense does it make?

"I'm hopeful [that the Neeman Commission will reach a compromise] because the alternative is so terrible. I've got to hope. What I'm fighting for—and here I'm against the majority of the Orthodox rabbinate probably—is in favor of the compromise I've heard so far, although it is far from perfect. Because when [Israeli Prime Minister Yitzhak] Shamir called me about ten or so years ago, the problem was his government was going to fall on the 'Who Is a Jew?' question. Then the problem was not about conversions done in Israel, but about conversions done in America. And I came up with a solution that almost worked. . . . I'm in favor of a compromise where Reform and Conservative rabbis or any kind of rabbis will be allowed to have some kind of a ceremonial function, but not part of a halakhic function. Therefore, what we have now with the recommendation of Neeman [is] that all rabbis will be permitted to teach, not only rabbis but laymen too, at a school for instructing potential converts, but that the actual conversion will be done by a panel of Orthodox rabbis who constitute an official bet din. I think it's a good compromise. What I had [proposed] about a decade ago was that there would be a panel of mixed rabbis and laymen of all denominations who would pass on the perceived integrity of the convert as to his or her intentions, and then it would be passed on to a panel of Orthodox rabbis, hopefully of more liberal bents, who would not throw the book at people, but try to look for the easiest way in. So if the halakhic functions remain with their integrity intact, then I see no reason for avoiding a compromise.

"The battle here is not over 'Who Is a Jew?' The battle is over 'Who Is a Rabbi?' That we can't yield on. I can't recognize the true rabbinic authentic credentials of a man who says, 'I do not accept the *halakha*.' With Conservative rabbis we face a problem because some do and some don't, and some say they do and really don't, and some say they don't but really do. It's a mish-mash. When you come to the Reform group, they're pretty clear. They have not accepted *halakha* for over 100 years now. So to say that I accept a Reform rabbi as halakhically authentic is to perpetuate an outright falsehood. Can I accept someone as a supreme court justice who refuses to pledge fealty and loyalty to the Constitution of the United States? You can't do such things. It's not logical."

What sort of lifestyle would he demand of a convert?

"In the development of *halakha* . . . strictly speaking you ask very few questions. You notify the potential convert of some of the major laws and some of the minor laws. Now, here comes the very interesting ticklish point. If the convert says 'I accept every-thing except one thing. I accept everything except a Passover seder,' or, 'I accept everything except for not smoking on Shab-bat,' you cannot convert him or her. But you don't tell him every-thing [about Judaism during the conversion process]—and you aren't required to tell him everything because no Jew in the world knows everything—you just impart the major things. Thus, there is no idolatry; you don't have to go into those areas that may be sticky. No one in the world observes all 613 commandments."

Therefore, I asked him, if I as a potential convert say I won't observe *kashrut* . . .

"Then I won't convert you," he said. "But I don't necessarily have to demand everything. Moreover, I can ask you to observe kashrut and you can say, 'I'll do it to the best of my ability'—and mean it; I'm not speaking of lying. I would accept that in Israel. But not here [in the United States]. I would accept it in Israel be-cause that to my mind means that you will keep up the major laws of *kashrut* but not the strictions that have been added by many people. But if you say, 'No, I will not accept *kashrut* at all and I'm going to eat pork and lobster together with a milkshake,' than I'll say 'Bon appetit,' but Judaism is not for you. In Israel I would feel at least there is a Jewish society into which you will assimilate. That society is more secular than we are led to believe in America. But, most people in Israel are somewhere in the middle. So at least you'll be Jewish. In the United States, I would be more strict. One of my teachers used to say when he had a young man or a young woman coming for conversion, he would say to him or her, 'Do you want to embrace Judaism or a Jewish boy or girl?' In this country, I would fear that once a Jewish boy or girl falls out of favor, or they get divorced, that you remain with someone who is nominally Jewish but has no intention of doing anything about it. In Israel, I would be more sure that the effects of society unconsciously would lead someone to a more Jewish way of life."

I asked if his being an American in some way informs his philosophy.

"I suppose it's impossible to avoid influences of your own background. Maybe because I've experienced a pluralistic society— and I am here using the term in its political and social sense, not in the religious sense—I learned that you can live in this kind of society. I really believe that, as [Winston] Churchill said [about Democracy], it's a terrible system, but the alternatives are far worse. So that must have some effect on me. And I grew up under a grandfather who was a great halakhic scholar, who always was moderate and leaning more to the permissive rather than to the restrictive pole."

It is precisely on this point that modern American Orthodox Rabbi Lamm is at odds with ultra-Orthodox American Jews whose influences lead them to a conclusion that the ship must be steered toward the "restrictive pole" to keep Judaism on course.

"We differ with Rabbi Lamm's approach to the political question of whether halakha should be enshrined as the official Jewish religion in Israel," said Rabbi Avi Shafran, spokesman for Agudath Israel in the United States. Lamm's hopes for a compromise through the Neeman Commission "is where he differs from many other people in the modern Orthodox community. In the '80s, in Denver, there was a joint Orthodox, Reform, and Conservative rabbinic group that had a set-up by which they converted people. For many reasons, it fell apart. The party line of the rabbis who were involved was that it fell apart because it was exposed and couldn't stand up to pressure from the outside, but people on the scene say it imploded, because it became clear it was just a Reform conversion factory. And even the Orthodox rabbis who were involved felt that they were basically processing converts of dubious candidacy for conversion. And doing it entirely for the Reform rabbis. The actual conversion was done by the Orthodox group, but it was overseen and the candidates were handed over [by non-Orthodox rabbis]. It was essentially a rubber-stamping set-up. On the one hand, it seemed like it was innocuous, that the [non-Orthodox rabbis were] just witnessing. But I think many Orthodox, including the right-wing Orthodox, feel that that is itself more than inadvisable, because it fosters an impression that is an extremely dangerous one. That is that the other movements—quasi-movements—are legitimate expressions of Jewish tradition. And to do that even in a way that doesn't technically violate any law is itself a violation of something even more essential—Jewish philosophy. So I think that right off the bat, and maybe this is a distinction between some of the modern Orthodox and [us] more right-wing Orthodox, for lack of a better term, is that anything that could be perceived by anyone as a recognition of the validity of non-Orthodox movements will automatically be an impossible thing to accept.

"But beyond that, the truth is that the Reform movement . . . says nothing is acceptable as a compromise unless it gives the Reform movement the right to decide who should be converted. In other words, they will not be satisfied with this sort of 'suggesting' of converts, and then overseeing it along with Orthodox rabbis. What they want is a rubber-stamp. They want to be able to say, 'This man John Smith has been deemed a candidate for conversion, so convert him!' And no questions asked. And regardless of what the Orthodox may or may not find out in an investigation of the intentions of this convert, that makes no difference.

"Mr. Neeman's ostensible plan won't even be accepted by the Reform movement. I don't impugn the idealism or the good will of anybody along the spectrum. I just disagree strongly with the contention that the Reform movement can lay claim to the mantle of Judaism. And I also contest the wisdom—even if they are idealistic and believe what they say—of insisting on conversion in situations where it has already created and is going to continue to create a whole quasi-Jewish people that's largely people considered Jewish by one movement and not by others. Is that a wise approach even for a movement that is convinced that it is correct in its interpretation of Judaism? But the [non-Orthodox] know that we're not going away. They know that there are these stubborn Orthodox Jews who they hoped perhaps at one point, thirty or forty years ago, would just give up the ghost. They clearly know that's not going to happen now. They see the intensity of Orthodoxy and the growth of Orthodoxy and the institutions and things that show we aren't going anywhere. So we are going to be a player on the scene at least.

"For [Reform Jews] to sort of single-mindedly go ahead and create a whole contested community of Jews who are semi-Jews, who are Jews to some people and not to others, is to be very irresponsible from a sociological view, from a Jewish unity perspective. But of course they'll come back and say, 'But what are we supposed to do? We want to convert people.' The answer of conversion is not one of the principles of Judaism. There isn't a need to create converts, and especially to do it in a wholesale fashion, as unfortunately it is done, where anybody who falls in love with a Jewish person is thereby a candidate for conversion. And anybody who expresses an interest in things Jewish is automatically a convert and accepted. That's a kind of lowering of standards that is bound to create disunity among the Jewish people as a people. That's what it has done in the United States already.

"[Patrilineal descent] is something [Reform Jews] have had ample time to back off of. And they are not backing off. The truth is, its just a magnification of the essential conversion crisis. Conversions create the same kind of thing as patrilineality does. Maybe on a lesser scale because [patrilineal descent] happened overnight. Suddenly every person born of a Jewish father and a non-Jewish mother was automatically Jewish, willy-nilly. It was a new definition, at least vis-à-vis *halakha* until the turn of the century. And I don't spare the Conservative movement this either, because that movement, also, although its a much more subtle departure from *halakha*, is clearly departed from *halakha*. Their claim that they once could make with some degree of integrity that they are a halakhic movement I don't believe can really be made anymore. . . . There is something of an assumption throughout the texts that even though everything can't be studied and spoken out with the potential convert, there has to be, at least in principle, acceptance of doing whatever it is that he or she will discover as necessary according to Jewish law. . . . We're talking about a whole fundamental attitude toward the binding nature of Jewish law. It's not just a question of, 'I accept to keep kosher.' If a person today says, 'I accept to keep kosher but its not a commandment of God, but as a sociological connection with fellow Jews,' I don't believe that any [halakhic scholar] would consider that to be a proper conversion. [A convert] has to accept commandments. Commandments have a meaning—someone commanded it, not acceptance of practice but acceptance of commandments. And if one does not believe in the commander or in the commandments having originated with the commander—and the movements themselves don't insist on that! Even the Conservative movement doesn't insist that its rabbis accept everything that the Talmud says or the [scholars] have said over the ages. And if they can't be held to that themselves, they certainly can't be expected to hold converts to that.

"I think that it's a little bit disingenuous to try to put forth those kind of plans which in and of themselves are probably not even satisfactory. But it's taking the focus away from the larger question here, which is that we have movements that are not committed to what—at least historically until the Enlightenment or the turn of the century—was considered Judaism. And to ask those who do maintain a link between the Judaism of old to accept in any which way contorting and creating situations and technicalities, to ask them to accept that these other movements' representatives will be part of the process on any level, is really going to be asking too much. I don't think there is a solution. . . . Nothing that could possibly satisfy the Reform movement in its declared or even undeclared foot-in-the-door goal would conceivably be acceptable to the right-wing leadership in Israel, who consider this an opportunity to make it clear once and for all that these are not Judaisms. And there are no Judaisms. There is only one Judaism, and it has many forms and there is pluralism, but all that pluralism has to be based upon the essential acceptance of *mitzvoth* as divine commandments.

"This thing has come to a head. We've let it go too long. I believe that the Orthodox world has been remiss in not strongly enough taking umbrage at the redefinition of Judaism that has taken place in America over the past half century. I don't think we've been clear enough. We've tried to be polite, and at the same time we've endangered truth. Every Jew is a Jew, but that doesn't mean that every Judaism is a Judaism. By not making that clear enough, we've inadvertently played a role in misleading other Jews. And here's an opportunity for us to say clearly whatever needs to be said. And, hopefully, to say it with love and to say it properly. But it does need to be said. And I don't think that that's something to bemoan. I think its just a necessary correction.

"I deal with ultra-Orthodox Jews day in and day out. I can only assure you that there is a true and sincere concern for their non-Orthodox brothers and sisters. And that is something that is so often lost in all the heat that goes on. We could be very fine and good on our own, we ultra-Orthodox. We live in our world, we have our own communities. We could just say, 'The hell with the rest of the Jewish world.' But we don't care just for ourselves, but for our fellow Jews as well."

After Words

When I told an Israeli that I had interviewed ultra-Orthodox rabbis for this book, he said, "How much did that cost you?" When I told a Conservative rabbi that I had learned there are no monsters in the "Who Is a Jew?" debate, he said, "There *are* monsters!" A Reform rabbi informed me that the Orthodox use theological arguments only to gain wealth and power. Not one Orthodox Jew with whom I spoke was willing to believe that many Reform conversions require the convert to be immersed in a traditional ritual bath. My people, whose strength is in large measure in their pursuit of learning, know very little about each other, and much of what they think they know is wrong.

In Beachwood, Ohio, a community composed primarily of non-Orthodox Jews near Cleveland, just a few miles from my childhood home, voters vetoed legislation in 1997 that would allow construction of two new Orthodox synagogues. It was not the proposed buildings they objected to, but the proposed occupants. The result was a continuing, highly public war: Jew against Jew.

In 1997, Secretary of State Madeleine Albright was "exposed" in the media as a Jew. Her grandparents were Jews. Three of them perished in the Holocaust. Her parents converted to Catholicism in Czechoslovakia. When they came to the United States, they told no one, including their own daughter, she said, about their past. If Albright was surprised to learn of her ancestry I was equally surprised by the hubbub that ensued. I thought the world had matured since I was a child and the conversions of entertainers Sammy Davis Jr. and Elizabeth Taylor were considered big news. Yet this was a new twist on an even older story harking back to the time when public figures sought to hide their ethnicity behind "acceptable" Christian-sounding names. Ostensibly, the question was whether Albright knew she was of Jewish descent and hid the knowledge. How could she not have known? But the underlying question was how she would handle the information, and how the rest of the country and the world would handle it, as though being discovered to have Jewish blood would influence her performance in the job.

In the face of our mistrust and ignorance of our fellow Jews, how must we appear to those outside of Judaism? And how have we managed to forge a new and remarkable understanding with a majority of the Christian world?

In the 1960s, the Second Vatican Council called for the end to the demonization of Jews in Roman Catholic thought. In the thirty years since, in great part under the guidance of Pope John Paul II, the Roman Catholic church has rewritten its textbooks to reflect the Jew as brother and friend of the Christian. It has reached back into its own history to find anew the people in whom, they believe, God entrusted his son. It has presented that new understanding to its 60 million U.S. members and to its vast membership across the world. The Catholic church has celebrated the spiritual link between Christianity and Judaism. It has condemned anti-Semitism and has accepted and apologized for its part in creating the societal fabric that allowed the Holocaust. At every turn, contemporary Catholics have reached out to Jews in unprecedented dialogue.

Too few of us know the extent to which Catholics and Jews have worked together and forged a remarkable, historic understanding. Yet from which Jews does the Catholic Church seek a Jewish viewpoint? How is it that though Jews cannot bring themselves to speak with each other, they can speak with non-Jews and cross theological bridges once thought uncrossable?

"It was easier to speak to Jews some years ago than it is today," said Dr. Eugene J. Fisher, associate director of the Secretariat for Ecumenical and Interreligious Affairs of the National Conference of Catholic Bishops, a point man for Catholics on Catholic-Jewish relations. Discussions were formerly held with the now-defunct Synagogue Council of America, which represented Orthodox, Conservative, and Reform Jews. Since that organization's demise, Catholic representatives have "a very good dialogue with the Orthodox" through the Orthodox Union and the Rabbinical Council of America, said Fisher, and with Conservative and Reform Jews through the National Council of Synagogues.

"It is more complex [to talk to Jews]," said Fisher. "On the other hand, one has to deal with the living community one deals with. If you want a dialogue with the Catholic Church, that's a fairly neat dialogue from the Jewish point of view because of our hierarchy. We're nice and organized. Within the Catholic community, we have a very diverse range of views, but the church as an institution can make commitments like it did at the Second Vatican Council, and it has the right to change the teachings. So changes begin.

"The Church considers itself a people, a people of God, and what it takes to belong to that people we argue over all the time. That's why there are so many splits in Christianity. It's different [from Jewish arguments] in that it's not a parentage issue. Christians split up over formulations of what makes a good Christian."

I asked him how it was possible for the Catholic Church to remain virtually intact in the face of its own inner dissension. He laughed and said, "Why can it hold together? Because every side still has a chance to win."

Then he was serious again. "The Synagogue Council of America broke down. I think within Orthodoxy there's a fissure now between the mainline Orthodox of Yeshiva University, and those to the right of it. The insult hurled by the rabbi of Agudath Israel against Norman Lamm, one would not have imagined that! In *public,* I mean."

Fisher was talking about an incident that occurred late in 1997. Before more than 2,000 ultra-Orthodox people meeting in New Jersey under the auspices of Agudath Israel, a speaker had denounced Norman Lamm, the Yeshiva University president, as "one who hates God." Lamm and Agudath Israel itself sought to minimize the outburst as an anomaly, but news of the family feud reached other ears.

"In a more private setting, Jews have always hurled verbal barbs," said Fisher. "It's part of the culture of the Talmud. It's nothing new. But one has to have the will to want to get along. I had predicted long ago that as peace escalated with Israel's neighbors, the internal situation would grow visibly more fractious. Israel right now is militarily pretty secure, and that's what's happening to people now; they are pushing for their traditions. In the United States, with its more pluralistic framework, one can have the arguments mostly on an intellectual level."

And though Fisher did not say it directly, it became clear that the "fractious" internal situation among Jews has, in some way, taken its toll on Catholic-Jewish dialogue. For while Catholics were able to agree among themselves on changes reflecting Jews in Catholic liturgy and education, Jews have yet to accept a standard of how Christians are portrayed by Jews, to Jews.

"An amazing number of misconceptions about Christians was handed down from the *shtetl*," said Fisher. "Jews would take the criticisms that Catholics threw at Protestants, and that Protestants used to throw at Catholics, and take the most negative of that and say, 'That is what Christianity is!' Then they'd contrast that with the best of Judaism. There is [among Jews] a very strongly held idea that Christians don't care about deed, just creed. There's a real stereotype of Christianity—a lot of it created in self-defense, but misinformed nonetheless. There is still a tremendous sense of distrust and mistrust. There is very little in Jewish textbooks about Christianity, and most of it tends toward the lachrymose. Most Jewish textbooks seem to say that the mindset of Christians is in about the fifteenth century. So there's a lot of stuff that simply is misunderstanding.

"It seems to me that Jewish education has a task, and a role, to bring Jewish kids up to some sort of awareness, especially in America, of where American Christians are coming from.

"One of the nice things about dialogue is that it pushes understanding, because you have to start articulating where you're coming from. Christians come away from dialogue knowing more about Christianity. I'm a great proponent of dialogue. There's been a lot of work done on reconciliation dialogue: We define ourselves; the other listens to that definition. I can't define you. We try to articulate our understanding in a way that the other can accept as being recognizable. People tend to project onto other people a stereotype quite often derived from several generations back. I would imagine there are many misunderstandings within Orthodox Judaism about how Reform Jews actually live.

"Dialogue opens up understanding, and humanizes people to each other. Once you've been through a process of dialogue with somebody, it's very hard to stereotype."

I learned that lesson myself over the year I spoke to rabbis and others across the spectrum of Jewish thought. Even those with whom I disagreed, even those who would not see me as a Jew, were outstanding in their compassion. Though Israel itself might not accept me, I know that all the people with whom I spoke would take me in and provide real help in time of spiritual, or physical, danger. They are good people. They merely disagree.

My Judaism has been tested in rather harsher ways than I believed it would be when I set out to write this book. For every door that was opened to me, another was closed. For every insight that brought me pleasure, another brought me pain. After traveling through Israel and England, I came home to the U.S. with great respect for those whose actions are in and of traditional Judaism. But the fact remains that, for most of them, I am not family.

Yet my father was right when he said, "A little bit Jewish is like a little bit pregnant." This certainly applies as far as the Christian majority in the United States is concerned, although Christians would never phrase it that way.

Among the American Christians who have reason to define "Who Is a Jew?" is Jim Sibley, the Coordinator of Jewish Ministries for the North American Mission Board of the Southern Baptist Convention. His life's work is to bring Jews to Jesus. "I have had a special love for the Jewish people since I was a child of fourteen years of age," he told me. "God's will" had told him to "take His message to the Jewish people." Sibley took that message to Israel for many years. In the United States, he continues to encourage Jews to see Jesus as the Messiah, though not for purposes of "conversion." It is impossible, he says, for a Jew to become anything other than a Jew.

And what is a Jew in the eyes of this Southern Baptist? "Probably the best thing for all of us would be to go back to scriptures—the Hebrew scriptures," he said. "See what they tell us about the subject, and that *should* settle it. I'm not naive. I don't think it will. According to scripture, a Jew is not one born to a Jewish mother. That's not a Biblical definition. That's a rabbinic definition. Biblically, the lineage was traced through the father. Secondly, a Jew is one who is a descendent of Abraham, Isaac, or Jacob, or who is identified with the Jewish people.

"And, of course, the Old Testament was written by Jews, in Israel. So I consider it Jewish literature. In the New Testament, Paul says that for a gentile who becomes a Christian and then tries to officially become a Jew is wrong. He also said that for a Jewish person to try to annul or revoke his Jewishness is equally wrong.

"The question isn't, 'Can a Jew become a Christian and still remain a Jew?' The question is, 'Is Jesus the Messiah of Israel? Or is he an impostor?'" If Jesus is the Messiah, as Sibley believes, he is the fulfillment of Jewish prophecy and therefore one need not, since he or she cannot, revoke Jewishness to believe in Christ.

"'Conversion' is one of those loaded terms," said Sibley. "Conversion is not something that man does. It's something that God does in a person's heart. . . . Our faith is, in that sense, really a Jewish faith."

Judaism is then, for Sibley and I think for most other Christians and a great many Jews, first a nationality from which there is no escape. It is *secondly* a faith.

When I spoke to Jews, I often heard Judaism referred to as a "club." I cannot see it that way, although I was at every stop invited to join. Many of the "clubhouses" were extremely comfortable, their causes laudable, administered by people who asked that I take the pledge according to a lovely script. Yet that was, for me, entirely too much to ask when I have already lived my life, and would give my life, for them.

Judaism is belief. I know that the Ten Commandments are God-given, though I am not sure God appeared on a mountain and handed them down. I am comfortable with the notion that the ideas were somehow put into our minds and hearts. We work at them, and the work can bring out the best in us and God's world, though our best is never perfect. It is never even good enough.

Judaism is, for me, also and equally, a peoplehood. I am no more or less Jewish than I am American. Combined, they have made me an American Jew, but only in the sense that the life I choose is best lived by me in a country where, because there is no single standard, everybody fits. My rhythms are Jewish—and American. My thoughts are Jewish—and American. My speech is Jewish—and American. My actions are Jewish—and American. Does this echo the lethal delusion of those Jews who also saw themselves as German? Will the United States, the country I chose to live in, someday deny my right to exist? If it does, will Judaism—or Israel—sustain me? Will my vast extended "family" in Israel, in England, in Russia and Poland and India and Spain take me in? And if they take me in, will they allow me to love and be, officially, of them?

The hard answer is that most will not. When my father asked me, all those years ago, if I should stand up to Hitler and tell him I was a Jew, though it would mean certain death, my answer was "yes." It still is "yes." My declaration to Hitler is my declaration to Jews: I can not sign away my Jewishness to please a court that would bestow on me what they think God has denied. The idea of conversion as rebirth is unacceptable to me. I will not attempt to save my skin by renouncing my biological connection to my father; I will not attempt to save my soul by renouncing my biological connection to my mother.

If I keep God's laws to the best of my ability, why must I suffer at the hand of human embellishers?

If I am not Jewish, why do I see my father in Rabbi Bulman's eyes, hear my father in Rabbi Richard Hirsch's voice, see myself in Rabbi Ramon's face? "I am a Jew because my DNA stood at the Western Wall thousands of years ago," a woman told me. So did mine.

If I have not been chosen for Judaism, why do I choose Judaism? If the Messiah is not for me, why do I know its spirit, and feel it hear my prayers, even when I do not know I am praying? I do not ask God for personal appointments, do not require signs of God's existence, do not ask God to help me win football games or lotteries, or even to keep my relationships intact and my loved ones alive. My prayers are those prayed by my community, offered in community, not so that God will hear them, but so that we may reinforce and remind ourselves of the life, the commandments, we have agreed to keep. God does not disallow the community's prayer because I, whose mother is Christian, take part. Nor does God invalidate my desire and commitment to be part of a people who subscribe to the conduct that uses the will God gave us.

I admire *halakha*, but I consider it to be a starting point. I simply cannot believe that God would have us reject all experience and learning of the past 2,000 years. I do not believe that God provides further learning and experience to taunt us. God does not expect us to reject reason in support of faith. God gave us brain, heart, experience, so that we might find our way closer to God through the centuries.

God has not kept me out. People cannot bring me in.

I live in the United States. Somewhere near my home is a congregation that sees things my way, a congregation that will take me in should I choose to ask for admission. Thank God.

The marvelous American spiritual leader and storyteller Rabbi Lawrence Kushner told me this story:

"It's a trans-Atlantic El Al flight. All of a sudden, 36,000 feet over the Atlantic, some guy in the front row reaches under his seat, pulls out an AK-47. Nobody knows how he got it through security. He spins around to a cabin full of terrified passengers and shouts, 'All right. Who is a Jew?!'"

"Some little guy in seat 34C raises his hand and says, 'That's a very difficult question.'"

Epilogue

"All government—indeed, every human benefit and enjoyment, every virtue and every prudent act—is founded on compromise and barter," wrote the Irish statesman and philosopher Edmund Burke in 1775. In this spirit, the Neeman Commission, composed of five men of faith conferring in good faith—three Orthodox, one Conservative and one Reform—proposed a compromise to the bill that would deny legitimacy to non-Orthodox conversions performed in Israel. The commission's proposal of January 1998 called for an Institute for Jewish Studies run by all three denominations under the auspices of the Jewish Agency, and for the Orthodox rabbinate to oversee the actual conversions. Even before the proposal was considered by the chief rabbis of Israel, Rabbi Eric H. Yoffie, the president of the Union of American Hebrew Congregations, assumed that "the proposals will be rejected by the Chief Rabbinate." The chief rabbis did not respond immediately. Ultra-Orthodox rabbis used the lull to attack the Neeman plan and, in a document printed in Israeli newspapers, said the Reform and Conservative movements were attempting to put "their claws in the Holy Land."

In early February, the Israeli Chief Rabbinate rejected the Neeman Commission proposals and called upon "all who are able to prevent the actions of those who . . . try to shake the foundations of the Jewish religion and by this separate the nation. . . . One cannot consider establishing a joint institute with them."

Rabbi Uri Regev, who sat on the commission as the Progressive, or Reform, movement's representative, joined with the Masorti movement in saying the chief rabbis had "declared war on the Jewish people." The next day, as Neeman battled to keep the original compromise alive, Chief Rabbi Yisrael Meir Lau accused the non-Orthodox of defrauding the public by claiming to be genuine forms of Judaism.

As the Neeman Commission was in its final stages of deliberation, Avraham Burg, the head of the Jewish Agency for Israel, led another group of Orthodox, Conservative, and Reform rabbis—including two who also sat on the Neeman Commission—in search of a "stopgap measure" to prevent passage of the conversion bill if the Neeman proposal failed. This group proposed changing the *Leom*, or nationality, portion of the identity card to include the date on which a person became a Jew: for Jews by birth, this would be their birth date; for Jews by choice, it would be the date of conversion. In this way the rabbinate could recognize a potential "problem case" when an individual wanted to get married. This was not a popular suggestion in all quarters because, as Neeman said, it was tantamount to "a scarlet letter" that would label converts as somehow inferior to other Jews.

The Burg group subsequently agreed on a plan to eliminate the *Leom* section completely, and to lodge conversion documents in the population registry where the rabbinate would have access to them. Because the group had not yet settled on the plan's details, Burg presented this second proposal in his own name to Prime Minister Binyamin Netanyahu. This second plan seemed to be gaining support in the Knesset as this book went to press.

I cannot say as I write these words whether the conversion bill, or a compromise, will be passed. But I can say, as have many before me in these pages, that even if a change is made—whether it appears to be a permanent change in the law or a stopgap measure that will "put the genie back in the bottle"—that will not be the end of the argument.

Appendices

Patrilineal Descent

This policy was adopted by the Central Conference of American Rabbis at its 94th Annual convention, March 15, 1983. Its acceptance of children of Jewish fathers and non-Jewish mothers as Jews is, without question, the single most controversial break from Jewish tradition in recent history. It is still a subject of discord among the movements, and among American Reform Jews themselves.

Report of the Committee on Patrilineal Descent on the Status of Children of Mixed Marriages[1]

The purpose of this document is to establish the Jewish status of the children of mixed marriages in the Reform Jewish community of North America.

One of the most pressing human issues for the North American Jewish community is mixed marriage, with all its attendant implications. For our purpose mixed marriage is defined as a union between a Jew and a non-Jew. A non-Jew who joins the Jewish people through conversion is recognized as a Jew in every respect. We deal here only with the Jewish identity of children born of a union in which one parent is Jewish and the other parent is non-Jewish.

This issue arises from the social forces set in motion by the Enlightenment and the Emancipation. They are the roots of our current struggle with mixed marriage. "Social change so drastic and far reaching could not but affect on several levels the psychology of being Jewish. . . . The result of Emancipation was to make

---

[1]Walter Jacob, ed., *American Reform Responsa: Collected Responsa of the Central Conference of American Rabbis, 1889–1983.* New York: Central Conference of American Rabbis, 1983.

223

Jewish identity a private commitment rather than a legal status, leaving it a complex mix of destiny and choice."[2] Since the Napoleonic Assembly of Notables of 1806, the Jewish community has struggled with the tension between modernity and tradition. This tension is now a major challenge, and it is within this specific context that the Reform Movement chooses to respond. Wherever there is ground to do so, our response seeks to establish Jewish identity of the children of mixed marriages.

According to the *Halacha* as interpreted by traditional Jews over many centuries, the offspring of a Jewish mother and a non-Jewish father is recognized as a Jew, while the offspring of a non-Jewish mother and a Jewish father is considered a non-Jew. To become a Jew, the child of a non-Jewish mother and a Jewish father must undergo conversion.

As a Reform community, the process of determining an appropriate response has taken us to an examination of the tradition, our own earlier responses, and the most current considerations. In doing so, we seek to be sensitive to the human dimensions of this issue.

Both the Biblical and Rabbinical traditions take for granted that ordinarily the paternal line is decisive in the tracing of descent within the Jewish people. The Biblical genealogies in Genesis and elsewhere in the Bible attest to this point. In intertribal marriage in ancient Israel, paternal descent was decisive. Numbers 1:2, etc., says: "By their families, by their fathers' houses" *(emishpechotam leveit avotam)*, which for the Rabbis means, "the line (literally: 'family') of the father is recognized; the line of the mother is not" *(Mishpachat av keruya mishpacha; mishpachat em einah keruya mishpacha; Bava Batra* 109b, *Yevamot* 54b; cf. *Yad, Nachalot* 1.6).

In the Rabbinic tradition, this tradition remains in force. The offspring of a male *Kohen* who marries a Levite or Israelite is considered a *Kohen*, and the child of an Israelite who marries a *Kohenet* is an Israelite. Thus: *yichus*, lineage, regards the male

---

[2]Robert Seltzer, *Jewish People, Jewish Thought.* (Upper Saddle River, N.J.: Prentice Hall, 1981).

line as absolutely dominant. This ruling is stated succinctly in *Mishna Kiddushin* 3.12 that when *kiddushin* (marriage) is licit and no transgression (*ein avera*) is involved, the line follows the father. Furthermore, the most important parental responsibility to teach Torah rested with the father (*Kiddushin* 29a; cf. *Shulchan Aruch, Yoreh De-a* 245.1).

When, in the tradition, the marriage was considered not to be licit, the child of that marriage followed the status of the mother (*Mishna Kiddushin* 3.12, *havalad kemotah*). The decisions of our ancestors thus to link the child inseparably to the mother, which makes the child of a Jewish mother Jewish and the child of a non-Jewish mother non-Jewish, regardless of the father, was based upon the fact that the woman with her child had no recourse but to return to her own people. A Jewish woman could not marry a non-Jewish man (cf. *Shulchan Aruch, Even Ha-ezer* 4.19, *la tafsei kiddushin*). A Jewish man could not marry a non-Jewish woman. The only recourse in Rabbinic law for the woman in either case was to return to her own community and people.

Since Emancipation, Jews have faced the problem of mixed marriage and the status of the offspring of mixed marriage. The Reform Movement responded to the issue. In 1947, the CCAR adopted a proposal made by the Committee on Mixed Marriage and Intermarriage:

> With regard to infants, the declaration of the parents to raise them as Jews shall be deemed sufficient for conversion. This could apply, for example, to adopted children. This decision is in line with the traditional procedure in which, according to the Talmud, the parents bring young children (The Talmud speaks of children earlier than the age of three) to be converted, and the Talmud comments that although an infant cannot give its consent, it is permissible to benefit somebody without his consent (or presence). On the same page the Talmud also speaks of a father bringing his children for conversion, and says that the children will be satisfied with the action of their father. If the parents therefore will make a declaration to the rabbi that it is their intention to raise the

child as a Jew, the child may, for the sake of impressive formality, be recorded in the Cradle-Roll of the religious school and thus be considered converted.

Children of religious school age should likewise not be required to undergo a special ceremony of conversion but should receive instruction as regular student in the school. The ceremony of Confirmation at the end of the school course shall be considered in lieu of a conversion ceremony.

Children older than confirmation age should not be converted without their own consent. The Talmudic law likewise gives the child who is converted in infancy by the court the right to reject the conversion when it becomes of religious age. Therefore the child above religious school age, if he or she consents sincerely to conversion, should receive regular instruction for that purpose and be converted in the regular conversion ceremony.

This issue was again addressed in the 1961 edition of the "Rabbi's Manual":

Jewish law recognizes a person as Jewish if his mother was Jewish, even though the father was not a Jew. One born of such mixed parentage may be admitted to membership in the synagogue and enter into a marital relationship with a Jew, provided he has not been reared in or formally admitted into some other faith. The child of a Jewish father and a non-Jewish mother, according to traditional law, is a Gentile; such a person would have to be formally converted in order to marry a Jew or become a synagogue member.

Reform Judaism, however, accepts such a child as Jewish without a formal conversion, if he attends a Jewish school and follows a course of studies leading to Confirmation. Such procedure is regarded as sufficient evidence that the parents and the child himself intend that he shall live as Jew ("Rabbi's Manual," p. 112).

We face today an unprecedented situation due to the changed conditions in which decisions concerning the status of the child of a mixed marriage are to be made. There are tens of thousands of mixed marriages. In a vast majority of these cases the non-Jewish extended family is a functioning part of the child's world, and may be decisive in shaping the life of the child. It can no longer be assumed a priori, therefore, that the child of a Jewish mother will be Jewish any more than that the child of a non-Jewish mother will not be.

This leads us to the conclusion the same requirements must be applied to establish the status of a child of a mixed marriage, regardless of whether the mother or the father is Jewish.

Therefore:

> The Central Conference of American Rabbis declares that the child of one Jewish parent is under the presumption of Jewish descent. This presumption of the Jewish status of the offspring of any mixed marriage is to be established through appropriate and timely public and formal acts of identification with the Jewish faith and people. The performance of these *mitzvot* serves to commit those who participate in them, both parent and child, to Jewish life.
>
> Depending on circumstances,[3] *mitzvot* leading toward a positive and exclusive Jewish identify will include entry into the covenant, acquisition of a Hebrew name, Torah study, Bar/Bar [sic] Mitzvah, and *Kabbalat Torah* (Confirmation).[4] For those beyond childhood claiming Jewish identity, other public acts or declarations may be added or substituted after consultation with their rabbi.

Law of Return

The Law of Return allows all Jews to live in Israel and become citizens as of right, without having to undergo a naturalization process. Enacted in 1950, it was amended in 1954 to exclude Jews with a criminal past. It was amended again in 1970 to in-

---

[3]According to the age or setting, parents should consult a rabbi to determine the specific *mitzvot* which are necessary.

[4]A full description of these and other *mitzvot* can be found in *Shaarei Mitzvah*.

clude, among other stipulations, a definition of a Jew: "a person who was born of a Jewish mother or has become converted to Judaism and who is not a member of another religion." It is notable that although attempts had been made to stipulate in the law that recognized conversions must be "halakhic," and therefore Orthodox, such attempts failed.

Rabbinical Courts Jurisdiction Bill

This bill, presented in the Knesset in 1997, sought to change conversion acceptability standards. The bill would not directly change the Law of Return, but it would change the Population Registry Law, so that conversions done within Israel would only be acceptable in Israel if they were approved by the president of the High Rabbinical Court, i.e. Orthodox.

Law of Return 5710-1950

Right of aliyah**
Oleh's visa

1. Every Jew has the right to come to this country as an oleh**.
2. (a) Aliyah shall be by oleh's visa.

(b) An oleh's visa shall be granted to every Jew who has expressed his desire to settle in Israel, unless the Minister of Immigration is satisfied that the applicant

(1) is engaged in an activity directed against the Jewish people; or

(2) is likely to endanger public health or the security of the State.

Oleh's certificate

3. (a) A Jew who has come to Israel and subsequent to his arrival has expressed his desire to settle in Israel may, while still in Israel, receive an oleh's certificate.

(b) The restrictions specified in section 2(b) shall apply also to the grant of an oleh's certificate, but a person shall not be regarded as endangering public health on account of an illness contracted after his arrival in Israel.

Residents and persons born in this country

4. Every Jew who has immigrated into this country before the coming into force of this Law, and every Jew who was born in this country, whether before or after the coming into force of this Law, shall be deemed to be a person who has come to this country as an oleh under this Law.

Implementation and regulations

5. The Minister of Immigration is charged with the implementation of this Law and may make regulations as to any matter relating to such implementation and also as to the grant of oleh's visas and oleh's certificates to minors up to the age of 18 years.

DAVID BEN-GURION
Prime Minister

MOSHE SHAPIRA
Minister of Immigration

YOSEF SPRINZAK
Acting President of the State
Chairman of the Knesset

* Passed by the Knesset on the 20th Tammuz, 5710 (5th July, 1950) and published in Sefer Ha-Chukkim No. 51 of the 21st Tammuz, 5710 (5th July. 1950), p. 159; the Bill and an Explanatory Note were published in Hatza'ot Chok No. 48 of the 12th Tammuz, 5710 (27th June, 1950), p. 189.

** Translator's Note: Aliyah means immigration of Jews, and oleh (plural: olim) means a Jew immigrating, into Israel.

Law of Return (Amendment 5714-1954)*

Amendment of section 2(b)

1. In section 2 (b) of the Law of Return, 5710-1950** -

(1) the full stop at the end of paragraph (2) shall be replaced by a semi-colon, and the word "or" shall be inserted thereafter ;

(2) the following paragraph shall be inserted after paragraph (2):

"(3) is a person with a criminal past, likely to endanger public welfare.".

Amendment of sections 2 and 5

2. In sections 2 and 5 of the Law, the words "the Minister of Immigration" shall be replaced by the words "the Minister of the Interior".

MOSHE SHARETT
Prime Minister

YOSEF SERLIN
Minister of Health
Acting Minister of the Interior

YITZCHAK BEN-ZVI
President of the State

* Passed by the Knesset on the 24th Av, 5714 (23rd August, 1954) and published in Sefer Ha-Chukkim No. 163 of the 3rd Elul, 5714 (1st September, 1954) p. 174; the Bill and an Explanatory Note were published in Hatza'ot Chok No. 192 of 5714, p. 88.

** Sefer Ha-Chukkim No. 51 of 5710, p. 159, LSI vol. IV, 114.

Law of Return (Amendment No. 2) 5730-1970*

Addition of sections 4A and 4B

1. In the Law of Return, 5710-1950**, the following sections shall be inserted after section 4:

"Rights of members of family

4A. (a) The rights of a Jew under this Law and the rights of an oleh under the Nationality Law, 5712-1952***, as well as the rights of an oleh under any other enactment, are also vested in a child and a grandchild of a Jew, the spouse of a Jew, the spouse of a child of a Jew and the spouse of a grandchild of a Jew, except for a person who has been a Jew and has voluntarily changed his religion.

(b) It shall be immaterial whether or not a Jew by whose right a right under subsection (a) is claimed is still alive and whether or not he has immigrated to Israel.

(c) The restrictions and conditions prescribed in respect of a Jew or an oleh by or under this Law or by the enactments referred to in subsection (a) shall also apply to a person who claims a right under subsection (a).

Definition

4B. For the purposes of this Law, "Jew" means a person who was born of a Jewish mother or has become converted to Judaism and who is not a member of another religion."

Amendment of section 5

2. In section 5 of the Law of Return, 5710-1950, the following shall be added at the end: "Regulations for the purposes of sections 4A and 4B require the approval of the Constitution, Legislation and Juridical Committee of the Knesset.".

Amendment of the Population Registry Law, 5725-1965

3. In the Population Registry Law, 5725-1965****, the following section shall be inserted after section 3:

"Power of registration and definition

3A. (a) A person shall not be registered as a Jew by ethnic affiliation or religion if a notification under this Law or another entry in the Registry or a public document indicates that he is not a Jew, so long as the said notification, entry or document has not been controverted to the satisfaction of the Chief Registration Officer or so long as declaratory judgment of a competent court or tribunal has not otherwise determined.

(b) For the purposes of this Law and of any registration or document thereunder, "Jew" has the same meaning as in section 4B of the Law of Return, 5710-1950.

(c) This section shall not derogate from a registration effected before its coming into force.".

GOLDA MEIR
Prime Minister
Acting Minister of the Interior

SHNEUR ZALMAN SHAZAR
President of the State

---

* Passed by the Knesset on 2nd Adar Bet, 5730 (10th March, 1970) and published in Sefer Ha-Chukkim No. 586 of the 11th Adar Bet, 5730 (19th March, 1970), p. 34; the Bill and an Explanatory Note were published in Hatza'ot Chok No. 866 of 5730, p. 36.

** Sefer Ha-Chukkim of 5710 p. 159 - LSI vol. IV, p. 114; Sefer Ha-Chukkim No. 5714, p. 174 - LSI vol. VIII, p. 144.

*** Sefer Ha-Chukkim of 5712, p. 146 ; LSI vol. VI, p. 50.

**** Sefer Ha-Chukkim of 5725, p. 270 ; LSI vol. XIX, p. 288.

Rabbinical Courts Jurisdiction (Marriage and Divorce) (Amendment-Conversion), 5757–1996

Changing the Name of the Law	1.	In the Rabbinical Courts' Jurisdiction (Marriage and Divorce) Law, 5713–1953 (hereafter "The principal Law"), the name of the Law, instead of "(Marriage and Divorce)" will be "(Marriage, Divorce and Conversion)".
Addition of clause 8A	2.	After Clause 8 of the Principal Law will come:
	"Jurisdiction in the matter of conversion"	8A (a) A conversion of a person in Israel will be performed according to the Halacha. (b) There shall be no legal validity given to a conversion that was performed in Israel unless the Chief Justice of the high Rabbinical Court certified that the conversion was performed according to sub-section (a)*.
Amending the Emergency Regulations (Judes, Samaria and Gaza Strip-Jurisdiction over Offenses and Legal Aid)	3.	After regulation 7B in the annex to the Law Extending the Validity of the Emergency Regulation (Judes, Samaria and Gaza Strip-Jurisdiction over Offenses and Legal Aid), 5738–1977 will come:
	"Conversion in the Territory"	7C "Clause 8A of the Rabbinical Jurisdiction (Marriage, Divorce and Conversion) will apply also for a conversion performed in the Territory, but the certification according to sub-section (b) of the aforementioned article, may be issued by a Rabbinical Court established by order of he Commissioner."
Amendment of the Population Registry Law	4.	In clause 15 of the Population registry Law, 5725–1865, after paragraph (3) will come: "(3A) Certification of conversions performed according to clause 8A of The Rabbinical Courts' Jurisdiction (Marriage, Divorce and Conversion), Law 5713–1953.

About JEWISH LIGHTS Publishing

People of all faiths and backgrounds yearn for books that attract, engage, educate and spiritually inspire.

Our principal goal is to stimulate thought and help all people learn about who the Jewish People are, where they come from, and what the future can be made to hold. While people of our diverse Jewish heritage are the primary audience, our books speak to people in the Christian world as well and will broaden their understanding of Judaism and the roots of their own faith.

We bring to you authors who are at the forefront of spiritual thought and experience. While each has something different to say, they all say it in a voice that you can hear.

Our books are designed to welcome you and then to engage, stimulate and inspire. We judge our success not only by whether or not our books are beautiful and commercially successful, but by whether or not they make a difference in your life.

We at Jewish Lights take great care to produce beautiful books that present meaningful spiritual content in a form that reflects the art of making high quality books. Therefore, we want to acknowledge those who contributed to the production of this book.

PRODUCTION
Maria O'Donnell

EDITORIAL & PROOFREADING
Sandra Korinchak / Jennifer Goneau

BOOK DESIGN
Sans Serif Inc., Saline, Michigan

TYPE
Set in Sabon
Sans Serif Inc., Saline, Michigan

COVER PRINTING
Phoenix Color Corp., Taunton, Massachusetts

PRINTING AND BINDING
Royal Book, Norwich, Connecticut

Spirituality

HOW TO BE A PERFECT STRANGER, In 2 Volumes
A Guide to Etiquette in Other People's Religious Ceremonies
Edited by *Stuart M. Matlins* & *Arthur J. Magida*

BEST REFERENCE BOOK OF THE YEAR

"A book that belongs in every living room, library and office!"

Explains the rituals and celebrations of America's major religions/denominations, helping an interested guest to feel comfortable, participate to the fullest extent possible, and avoid violating anyone's religious principles. Answers practical questions from the perspective of *any* other faith.

VOL. 1: America's Largest Faiths

VOL. 1 COVERS: Assemblies of God • Baptist • Buddhist • Christian Science • Churches of Christ • Disciples of Christ • Episcopalian • Greek Orthodox • Hindu • Islam • Jehovah's Witnesses • Jewish • Lutheran • Methodist • Mormon • Presbyterian • Quaker • Roman Catholic • Seventh-day Adventist • United Church of Christ

6" x 9", 432 pp. Hardcover, ISBN 1-879045-39-7 **$24.95**

VOL. 2: Other Faiths in America

VOL. 2 COVERS: African American Methodist Churches • Baha'i • Christian and Missionary Alliance • Christian Congregation • Church of the Brethren • Church of the Nazarene • Evangelical Free Church of America • International Church of the Foursquare Gospel • International Pentecostal Holiness Church • Mennonite/Amish • Native American • Orthodox Churches • Pentecostal Church of God • Reformed Church of America • Sikh • Unitarian Universalist • Wesleyan

6" x 9", 416 pp. HC, ISBN 1-879045-63-X **$24.95**

GOD & THE BIG BANG
Discovering Harmony Between Science & Spirituality
by *Daniel C. Matt*

Mysticism and science: What do they have in common? How can one enlighten the other? By drawing on modern cosmology and ancient Kabbalah, Matt shows how science and religion can together enrich our spiritual awareness and help us recover a sense of wonder and find our place in the universe.

"This poetic new book...helps us to understand the human meaning of creation."
—*Joel Primack, leading cosmologist, Professor of Physics, University of California, Santa Cruz*

6" x 9", 216 pp. Quality Paperback, ISBN 1-879045-89-3 **$16.95** HC, ISBN-48-6 **$21.95**

MINDING THE TEMPLE OF THE SOUL
Balancing Body, Mind, & Spirit through Traditional Jewish Prayer, Movement, & Meditation
by *Tamar Frankiel* and *Judy Greenfeld*

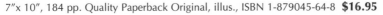

This new spiritual approach to physical health introduces readers to a spiritual tradition that affirms the body and enables them to reconceive their bodies in a more positive light. Relying on Kabbalistic teachings and other Jewish traditions, it shows us how to be more responsible for our own psychological and physical health. Focuses on the discipline of prayer, simple Tai Chi–like exercises and body positions, and guides the reader throughout, step by step, with diagrams, sketches and meditations.

7"x 10", 184 pp. Quality Paperback Original, illus., ISBN 1-879045-64-8 **$16.95**

Audiotape of the Prayers, Movements & Meditations (60-min. cassette) **$9.95**
Videotape of the Blessings & Meditations (46-min. VHS) **$20.00**

Spirituality

MEDITATION FROM THE HEART OF JUDAISM
Today's Teachers Share Their Practices, Techniques, and Faith
Edited by *Avram Davis*

A "how-to" guide for both beginning and experienced meditators, it will help you start meditating or help you enhance your practice.

Twenty-two masters of meditation explain why and how they meditate. *A detailed compendium of the experts' "Best Practices"* offers practical advice and starting points.

"A treasury of meditative insights and techniques....Each page is a meditative experience that brings you closer to God."
—*Rabbi Shoni Labowitz, author of* Miraculous Living: A Guided Journey in Kabbalah through the Ten Gates of the Tree of Life

6" x 9", 256 pp. Hardcover, ISBN 1-879045-77-X **$21.95**

SELF, STRUGGLE & CHANGE
Family Conflict Stories in Genesis and Their Healing Insights for Our Lives
by *Norman J. Cohen*

How do I find greater wholeness in my life and in my family's life?

The people described by the biblical writers of Genesis were in situations and relationships very much like our own. We identify with them. Their stories still speak to us because they are about the same problems we deal with every day. Here a modern master of biblical interpretation brings us greater understanding of the ancient text and of ourselves in this intriguing re-telling of conflict between husband and wife, father and son, brothers, and sisters.

"Delightfully written...rare erudition, sensitivity and insight." —*Elie Wiesel*
6" x 9", 224 pp. Quality Paperback, ISBN 1-879045-66-4 **$16.95**; HC, ISBN-19-2 **$21.95**

ECOLOGY & THE JEWISH SPIRIT
Where Nature & the Sacred Meet
Edited and with Introductions by *Ellen Bernstein*

What is nature's place in our spiritual lives?

A focus on nature is part of the fabric of Jewish thought. Here, experts bring us a richer understanding of the long-neglected themes of nature that are woven through the biblical creation story, ancient texts, traditional law, the holiday cycles, prayer, *mitzvot* (good deeds), and community.

For people of all faiths, all backgrounds, this book helps us to make nature a sacred, spiritual part of our own lives.

"A great resource for anyone seeking to explore the connection between their faith and caring for God's good creation, our environment."
—*Paul Gorman, Executive Director, National Religious Partnership for the Environment*

6" x 9", 288 pp. HC, ISBN 1-879045-88-5 **$23.95**

ISRAEL—A SPIRITUAL TRAVEL GUIDE
A Companion for the Modern Jewish Pilgrim
by *Rabbi Lawrence A. Hoffman*

Be spiritually prepared for your journey to Israel.

A Jewish spiritual travel guide to Israel, helping today's pilgrim tap into the deep spiritual meaning of the ancient—and modern—sites of the Holy Land. Combines in quick reference format ancient blessings, medieval prayers, biblical and historical references, and modern poetry. The only guidebook that helps readers to prepare spiritually for the occasion. More than a guide book: It is a spiritual map.

"At last, the missing guide book—one that can spiritually deepen any trip to Israel."
—*Rabbi Richard Jacobs, Westchester Reform Temple; member, Board of the New Israel Fund*

4 3/4" x 10 1/8", 192 pp. (est.) Quality Paperback Original, ISBN 1-879045-56-7 **$18.95**

Spirituality—The Kushner Series

INVISIBLE LINES OF CONNECTION
Sacred Stories of the Ordinary
by *Lawrence Kushner*

Through his everyday encounters with family, friends, colleagues and strangers, Kushner takes us deeply into our lives, finding flashes of spiritual insight in the process. This is a book where literature meets spirituality, where the sacred meets the ordinary, and, above all, where people of all faiths, all backgrounds can meet one another and themselves.

"Does something both more and different than instruct—it inspirits. Wonderful stories, from the best storyteller I know."
— *David Mamet*

•AWARD WINNER•

5 1/2" x 8 1/2", 160 pp. Quality Paperback, ISBN 1-879045-98-2 **$15.95** HC, -52-4 **$21.95**

HONEY FROM THE ROCK
An Easy Introduction to Jewish Mysticism
by *Lawrence Kushner*

"Quite simply the easiest introduction to Jewish mysticism you can read."

An introduction to the ten gates of Jewish mysticism and how it applies to daily life.

"Captures the flavor and spark of Jewish mysticism. . . . Read it and be rewarded." —*Elie Wiesel*

6" x 9", 168 pp. Quality Paperback, ISBN 1-879045-02-8 **$14.95**

THE BOOK OF WORDS
Talking Spiritual Life, Living Spiritual Talk
by *Lawrence Kushner*

In the incomparable manner of his extraordinary *The Book of Letters*, Kushner now lifts up and shakes the dust off primary religious words we use to describe the spiritual dimension of life. For each word Kushner offers us a startling, moving and insightful explication, and pointed readings from classical Jewish sources that further illuminate the concept. He concludes with a short exercise that helps unite the spirit of the word with our actions in the world.

"This is a powerful and holy book."
—*M. Scott Peck, M.D., author of* The Road Less Traveled *and other books*

"What a delightful wholeness of intellectual vigor and meditative playfulness, and all in a tone of gentleness that speaks to this gentile."
—*Rt. Rev. Krister Stendahl, formerly Dean, Harvard Divinity School/Bishop of Stockholm*

6" x 9", 152 pp. HC, beautiful two-color text, ISBN 1-879045-35-4 **$21.95**

THE BOOK OF LETTERS
A Mystical Hebrew Alphabet
by *Rabbi Lawrence Kushner*

In calligraphy by the author. Folktales about and exploration of the mystical meanings of the Hebrew Alphabet. Open the old prayerbook-like pages of *The Book of Letters* and you will enter a special world of sacred tradition and religious feeling. Rabbi Kushner draws from ancient Judaic sources, weaving talmudic commentary, Hasidic folktales, and kabbalistic mysteries around the letters.

"A book which is in love with Jewish letters."
— *Isaac Bashevis Singer* (ז'ל)

•AWARD WINNER•

• **Popular Hardcover Edition** 6"x 9", 80 pp. HC, two colors, inspiring new Foreword. ISBN 1-879045-00-1 **$24.95**

• **Deluxe Gift Edition** 9"x 12", 80 pp. HC, four-color text, ornamentation, in a beautiful slipcase. ISBN 1-879045-01-X **$79.95**

• **Collector's Limited Edition** 9"x 12", 80 pp. HC, gold-embossed pages, hand-assembled slipcase. With silkscreened print. **Limited to 500 signed and numbered copies.** ISBN 1-879045-04-4 **$349.00**

To see a sample page at no obligation, call us

Spirituality

GOD WAS IN THIS PLACE & I, i DID NOT KNOW
Finding Self, Spirituality & Ultimate Meaning
by Lawrence Kushner

Who am I? Who is God? Kushner creates inspiring interpretations of Jacob's dream in Genesis, opening a window into Jewish spirituality for people of all faiths and backgrounds.

In this fascinating blend of scholarship, imagination, psychology and history, seven Jewish spiritual masters ask and answer fundamental questions of human experience.

"Rich and intriguing."
—*M. Scott Peck, M.D., author of* The Road Less Traveled *and other books*

6" x 9", 192 pp. Quality Paperback, ISBN 1-879045-33-8 **$16.95**

THE RIVER OF LIGHT
Spirituality, Judaism, Consciousness
by Lawrence Kushner

A "manual" for all spiritual travelers who would attempt a spiritual journey in our times. Taking us step by step, Kushner allows us to discover the meaning of our own quest: "to allow the river of light—the deepest currents of consciousness—to rise to the surface and animate our lives."

"Philosophy and mystical fantasy....Anybody—Jewish, Christian, or otherwise...will find this book an intriguing experience."
—*Kirkus Reviews*

6" x 9", 180 pp. Quality Paperback, ISBN 1-879045-03-6 **$14.95**

GODWRESTLING—ROUND 2
Ancient Wisdom, Future Paths
by *Arthur Waskow*

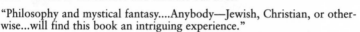
BEST RELIGION BOOK OF THE YEAR

This 20th-anniversary sequel to a seminal book of the Jewish renewal movement deals with spirituality in relation to personal growth, marriage, ecology, feminism, politics, and more. Including new chapters on recent issues and concerns, Waskow outlines original ways to merge "religious" life and "personal" life in our society today.

"A delicious read and a soaring meditation."
—*Rabbi Zalman M. Schachter-Shalomi*

"Vivid as a novel, sharp, eccentric, loud....An important book for anyone who wants to bring Judaism alive."
—*Marge Piercy*

6" x 9", 352 pp. Quality Paperback, ISBN 1-879045-72-9 **$18.95** HC, ISBN-45-1 **$23.95**

BEING GOD'S PARTNER
How to Find the Hidden Link Between Spirituality and Your Work
by *Jeffrey K. Salkin* Introduction by *Norman Lear*

Will challenge people of every denomination to reconcile the cares of work and soul. A groundbreaking book about spirituality and the work world, from a Jewish perspective. Helps the reader find God in the ethical striving and search for meaning in the professions and in business and offers practical suggestions for balancing your professional life and spiritual self.

"This engaging meditation on the spirituality of work is grounded in Judaism but is relevant well beyond the boundaries of that tradition."
—*American Library Association's* Booklist

6" x 9", 192 pp. Quality Paperback, ISBN 1-879045-65-6 **$16.95** HC, ISBN-37-0 **$19.95**

Spirituality

MY PEOPLE'S PRAYER BOOK
Traditional Prayers, Modern Commentaries
Vol. 1—The Sh'ma and Its Blessings
Edited by *Rabbi Lawrence A. Hoffman*

Provides a diverse and exciting commentary to the traditional liturgy, written by 10 of today's most respected scholars and teachers from all perspectives of the Jewish world.

This groundbreaking first of seven volumes examines the oldest and best-known of Jewish prayers. Often the first prayer memorized by children and the last prayer recited on a deathbed, the *Sh'ma* frames a Jewish life.

7" x 10", 168 pp. HC, ISBN 1-879045-79-6 **$19.95**

FINDING JOY
A Practical Spiritual Guide to Happiness
by *Dannel I. Schwartz* with *Mark Hass*

Searching for happiness in our modern world of stress and struggle is common; *finding* it is more unusual. This guide explores and explains how to find joy through a time-honored, creative—and surprisingly practical—approach based on the teachings of Jewish mysticism and Kabbalah.

"Lovely, simple introduction to Kabbalah....a singular contribution...."
—*American Library Association's* Booklist

•AWARD WINNER•   6" x 9", 192 pp. HC, ISBN 1-879045-53-2 **$19.95**

THE DEATH OF DEATH
Resurrection and Immortality in Jewish Thought
by *Neil Gillman*

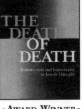

Noted theologian Neil Gillman explores the original and compelling argument that Judaism, a religion often thought to pay little attention to the afterlife, not only offers us rich ideas on the subject—but delivers a deathblow to death itself. By exploring Jewish thought about death and the afterlife, this fascinating work presents us with challenging new ideas about our lives.

"Enables us to recover our tradition's understanding of the afterlife and breaks through the silence of modern Jewish thought on immortality.... A work of major •AWARD WINNER• significance."
—*Rabbi Sheldon Zimmerman, President, Hebrew Union College–Jewish Institute of Religion*

6" x 9", 336 pp., HC, ISBN 1-879045-61-3 **$23.95**

THE EMPTY CHAIR: FINDING HOPE & JOY
Timeless Wisdom from a Hasidic Master,
Rebbe Nachman of Breslov
Adapted by Moshe Mykoff and the Breslov Research Institute

A "little treasure" of aphorisms and advice for living joyously and spiritually today, written 200 years ago, but startlingly fresh in meaning and use. Challenges and helps us to move from stress and sadness to hope and joy.

Teacher, guide and spiritual master—Rebbe Nachman provides vital words of inspiration and wisdom for life today for people of any faith, or of no faith.

•AWARD WINNER•

"For anyone of any faith, this is a book of healing and wholeness, of being alive!"
— *Bookviews*

4" x 6", 128 pp., 2-color text, Deluxe Paperback, ISBN 1-879045-67-2 **$9.95**

Theology/Philosophy

•AWARD WINNER•

A LIVING COVENANT
The Innovative Spirit in Traditional Judaism
by *David Hartman*

WINNER,
National Jewish
Book Award

The Judaic tradition is often seen as being more concerned with uncritical obedience to law than with individual freedom and responsibility. Hartman challenges this approach by revealing a Judaism grounded in a covenant—a relational framework—informed by the metaphor of marital love rather than that of parent-child dependency.

"Jews and non-Jews, liberals and traditionalists will see classic Judaism anew in these pages."
—*Dr. Eugene B. Borowitz, Hebrew Union College–Jewish Institute of Religion*
6" x 9", 368 pp. Quality Paperback, ISBN 1-58023-011-3 **$18.95**

THE SPIRIT OF RENEWAL
Finding Faith after the Holocaust
by *Edward Feld*

Trying to understand the Holocaust and addressing the question of faith after the Holocaust, Rabbi Feld explores three key cycles of destruction and recovery in Jewish history, each of which radically reshaped Jewish understanding of God, people, and the world.

"A profound meditation on Jewish history [and the Holocaust]....Christians, as well as many others, need to share in this story."
—*The Rt. Rev. Frederick H. Borsch, Ph.D., Episcopal Bishop of L.A.*

•AWARD WINNER•

6" x 9", 224 pp. Quality Paperback, ISBN 1-879045-40-0 **$16.95**

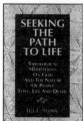

•AWARD WINNER•

SEEKING THE PATH TO LIFE
Theological Meditations On God
and the Nature of People, Love, Life and Death
by *Rabbi Ira F. Stone*

For people who never thought they would read a book of theology—let alone understand it, enjoy it, savor it and have it affect the way they think about their lives. In 45 intense meditations, each a page or two in length, Stone takes us on explorations of the most basic human struggles: Life and death, love and anger, peace and war, covenant and exile.

"A bold book....The reader of any faith will be inspired...."
— *The Rev. Carla V. Berkedal, Episcopal Priest*

6" x 9", 132 pp. Quality Paperback, ISBN 1-879045-47-8 **$14.95**   HC, ISBN-17-6 **$19.95**

THEOLOGY & PHILOSOPHY...Other books—Classic Reprints

Aspects of Rabbinic Theology by Solomon Schechter, with a new Introduction by Neil Gillman 6" x 9", 440 pp, Quality Paperback, ISBN 1-879045-24-9 **$18.95**

The Last Trial: On the Legends and Lore of the Command to Abraham to Offer Isaac as a Sacrifice by Shalom Spiegel, with a new Introduction by Judah Goldin
6" x 9", 208 pp, Quality Paperback, ISBN 1-879045-29-X **$17.95**

Judaism and Modern Man: An Interpretation of Jewish Religion by Will Herberg; new Introduction by Neil Gillman 5.5" x 8.5", 336 pp, Quality Paperback, ISBN 1-879045-87-7 **$18.95**

Tormented Master: The Life and Spiritual Quest of Rabbi Nahman of Bratslav by Arthur Green 6" x 9", 408 pp, Quality Paperback, ISBN 1-879045-11-7 **$18.95**

Your Word Is Fire Edited and translated with a new Introduction by Arthur Green and Barry W. Holtz 6" x 9", 152 pp, Quality Paperback, ISBN 1-879045-25-7 **$14.95**

CLASSICS BY ABRAHAM JOSHUA HESCHEL

The Earth Is the Lord's: The Inner World of the Jew in Eastern Europe
5 1/2" x 8", 112 pp, Quality Paperback, ISBN 1-879045-42-7 **$13.95**

Israel: An Echo of Eternity with new Introduction by Susannah Heschel
5 1/2" x 8", 272 pp, Quality Paperback, ISBN 1-879045-70-2 **$18.95**

A Passion for Truth: Despair and Hope in Hasidism
5 1/2" x 8", 352 pp, Quality Paperback, ISBN 1-879045-41-9 **$18.95**

Life Cycle

GRIEF IN OUR SEASONS
A Mourner's Kaddish Companion
by Rabbi Kerry M. Olitzky

Strength from the Jewish tradition for the first year of mourning.

Provides a wise and inspiring selection of sacred Jewish writings and a simple, powerful ancient ritual for mourners to read each day, to help hold the memory of their loved ones in their hearts. It offers a comforting, step-by-step daily link to saying *Kaddish.*

"A hopeful, compassionate guide along the journey from grief to rebirth from mourning to a new morning."
> —*Rabbi Levi Meier, Ph.D., Chaplain, Cedars–Sinai Medical Center, Los Angeles*

4 1/2" x 6 1/2", 448 pp., Quality Paperback Original, ISBN 1-879045-55-9 **$15.95**

MOURNING & MITZVAH
A Guided Journal for Walking the Mourner's Path Through Grief to Healing

• WITH OVER **60** GUIDED EXERCISES •

by Anne Brener, L.C.S.W.; Foreword *by Rabbi Jack Riemer;* Introduction *by Rabbi William Cutter*

"Fully engaging in mourning means you will be a different person than before you began." **For those who mourn a death, for those who would help them,** for those who face a loss of any kind, Brener teaches us the power and strength available to us in the fully experienced mourning process. Guided writing exercises help stimulate the processes of both conscious and unconscious healing.

"A stunning book! It offers an exploration in depth of the place where psychology and religious ritual intersect, and the name of that place is Truth."
> —*Rabbi Harold Kushner, author of* When Bad Things Happen to Good People

7 1/2" x 9", 288 pp. Quality Paperback Original, ISBN 1-879045-23-0 **$19.95**

Healing/Recovery/Wellness

Healing of Soul, Healing of Body: Spiritual Leaders Unfold the Strength & Solace in Psalms
Edited by Rabbi Simkha Y. Weintraub, CSW, for the Jewish Healing Center. 6 x 9, 2-color text, 128 pp, Quality Paperback, ISBN 1-879045-31-1 **$14.95**

One Hundred Blessings Every Day: Daily Twelve Step Recovery Affirmations, Exercises for Personal Growth & Renewal Reflecting Seasons of the Jewish Year
by Rabbi Kerry M. Olitzky. 4.5 x 6.5, 432 pp, Quality Paperback, ISBN 1-879045-30-3 **$14.95**

Recovery from Codependence: A Jewish Twelve Steps Guide to Healing Your Soul
by Rabbi Kerry M. Olitzky. 6 x 9, 160 pp, Quality Paperback, ISBN 1-879045-32-X **$13.95**
HC, ISBN 1-879045-27-3 **$21.95**

Renewed Each Day: Daily Twelve Step Recovery Meditations Based on the Bible
by Rabbi Kerry M. Olitzky & Aaron Z. 6 x 9, Quality Paperback; Vol. I: Genesis & Exodus, 224 pp, **$14.95**; Vol. II: Leviticus, Numbers & Deuteronomy, 280 pp, **$16.95**; Two-Volume Set, Quality Paperback, ISBN 1-879045-21-4 **$27.90**

Twelve Jewish Steps to Recovery: A Personal Guide to Turning from Alcoholism & Other Addictions
by Rabbi Kerry M. Olitzky & Stuart A. Copans, M.D. 6 x 9, 136 pp, Quality Paperback, ISBN 1-879045-09-5 **$13.95**

Life Cycle

A Time to Mourn, A Time to Comfort: A Guide to Jewish Bereavement and Comfort
by Dr. Ron Wolfson. 7 x 9, 320 pp, Quality Paperback, ISBN 1-879045-96-6 **$16.95**

When a Grandparent Dies: A Kid's Own Remembering Workbook for Dealing with Shiva and the Year Beyond by Nechama Liss-Levinson, Ph.D. 8 x 10, 2-color text, 48 pp, HC, ISBN 1-879045-44-3 **$15.95**

Life Cycle

A HEART OF WISDOM
Making the Jewish Journey from Midlife Through the Elder Years
Edited by *Susan Berrin*

We are all growing older. *A Heart of Wisdom* shows us how to understand our own process of aging—and the aging of those we care about—from a Jewish perspective, from midlife through the elder years.

How does Jewish tradition influence our own aging? How does living, thinking and worshipping as a Jew affect us as we age? How can Jewish tradition help us retain our dignity as we age? Offers insights and enlightenment from Jewish tradition.

"A thoughtfully orchestrated collection of pieces that deal candidly and compassionately with a period of growing concern to us all: midlife through old age."

—*Chaim Potok*

6" x 9", 384 pp. HC, ISBN 1-879045-73-7 **$24.95**

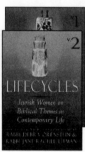

LIFECYCLES
V. 1: Jewish Women on Life Passages & Personal Milestones
Edited and with Introductions by *Rabbi Debra Orenstein*
V. 2: Jewish Women on Biblical Themes in Contemporary Life
Edited and with Introductions by
Rabbi Debra Orenstein and *Rabbi Jane Rachel Litman*

This unique multivolume collaboration brings together over one hundred women writers, rabbis, and scholars to create the first comprehensive work on Jewish life cycle that fully includes women's perspectives.

"Nothing is missing from this marvelous collection. You will turn to it for rituals and inspiration, prayer and poetry, comfort and community. *Lifecycles* is a gift to the Jewish woman in America."
—*Letty Cottin Pogrebin, author of* Deborah, Golda, and Me: Being Female and Jewish in America

V. 1: 6" x 9", 480 pp. HC, ISBN 1-879045-14-1, **$24.95**; **V. 2:** 6" x 9", 464 pp. HC, ISBN 1-879045-15-X, **$24.95**

LIFE CYCLE— The Art of Jewish Living Series for Holiday Observance
by Dr. Ron Wolfson

Hanukkah—7" x 9", 192 pp. Quality Paperback, ISBN 1-879045-97-4 **$16.95**

The Shabbat Seder—7" x 9", 272 pp. Quality Paperback, ISBN 1-879045-90-7 **$16.95**; Booklet of Blessings **$5.00**; Audiocassette of Blessings **$6.00**; Teacher's Guide **$4.95**

The Passover Seder—7" x 9", 336 pp. Quality Paperback, ISBN 1-879045-93-1 **$16.95**; Passover Workbook, **$6.95**; Audiocassette of Blessings, **$6.00**; Teacher's Guide, **$4.95**

LIFE CYCLE...Other Books

Bar/Bat Mitzvah Basics: A Practical Family Guide to Coming of Age Together
Ed. by Cantor Helen Leneman 6" x 9", 240 pp. Quality Paperback, ISBN 1-879045-54-0 **$16.95**

Embracing the Covenant: Converts to Judaism Talk About Why & How
Ed. and with Intros. by Rabbi Allan L. Berkowitz and Patti Moskovitz
6" x 9", 192 pp. Quality Paperback, ISBN 1-879045-50-8 **$15.95**

The New Jewish Baby Book: Names, Ceremonies, Customs—A Guide for Today's Families by Anita Diamant 6" x 9", 328 pp. Quality Paperback, ISBN 1-879045-28-1 **$16.95**

Putting God on the Guest List, 2nd Ed.: How to Reclaim the Spiritual Meaning of Your Child's Bar or Bat Mitzvah by Rabbi Jeffrey K. Salkin 6" x 9", 224 pp. Quality Paperback, ISBN 1-897045-59-1 **$16.95**; HC, ISBN 1-879045-58-3 **$24.95**

So That Your Values Live On: Ethical Wills & How to Prepare Them
Ed. by Rabbi Jack Riemer & Professor Nathaniel Stampfer
6" x 9", 272 pp. Quality Paperback, ISBN 1-879045-34-6 **$17.95**

Children's

IN GOD'S NAME
AWARD WINNER

by *Sandy Eisenberg Sasso*
Full-color illustrations by *Phoebe Stone*   **For ages 4 and up**

MULTICULTURAL, NONDENOMINATIONAL, NONSECTARIAN. This modern fable about the search for God's name celebrates the diversity and, at the same time, the unity of all the people of the world. "What a lovely, healing book!" —*Madeleine L'Engle*

9″ x 12″, 32 pp. HC, Full-color illus., ISBN 1-879045-26-5 **$16.95**

AWARD WINNER   ## GOD'S PAINTBRUSH
by *Sandy Eisenberg Sasso*
For ages 4–8   Full-color illustrations by *Annette Compton*

MULTICULTURAL, NONDENOMINATIONAL, NONSECTARIAN. Invites children of all faiths and backgrounds to encounter God openly in their own lives. Wonderfully interactive, provides questions adult and child can explore together at the end of each episode. "An excellent way to honor the imaginative breadth and depth of the spiritual life of the young." —*Dr. Robert Coles, Harvard University*

11″ x 8½″, 32 pp. HC, Full-color illus., ISBN 1-879045-22-2 **$16.95**

SHARING BLESSINGS
Children's Stories for Exploring the Spirit of the Jewish Holidays
by *Rahel Musleah* and *Rabbi Michael Klayman*
Full color illustrations by *Mary O'Keefe Young*   **For ages 6–10**

What is the spiritual message of each of the Jewish holidays? How do we teach it to our children? Many books tell children about the historical significance and customs of the holidays. Now, through engaging, creative stories about one family's spiritual preparation, *Sharing Blessings* explores ways to get into the spirit of the holidays all year long.

"A beguiling introduction to important Jewish values by way of the holidays."
—*Rabbi Harold Kushner*

7″ x 10″, 64 pp. HC, Full-color illus., ISBN 1-879045-71-0 **$18.95**

A PRAYER FOR THE EARTH: The Story of Naamah, Noah's Wife
by *Sandy Eisenberg Sasso*   **AWARD WINNER**
Full-color illustrations by *Bethanne Andersen*   **For ages 4–8**

9 x 12, 32 pp. HC, Full-color illus., ISBN 1-879045-60-5 **$16.95**

BUT GOD REMEMBERED: **AWARD WINNER**
Stories of Women from Creation to the Promised Land
by *Sandy Eisenberg Sasso*
Full-color illustrations by *Bethanne Andersen*   **For ages 8 and up**

9 x 12, 32 pp. HC, Full-color illus., ISBN 1-879045-43-5 **$16.95**

THE 11TH COMMANDMENT: Wisdom from Our Children
by *The Children of America*   **For all ages**

8 x 10, 48 pp. HC, Full-color illus., ISBN 1-879045-46-X **$16.95**

THE BOOK OF MIRACLES: A Young Person's Guide to Jewish Spiritual Awareness
by *Lawrence Kushner*   **For ages 9–13**

6 x 9, 96 pp. HC, 2-color illus., ISBN 1-879045-78-8 **$16.95**

Order Information

# of Copies	Book Title / ISBN (Last 3 digits)	$ Amount
_____	_____	_____
_____	_____	_____
_____	_____	_____
_____	_____	_____
_____	_____	_____
_____	_____	_____
_____	_____	_____
_____	_____	_____
_____	_____	_____
_____	_____	_____
_____	_____	_____
_____	_____	_____
_____	_____	_____

For shipping/handling, add $3.50 for the first book, $2.00 each
add'l book (to a max of $15.00) $ **S/H** _____

TOTAL _____

Check enclosed for $_____ *payable to:* JEWISH LIGHTS Publishing

Charge my credit card: ❏ MasterCard   ❏ Visa

Credit Card #_____Expires _____

Signature _____Phone (_____)_____

Your Name _____

Street_____

City / State / Zip _____

Ship To:

Name _____

Street_____

City / State / Zip _____

Phone, fax or mail to: **JEWISH LIGHTS Publishing**
Sunset Farm Offices, Route 4 • P.O. Box 237 • Woodstock, Vermont 05091
Tel (802) 457-4000   Fax (802) 457-4004   www.jewishlights.com
Credit card orders **(800) 962-4544** (9AM–5PM ET Monday–Friday)
Generous discounts on quantity orders. SATISFACTION GUARANTEED. Prices subject to change.